First World War

and Army of Occupation

War Diary

France, Belgium and Germany

63 (ROYAL NAVAL) DIVISION
188 Infantry Brigade
Howe Battalion
1 May 1916 - 28 February 1918

WO95/3111/2

The Naval & Military Press Ltd
www.nmarchive.com
Published in association with The National Archives

Published by

The Naval & Military Press Ltd

Unit 10 Ridgewood Industrial Park,

Uckfield, East Sussex,

TN22 5QE England

Tel: +44 (0) 1825 749494

www.naval-military-press.com

www.nmarchive.com

This diary has been reprinted in facsimile from the original. Any imperfections are inevitably reproduced and the quality may fall short of modern type and cartographic standards.

Contents

Document type	Place/Title	Date From	Date To
Heading	WO95/3111-2		
Heading	63rd Division 188th Infy Bde Howe Bn R.N. Divn May 1916-Feb 1918		
War Diary	Mudros	01/05/1916	13/05/1916
War Diary	Marseilles	14/05/1916	17/05/1916
War Diary	Huppy	17/05/1916	28/05/1916
War Diary	Houdain	29/05/1916	05/06/1916
War Diary	Bois de la Haie	06/06/1916	13/06/1916
War Diary	Hersin	14/06/1916	23/06/1916
War Diary	Trenches	24/06/1916	26/06/1916
War Diary	Coupigny	27/06/1916	28/06/1916
War Diary	Camblain	29/06/1916	29/06/1916
War Diary	Chatelain	30/06/1916	30/06/1916
Miscellaneous	March Orders		
Miscellaneous	War Diary		
War Diary	Camblain Chatelain	01/07/1916	01/07/1916
War Diary	Hermin	03/07/1916	13/07/1916
War Diary	Sains	13/07/1916	13/07/1916
War Diary	Angres I	14/07/1916	20/07/1916
War Diary	Fosse 10	21/07/1916	24/07/1916
War Diary	Angres I	25/07/1916	29/07/1916
War Diary	Fosse 10	30/07/1916	31/07/1916
War Diary	Bully	01/08/1916	01/08/1916
War Diary	Angres I	02/08/1916	06/08/1916
War Diary	Bully	06/08/1916	09/08/1916
War Diary	Angres I	10/08/1916	13/08/1916
War Diary	Bully	14/08/1916	16/08/1916
War Diary	Fosse 10	17/08/1916	17/08/1916
War Diary	Angres I	18/08/1916	24/08/1916
War Diary	Fosse 10	25/08/1916	25/08/1916
War Diary	Angres I	26/08/1916	29/08/1916
War Diary	Fosse 10	30/08/1916	31/08/1916
Miscellaneous	Report "A"		
Miscellaneous	Report "B"		
War Diary	Sains En Gohelle Fosse 10	01/09/1916	02/09/1916
War Diary	Angres I	03/09/1916	06/09/1916
War Diary	Bully	07/09/1916	10/09/1916
War Diary	Angres I	11/09/1916	14/09/1916
War Diary	Bully	15/09/1916	19/09/1916
War Diary	Hersin	19/09/1916	19/09/1916
War Diary	Lacomte	20/09/1916	23/09/1916
War Diary	La. Thieuloye	24/09/1916	05/10/1916
War Diary	Mailly Maillet	06/10/1916	08/10/1916
War Diary	Varennes	09/10/1916	17/10/1916
War Diary	The Line	18/10/1916	21/10/1916
War Diary	Englebelmer	22/10/1916	24/10/1916
War Diary	Trenches	25/10/1916	26/10/1916
War Diary	Trenches Near Englebelmer	26/10/1916	26/10/1916
War Diary	Englebelmer	26/10/1916	31/10/1916
Miscellaneous	Narrative of Events	27/10/1916	27/10/1916

Miscellaneous	Report On Raid Carried Out On The Night	26/10/1916	26/10/1916
Operation(al) Order(s)	Operation Order No.3 by Commander W.G. Ramsay Fairfax RN Commanding Howe Bn		
Miscellaneous	Headquarters 63rd (RN) Division	27/10/1916	27/10/1916
Heading	Howe B R N D Vol 6 Novbr 1916		
War Diary	Englebelmer	01/11/1916	04/11/1916
War Diary	Puchevillers	05/11/1916	06/11/1916
War Diary	Hedauville	07/11/1916	10/11/1916
War Diary	Englebelmer	11/11/1916	15/11/1916
War Diary	Puchevillers	16/11/1916	16/11/1916
War Diary	Gezaincourt	17/11/1916	17/11/1916
War Diary	Bernaville	18/11/1916	20/11/1916
War Diary	Cramont	21/11/1916	21/11/1916
War Diary	Marcheville	22/11/1916	24/11/1916
War Diary	Favieres	25/11/1916	30/11/1916
Operation(al) Order(s)	188th. Infantry Brigade Order No.56	09/11/1916	09/11/1916
Miscellaneous	Appendix "A" Notes on Operation Orders	09/11/1916	09/11/1916
Miscellaneous	Appendix "B" Orders for A Company No.2 Field Company Divisional Engineers and 1/2 "C" Company 14th Worcestershire Regiment	09/11/1916	09/11/1916
Miscellaneous	Appendix "C" Orders for 188th Machine Gun Company	09/11/1916	09/11/1916
Miscellaneous	Notes on Tanks		
Miscellaneous	Notes by The Divisional Commander	23/10/1916	23/10/1916
Miscellaneous	1 Number To Report Centre No 1 Guide To Nations		
Miscellaneous	Assembly Move Orders. Order 56	09/11/1916	09/11/1916
Miscellaneous	Memorandum Issued With 188th Infantry Brigade Order No 57	11/11/1916	11/11/1916
Miscellaneous	Appendix "D" Orders for 188th Light Trench Mortar Battery	11/11/1916	11/11/1916
Miscellaneous	Appendix "D" (Contd.)	10/11/1916	10/11/1916
Miscellaneous	Amended Time Table Of 63rd (RN) Division Attack	10/11/1916	10/11/1916
Miscellaneous	Supplementary		
Miscellaneous	With Reference To Barrage Table Issued With Operation Order No.44	04/11/1916	04/11/1916
Operation(al) Order(s)	Operation Orders No. 19		
Miscellaneous	Howe Battalion Time Table		
Miscellaneous	Pack Transport		
Miscellaneous	Pack Transport Table Shewing Distribution of Echelon "B"		
Miscellaneous	The Following Amendments To Operation Order No.19		
Miscellaneous	Ration On 'Z' Day		
Miscellaneous	Operation Order S.0.0.1/4		
Miscellaneous	188th Inf. Brigade No.G.2/60	29/10/1916	29/10/1916
Miscellaneous	Signal Officer Supplementary O.O. 1/3		
Miscellaneous	Supplementary Operation S.O.O.1/2		
Map	Map		
Miscellaneous		11/10/1916	11/10/1916
Operation(al) Order(s)	188th Infantry Brigade Order No.57	11/11/1916	11/11/1916
Miscellaneous			
War Diary	Favieres	01/12/1916	09/12/1916
War Diary	Vercourt	12/12/1916	12/01/1917
War Diary	Nouvion	13/01/1917	13/01/1917
War Diary	Marcheville	14/01/1917	14/01/1917
War Diary	Le Meillard	15/01/1917	16/01/1917
War Diary	Raincheval	17/01/1917	17/01/1917

War Diary	Englebelmer	18/01/1917	18/01/1917
War Diary	Trenches	19/01/1917	25/01/1917
War Diary	Englebelmer	26/01/1917	31/01/1917
War Diary	Trenches	31/01/1917	08/02/1917
War Diary	Thiepval	09/02/1917	09/02/1917
War Diary	Forceville	10/02/1917	12/02/1917
War Diary	Englebelmer	13/02/1917	14/02/1917
War Diary	Trenches	14/02/1917	18/02/1917
War Diary	Trenche	18/02/1917	21/02/1917
War Diary	Hedauville	22/02/1917	28/02/1917
Map	Trench Map		
Heading	Sheet Feb 17th 1917 Vol 9		
Miscellaneous	Appendix "A" Action by 188th and 190th. Machine Gun Companies	15/02/1917	15/02/1917
Miscellaneous	Memorandum	16/02/1917	16/02/1917
Miscellaneous	Ration Supply	16/02/1917	16/02/1917
Miscellaneous	Appendix "B" Action by 189th Light Trench Mortar Battery	15/02/1917	15/02/1917
Miscellaneous	Ration Supply	16/02/1917	16/02/1917
Miscellaneous	Amendment B.O.82/1	15/02/1917	15/02/1917
Miscellaneous	Appendix "C" R.A. Barrage	15/02/1917	15/02/1917
Miscellaneous	Artillery Time Table B.O.82		
Operation(al) Order(s)	188th. Infantry Brigade Order No.82	15/02/1917	15/02/1917
Miscellaneous	Amendment To Paras 17 And 18		
Miscellaneous	Amendment To Para 16 (b)		
Miscellaneous	Appendix "D"	15/02/1917	15/02/1917
Miscellaneous	Amendment B.O.82/2	15/02/1917	15/02/1917
Miscellaneous	Amendment B.O.82/5	16/02/1917	16/02/1917
Miscellaneous	B.O.82/3	16/02/1917	16/02/1917
Miscellaneous	Amendment B.O.82/4	16/02/1917	16/02/1917
Miscellaneous	C Form Messages And Signals	15/02/1917	15/02/1917
War Diary	Hedauville	01/03/1917	18/03/1917
War Diary	Rubempre	19/03/1917	19/03/1917
War Diary	Gezaincourt	20/03/1917	20/03/1917
War Diary	Ligny	21/03/1917	21/03/1917
War Diary	Hernicourt	22/03/1917	23/03/1917
War Diary	Bailleul-Lepernes	24/03/1917	24/03/1917
War Diary	Les Presses	25/03/1917	25/03/1917
War Diary	Le Cornet Halo	26/03/1917	26/03/1917
War Diary	Noeux Les Mines	27/03/1917	14/04/1917
War Diary	Ecoivres	17/04/1917	21/04/1917
War Diary	Maroeuil	21/04/1917	21/04/1917
War Diary	In The Line	22/04/1917	23/04/1917
War Diary	Gavrelle	23/04/1917	26/04/1917
War Diary	Point Du Jour	27/04/1917	27/04/1917
War Diary	Near Gavrelle	28/04/1917	30/04/1917
War Diary	Caucourt	01/05/1917	07/05/1917
War Diary	Mont-St-Eloy	08/05/1917	09/05/1917
War Diary	Roclincourt	10/05/1917	19/05/1917
War Diary	Gavrelle	19/05/1917	10/06/1917
War Diary	Bray	10/06/1917	12/06/1917
War Diary	St Aubin	13/06/1917	15/06/1917
War Diary	Maroeuil	16/06/1917	20/06/1917
War Diary	Roclincourt	22/06/1917	30/06/1917
War Diary	Bray	01/07/1917	01/07/1917
War Diary	St. Cathrine	02/07/1917	02/07/1917

War Diary	Gavrelle	03/07/1917	08/07/1917
War Diary	Reserve	11/07/1917	17/07/1917
War Diary	Gavrelle	18/07/1917	20/07/1917
War Diary	Support	20/07/1917	26/07/1917
War Diary	Gayrelle	26/07/1917	31/07/1917
War Diary	St. Aubin	31/07/1917	31/07/1917
Miscellaneous	H.Q. 188th Brigade	20/07/1917	20/07/1917
Diagram etc	Diagram		
War Diary	St. Aubin	01/08/1917	01/08/1917
War Diary	Maison Blanche	08/08/1917	08/08/1917
War Diary	Reserve	11/08/1917	11/08/1917
War Diary	Gayrelle	11/08/1917	15/08/1917
War Diary	Support	15/08/1917	15/08/1917
War Diary	Gavrelle	19/08/1917	25/08/1917
War Diary	St. Aubin	25/08/1917	02/09/1917
War Diary	Reserve	03/09/1917	06/09/1917
War Diary	Support	09/09/1917	09/09/1917
War Diary	Gavrelle	09/09/1917	17/09/1917
War Diary	Roclincourt	18/09/1917	30/09/1917
War Diary	Monchy Le Buton	01/10/1917	03/10/1917
War Diary	Dirty Bucket Camp	03/10/1917	05/10/1917
War Diary	Herzeele	06/10/1917	23/10/1917
War Diary	Reigersburg	24/10/1917	24/10/1917
War Diary	Irish Farm	25/10/1917	28/10/1917
War Diary	Dambre Camp	29/10/1917	31/10/1917
Miscellaneous	Operation Orders By Commander C.S. West D.S.O. R.N.V.R	23/10/1917	23/10/1917
Miscellaneous	Ref Operation Order		
War Diary	Dambre Camp	01/11/1917	04/11/1917
War Diary	Line	05/11/1917	08/11/1917
War Diary	School Camp	08/11/1917	11/11/1917
War Diary	Winnezeele	12/11/1917	12/11/1917
War Diary	Rubrouck	13/11/1917	21/11/1917
War Diary	Reigersburg	22/11/1917	05/12/1917
War Diary	School Camp	06/12/1917	09/12/1917
War Diary	Braulencourt	10/12/1917	13/12/1917
War Diary	Rocquigny	14/12/1917	14/12/1917
War Diary	Etricourt	15/12/1917	15/12/1917
War Diary	Lechelle	16/12/1917	21/12/1917
War Diary	Villiers Puich	22/12/1917	31/12/1917
Miscellaneous	Amendment To 188th Inf. Brigade Order No. 158	05/12/1917	05/12/1917
Miscellaneous	Reference Attached Warning Order	05/12/1917	05/12/1917
Miscellaneous	Warning Order	05/12/1917	05/12/1917
Operation(al) Order(s)	186th Infantry Brigade Order No.158	05/12/1917	05/12/1917
Miscellaneous	Amendment No.2 To 188th Infantry Brigade Order No.159	08/12/1917	08/12/1917
Miscellaneous	Amendment No.1 To 188th Infantry Brigade Order No. 159	07/12/1917	07/12/1917
Map	Plan To Accompany		
Miscellaneous	A Form Messages And Signals		
Miscellaneous	Amended Time Table To Accompany 188th Brigade Order 159		
Miscellaneous	63rd (R.N.) Division Administrative Instructions No.6 With Reference To 63rd Divn. Order No.185	05/12/1917	05/12/1917
Miscellaneous	Table "A" Issued With 63rd (R.N.) Division Administrative Instructions No.6		

Operation(al) Order(s)	188th Infantry Brigade Order No.159	06/12/1917	06/12/1917
Miscellaneous	Time Table To Accompany Brigade Order No.159		
Miscellaneous	Lorries	06/12/1917	06/12/1917
Miscellaneous	Rations	08/12/1917	08/12/1917
Operation(al) Order(s)	188th Infantry Brigade Order No.160	13/12/1917	13/12/1917
Operation(al) Order(s)	188th Infantry Brigade Order No.161	14/12/1917	14/12/1917
Miscellaneous	Warning Order	15/12/1917	15/12/1917
Operation(al) Order(s)	188th Infantry Brigade Order No.163	15/12/1917	15/12/1917
Miscellaneous	Amendment No.1 To 188th Inf. Bde Order No.164	17/12/1917	17/12/1917
Operation(al) Order(s)	188th Infantry Brigade Order No.164	16/12/1917	16/12/1917
Miscellaneous	Warning Order	19/12/1916	19/12/1916
Operation(al) Order(s)	188th Infantry Brigade Order No.165	20/12/1917	20/12/1917
Miscellaneous	Table To Accompany 188th Infantry Brigade Order No.165		
Miscellaneous	Reference 188th Inf. Bde Order No 165	21/12/1917	21/12/1917
Miscellaneous	Move Orders by Commander C.S. West D.S.O., R.N.V.R. in the Field	21/12/1917	21/12/1917
Operation(al) Order(s)	188th Infantry Brigade Order No.166	24/12/1917	24/12/1917
Miscellaneous	Relief Orders by Commander C.S. West D.S.O. R.N.V.R.	25/12/1917	25/12/1917
Operation(al) Order(s)	188th Infantry Brigade Order No.167	29/12/1917	29/12/1917
Miscellaneous	Move Orders by Lieut J. Coote" R.N.V.R.	31/12/1917	31/12/1917
War Diary	Metz	01/01/1918	04/01/1918
War Diary	Villers Pluich	04/01/1918	16/01/1918
War Diary	Metz	17/01/1918	20/01/1918
War Diary	Villers Pluich	21/01/1918	22/01/1918
War Diary	Metz	23/01/1918	24/01/1918
War Diary	Rocquigny	25/01/1918	13/02/1918
War Diary	Lechelle	14/02/1918	22/02/1918
War Diary	Ruyualcourt	22/02/1918	28/02/1918
Miscellaneous	Howe Battn		

63RD DIVISION
188TH INFY BDE

HOWE BN R.N.DIVN
MAY 1916-FEB 1918

DISBANDED

Feb 18 63 Army Form

Instructions regarding War Diaries and Intelligence Summaries are contained in F. S. Regs., Part II. and the Staff Manual respectively. Title pages will be prepared in manuscript.

WAR DIARY
or
~~INTELLIGENCE SUMMARY.~~
(Erase heading not required.)

May 1916 HOWE Bn RND. Vol

Place	Date	Hour	Summary of Events and Information	Remarks and references to Appendices
MUDROS	1st		1st to 6th. Ordinary routine, bathed Bn and got musketry course through except D Coy. at 100, 200 and 400 yards under Lieut DEWHURST.	
	7th		Bye Election held to fill vacancy in Greek Chamber of Deputies. M. VENIZELOS candidate in constituency of LEMNOS and MITYLENE.	
		3 pm.	Received order to hold Bn in readiness for immediate embarkation.	
		6 pm.	Bn moved off, less A Coy. Embarked less transport animals and vehicles on H.M.T. BRITON. (Union Castle Line). 2/RM Bn complete also on board.	
	8th		Sailed very early	
	12th		Arrived MARSEILLES daybreak. Landed 1 pm. Baggage stowed in hangars on quay, one platoon B Coy left on board for guards etc: Rest marched to LA VALENTINE camp. Carried full gear, 1 blanket waterproof sheet. Men soft after voyage, many fell out. Distance said to be 11 miles. Quartered in tents in Remount camp chiefly tenanted by Indians	
	13th		Camp routine. moved camp 50 yards + repitched tents. Leave till 9 pm to 10% of Bn.	

T2134. Wt. W708—776. 500000. 4/15. Sir J. C. & S.

Instructions regarding War Diaries and Intelligence Summaries are contained in F. S. Regs., Part II. and the Staff Manual respectively. Title pages will be prepared in manuscript.

WAR DIARY
or
INTELLIGENCE SUMMARY.
(Erase heading not required.)

Army Form C. 2118.

May 1916 — HOWE Bn

Place	Date	Hour	Summary of Events and Information	Remarks and references to Appendices
MARSEILLES	14		Got order stand by to entrain. Leave cancelled. About 2 pm got order not to entrain till 15th. Many men broke camp with no pass, 51 absent at 11 p.m.	
	15th		Fell in 7 a.m. Seven men still absent and two more absented themselves from a working party clearing up lines. By tram to centre of town, marched to GUIBAL station. Entrained 12 noon. Less 9 absentees and 4 men left as guard on baggage who were also required as witnesses. The platoon of B Coy that had been left as guard on ship had later been quartered at FOURNIER camp and also entrained with Bn. Train left 1.30 p.m. HALTS made for food at ORANGE.	
	16th		Halts at MACON. LESLAUMES and MONTEREAU.	
	17th		Halt at EPLUCHES about 7 am. reached PONT REMY about 2 pm. Marched to HUPPY arriving about 8 p.m. Billetting party consisting of Sub Lieut GILSON had been sent ahead on 12th. March was about 7 miles, no one fell out.	

[illegible signature]
Comdg. [illegible]

T2134. Wt. W708—776. 500000. 4/15. Sir J. C. & S.

Instructions regarding War Diaries and Intelligence Summaries are contained in F. S. Regs., Part II. and the Staff Manual respectively. Title pages will be prepared in manuscript.

WAR DIARY
or
~~INTELLIGENCE SUMMARY.~~
(*Erase heading not required.*)

Army Form C. 2118.

May 1916 HOWE Bn

Place	Date	Hour	Summary of Events and Information	Remarks and references to Appendices
HUPPY	17th		Lieut Comdr C.S. WEST RNVR rejoined from English leave (left Bn 28.2.16) and assumed Command. Lieut H.E. FUNNELL also rejoined and took command M.G. Section.	
"	18th		Dealt with MARSEILLES defaulters.	
	20th		Drew new H.V. MK III rifles and S.A.A. Officers and P.O.'s visited 4th Army School of Instruction at FLEXICOURT to see demonstration on last day of course.	
	21st	to 26th	Routine training. Constructed two ranges and D Coy fired one day. Returned Heavy Maxim Guns to Ordnance.	
	27th		Sergt Presland RMLI took on duty Bn S.M. Major A H French DSO RMLI took command of Bn. Billetting party of 4 Officers and 4 men sent ahead to arrange billets at HOUDAIN.	
	28th		Marched PONT REMY. Entrained complete Bn, transport + horses, by 1.30 p.m. arrived BARLIN about 9 p.m. Troops taken to HOUDAIN in motor lorries, 25 men per lorry. Transport followed.	
HOUDAIN	29th		Detailed for school Courses at IV Corps School at PERNES, officers	[illegible] Ward Major Comdg Howe

T2134. Wt. W768–776. 500000. 4/15. Sir J. C. & S.

Instructions regarding War Diaries and Intelligence Summaries are contained in F. S. Regs., Part II. and the Staff Manual respectively. Title pages will be prepared in manuscript.

WAR DIARY
or
INTELLIGENCE SUMMARY.
(Erase heading not required.)

Army Form C. 2118.

HOWE Bn R.N.D.

Place	Date	Hour	Summary of Events and Information — May 1916	Remarks and references to Appendices
HOUDAIN	29th		and men for Courses in Trench Warfare (14 Days) Light Trench Mortars, Lewis Guns, in all 11 officers and 56 OR.	
	30th 31st		Carried on training, got out standing orders.	A Lambert Ward Major Comdg. Howe

T2134. Wt. W708—776. 500000. 4/15. Sir J. C. & S.

Instructions regarding War Diaries and Intelligence Summaries are contained in F. S. Regs., Part II. and the Staff Manual respectively. Title pages will be prepared in manuscript.

WAR DIARY
or
INTELLIGENCE SUMMARY.
(Erase heading not required.)

June 1916 HOWE Bn 63rd JUNE Vol

Army Form C. 2118.

Place	Date	Hour	Summary of Events and Information	Remarks and references to Appendices
HOUDAIN	1st		1st & 2nd Bn was at Musketry on a 30 yds range. Did grouping 5 rounds + application 5 rds.	
	3rd	pm	Inspection by Sir C. Munro & Sir H. Wilson, commanding 1st Army & IV Corps respectively	
	4th		Completed musketry. Sent classes to IV Corps School at PERNES as follows:- i Physical Training and Bayonet Fighting ii Light Trench Mortars iii Lewis Guns and to 47th Div bomb School another class. Following Officers were detailed i Sub Lieuts Connell and Gilson ii Lieut Mackinlay Sub Lieuts Walker and Lieut de la Mothe iii Lieut Comdrs Edwards and Edgar iv Sub Lieuts Fry, Stokes, Meadmore and WAGNER.	
	5th		Bn moved to BOIS DE LA HAIE by route march. Moved 5.30 pm. 1 platoon A Coy as advance guard had erected 4 tents per Coy Bn in by 9 pm (first platoon). Tents up for all by 11 pm	
BOIS de la HAIE	6th	4 am	All tents down for painting. Done by 9 am. Wood being within range of enemy guns, orders were issued forbidding unauthorized fires & cutting of trees or walking outside wood. Whole Bn out digging at [illegible]	

T2134. Wt. W708—776. 500000. 4/15. Sir J. C. & S.

Army Form C. 2118.

Instructions regarding War Diaries and Intelligence Summaries are contained in F. S. Regs., Part II. and the Staff Manual respectively. Title pages will be prepared in manuscript.

WAR DIARY
or
INTELLIGENCE SUMMARY.
(*Erase heading not required.*)

Howe Bn R.N.D.

Place	Date	Hour	Summary of Events and Information	Remarks and references to Appendices
	June		June 1916	
BOIS de la HAIE	6-7		7.30 p.m till 2.30 or 3 a.m. C & D Coys S of CARENCY and A + B North of same village. Work on communication & rearward defence trenches, D coy improving old French & enemy trenches, this being ground fought over when French pushed enemy off LORETTE spur.	
	7th		Detailed carpenter parties to help in dugout construction. Night work as before. B coy moved to a wood S.W of VILLERS AU BOIS at 2 p.m to work in constant reliefs under 2nd Field Coy RNDE (Capt MARSHALL)	
	8th		Rain same work.	
	9th		Rain same work	
	10th		Rain no work, everyone being already wet through.	
	11th		Worked as usual but very wet. Sent to 47th (Divn) Gas school 1 officer Sub Lt Gray & two L.S and to 1st Army Anti gas School at AIRE 1 CPO and 2 P.O.	
	12th		A and D Coys left for HERSIN where they occupied billets [illegible]	[illegible] Major Comdg Howe

T2134. Wt. W708—776. 500000. 4/15. Sir J. C. & S.

Instructions regarding War Diaries and Intelligence Summaries are contained in F. S. Regs., Part II. and the Staff Manual respectively. Title pages will be prepared in manuscript.

WAR DIARY
or
~~INTELLIGENCE SUMMARY.~~
(Erase heading not required.)

Army Form C. 2118.

June 1916 — Howe Bn

Place	Date	Hour	Summary of Events and Information	Remarks and references to Appendices
			by 1st R.M. Bn who came down direct from trenches to the wood and took over our tents. Their first Coy arrived about 11 pm & 2nd went astray and got to CHATEAU DE LA HAIE about 2 am.	
			Howe B & C Coys dug as usual. Very wet and rained most of the time.	
	13		B & C Coys and Hqrs moved to billets at HERSIN. moved 1030 am. Transport 1½ hrs late.	
			A & D Coys got bathed	
HERSIN	14		A & D Coys went up to trenches. First platoon left 8.30 pm. Rest followed 10 minutes interval. Met guides at 140th Bde Hqrs at AIX NOULETTE at ~~of~~ 9.30 pm. Companies were attached by platoons to different Coys of 140th Bde. A Coy to 6th London Regt D Coy to 15th London Regt, Colonels MILDREN and WARRENDER.	
			D Coy was near SOLFERINO sap and A Coy to the right.	
	15th	1030	C.O. & Adjt visited A & D Coys B Coy bathed.	
			Time advanced 1 hour at 11 pm. which became midnight.	
			Learnt that A and D Coys going into trenches made a noise and so drew fire, but with no casualties.	[illegible]

T2134. Wt. W708–776. 500000. 4/15. Sir J. C. & S.

Instructions regarding War Diaries and Intelligence Summaries are contained in F. S. Regs., Part II. and the Staff Manual respectively. Title pages will be prepared in manuscript.

WAR DIARY
or
~~INTELLIGENCE SUMMARY.~~
(Erase heading not required.)

HOWE Bn RND

Army Form C. 2118.

Place	Date	Hour	June 1916 — Summary of Events and Information	Remarks and references to Appendices
HERSIN	June 16	5pm	Leave party of 3 men away. Gas parties returned. men returned yesterday from MARSEILLES, including 5 who have been sentenced to terms of I.H.L. by F.G.C.M. at MARSEILLES on 29.5.16. Lieut E.R. ASTON rejoined from Leave. Gas Alert on.	
		7.10pm	Received orders to send 250 men and 2 officers out on digging party. Not possible comply less than 1 hour late. Party was engaged on digging sap 160 yards long out from front line held by 18th London Regt ((London Irish). One man slightly wounded in arm. First casualty of Bn in France [M2ll AB KELLY G.H.] Party back 5 am 17th.	
HERSIN	17th		B and C Companies went up to trenches to relieve A + D. First platoon left 9.5 pm. rest at 10 minute intervals. A lot of aeroplanes about in the evening, all ours. About 8. Wind from North ~~by~~ but Gas Alert on.	
	18th 19th		Carrying parties required at night	
	20th		B + C Coys came down, arriving about midnight. No casualties but had a warm time with plenty of	

R. Lambert Ward
Major
Commdg Howe

Instructions regarding War Diaries and Intelligence Summaries are contained in F. S. Regs., Part II. and the Staff Manual respectively. Title pages will be prepared in manuscript.

WAR DIARY
or
~~INTELLIGENCE SUMMARY.~~
(Erase heading not required.)

Army Form C. 2118.

June 1916 — HOWE Bn RND.

Place	Date	Hour	Summary of Events and Information	Remarks and references to Appendices
HERSIN	20th		Minenwerfer bombs blowing trench in.	
	21st		Carrying parties at night, 390 men. These and previous parties were carrying gas cylinders which were later used with good result.	
	22nd		No fatigues	
	23rd		Went to trenches in evening, Souchez 2 Sub sector, Relieved 2nd R.M. Bn. Relief complete at 4 am 24th. Left 8 men behind to go through a P.T.I. course at PERNES. only 4 went.	copy of march orders
Trenches	24th		B Coy in reserve in a wood. A on right, C in centre, D on left. on our left were 7th London, later relieved by 21st	
			Dugout parties worked from 9 am in continuous shifts on deep dugouts under R.E.	
	25th		The following were detailed as part of the staff of 2nd Bde bomb School, Sub Lieut W.C. HAKEN. 2/19 M. P.O. HA CASSIDY KW456 P.O. P. WEST. Two casualties. TZ105 L.S. J. GIBSON who died of wounds and AB D. LEWIS. At about 1045 pm the	

T2134. Wt. W768–776. 500000. 4/15. Sir J. C. & S.

Army Form C. 2118.

Instructions regarding War Diaries and Intelligence Summaries are contained in F. S. Regs., Part II. and the Staff Manual respectively. Title pages will be prepared in manuscript.

WAR DIARY
or
~~INTELLIGENCE SUMMARY.~~
(Erase heading not required.)

June 1916 HOWE Bn

Place	Date	Hour	Summary of Events and Information	Remarks and references to Appendices
Trenches	25th		ration party from B Coy got shelled, 4 men being hit, of whom P.O. J.H.R SMITH later died.	
	26th		Relieved at night by HAWKE Bn. Lewis gunners and bombers relieved early. Bulk of Bn relief began 11.30 p.m. and Finished 3.30	
	27th		am. Again the presence of only one backward Communication trench was painfully evident and an ingoing company met an outgoing one in the narrowest bit of trench. Half the outgoing lot went over the open.	
			The work done while in the trenches was severely limited by two things, first the weather which was so bad that at all times there was a foot and a half of water in the Communication trench in places and plenty elsewhere as well, secondly our medium T.Ms were cutting wire and it was necessary to clear parts of the trenches at these times to avoid casualties caused by Bosch retaliation. It was our duty to prevent repair of the gaps. The said retaliation blew in certain trenches which had to be repaired, notably KELLET	

T2134. Wt. W708—776. 500000. 4/15. Sir J. C. & S.

Army Form C. 2118.

Instructions regarding War Diaries and Intelligence Summaries are contained in F. S. Regs., Part II. and the Staff Manual respectively. Title pages will be prepared in manuscript.

WAR DIARY
or
~~INTELLIGENCE SUMMARY.~~
(Erase heading not required.)

Place	Date	Hour	Summary of Events and Information — June 1916 — Howe Bn	Remarks and references to Appendices
Trenches	26th		LINE and SOLFERINO SAP.	
COUPIGNY	27th		Last of Bn got back to billets at HERSIN-COUPIGNY at about 5 a.m. In afternoon a lecture by Major CAMPBELL on P.T.I. and B.F. Had to detail two parties to relieve working parties of NELSON Bn. 1 officer and 50 to go to AIX NOULETTE and 1 officer and 75 men to go to MARQUEFFLES FARM.	
	28th		Marched to CAMBLAIN CHATELAIN to very comfortable billets. Told off more parties for instruction courses. Trench Warfare 1 off + 3 men P.T.I. 2 off and 8 men Lewis Gun, 2 officers and 6 men. 1st + 3rd at Pernes on ~~2nd~~ 1st July, 2nd at AUXI LE CHATEAU on 2nd July.	
CAMBLAIN	29		Training. 1 officer and 16 O.R. sent to 2nd Bde Bomb School at OURTON on 2nd July.	
CHATELAIN	30			

A. Lambert Ward
Comdg Howe

T2134. Wt. W708–776. 500000. 4/15. Sir J. C. & S.

10 SECRET.

[illegible]

1. [illegible] Battalion [illegible]
[illegible]

2. Parade [illegible]
"A" Coy [illegible]
"B" Coy [illegible]
"D" [illegible]
"C" [illegible]

3. [illegible]
[illegible]

4. Route. [illegible]
at R 5 D [illegible]
[illegible] -EN- GOHELLE - R 3 C 10
[illegible] IX - NOULETTE [illegible]
[illegible]

5. Intervals for March.
Companies will pass [illegible] intervals
with [illegible]
[illegible]
[illegible] -EN- GOHELLE [illegible]
[illegible]

File

11 SECRET. War diary

Secret Orders [illegible]

1. The above Battalion will [illegible] the trenches tonight.
2. Parade as follows.
   "A" Coy [illegible] 8.10 p.m.
   "B" "C" Coy [illegible] 8.20
   "D" Coy [illegible] 8.30
   "B" Coy will take [illegible]
3. Dress Marching Order.
   [illegible]
   [illegible]
   Smoke Helmets [illegible]
   [illegible]
4. Route. "A" "C" and "D" Coys will [illegible] at R.10.B.2.1 [illegible]
   "B" Coy [illegible] BAINS-EN-GOHELLE [illegible]
   to AIX-NOULETTE [illegible]
   [illegible]
   [illegible]
5. Intervals on March.
   Companies will march at [illegible] with 50 yds between [illegible]
   [illegible]
   to BAINS-EN-GOHELLE [illegible]
6. [illegible]

7. The following will proceed in advance & [illegible] at [illegible] there at times stated.

Battalion Sgt. Major — C.S.Ms. [illegible] & [illegible] and Signallers at [illegible] p.m. [illegible]

Bombers [illegible] at [illegible] p.m. [illegible]

Lewis Gun Personnel with Guns [illegible] at [illegible] 15 [illegible]

The Lewis Guns will proceed [illegible] as far as AIX NOULETTE. Thence by hand.

8. Os C Coys. will report Relief Completed [illegible] to H.Q. O.C. B Coy. will report on telephone direct to [illegible] [illegible]. The Code words will be given personally to O.C. "B" Coy.

9. Patrols. The Patrols from "A" & "B" [illegible] referred to in para 7 will proceed at time stated [illegible] [illegible] with their [illegible] routes etc. [illegible] and be ready to relieve [illegible] Patrols punctually at time to be arranged [illegible] [illegible].

10. The Dug-out Parties of each Coy. will be [illegible] [illegible] on that work. B Coy. party [illegible] with [illegible] be attached for rations to "C" Coy. They will report to O.C. "C" Coy. on parade.

11. Each Coy. will take [illegible] stretchers.

12. The Telephone from [illegible] Coy. [illegible] will only be used by an Officer and only in emergency. Each Coy. [illegible] will keep 2 Runners ready to carry messages.

13. "B" Coy. will carry [illegible] to the [illegible] tonight. The [illegible] will arrive at FRENCH DUMP [illegible] at [illegible].

14. Rations for 25th inst. will be carried in the [illegible]. Os C Coys. to arrange with Q.M. for [illegible] 24/25. [illegible] 25/26 Rations will be brought [illegible] FRENCH Dump [illegible] 11 p.m. [illegible] will [illegible] Trenches in Sectional Sandbags [illegible].

15. Water in [illegible] [illegible] Companies [illegible] from [illegible] at FRENCH Dump.

[illegible]

War Diary.

Instructions regarding War Diaries and Intelligence Summaries are contained in F. S. Regs., Part II. and the Staff Manual respectively. Title pages will be prepared in manuscript.

WAR DIARY
or
~~INTELLIGENCE SUMMARY.~~
(Erase heading not required.)

JULY

63 Feb Vol 2 HOWE Bn.

Army Form C. 2118.

Place	Date	Hour	Summary of Events and Information	Remarks and references to Appendices
CAMBLAIN CHATELAIN	1st		to 2nd Training. Made a 30 yards range.	
HERMIN	3rd		Bn is transferred to 3rd Bde and marches to HERMIN Court Martial occupies most of the day.	
	4th		Choosing training grounds. Class for T. M. instruction.	
	5th 6th		Preparing training ground. making ranges. digging bombing trenches, setting up P.T.I. gear.	
	7th		Brigadier and Bde Staff go to the new Bde. Col E.J. Stroude RMLI takes over 3rd Bde in which besides ourselves are ANSON and 1st and 2nd R M Battalions.	
	8th to 10th		Preparing training grounds. making range, dug bombing trenches, and erected bayonet fighting gallows etc. As about finished received move orders, 1st Inf Bde RND is to relieve 142 Bde in ANGRES sector of line	
	12th		Bathed Bn at FRESNICOURT	
	13th		Moved to billets at Fosse 10, SAINS EN GOHELLE. R9a. where	A. Lambert Ward Major Comdg Howe

T2134. Wt. W708—776. 500000. 4/15. Sir J. C. & S.

Instructions regarding War Diaries and Intelligence Summaries are contained in F. S. Regs., Part II. and the Staff Manual respectively. Title pages will be prepared in manuscript.

WAR DIARY
or
~~INTELLIGENCE SUMMARY.~~
(Erase heading not required.)

Army Form C. 2118.

July — HOWE BN.

Place	Date	Hour	Summary of Events and Information	Remarks and references to Appendices
SAINS	~~#~~13th		we relieved 7th London. Arrived 2.45 pm.	
ANGRES I	14th		Proceeded to trenches in ANGRES I Sub sector, relieving 23rd London who took over our billets. 23 officers only went up the line. First platoon left at 1.15 pm. last at 2.12 pm, via BULLY GRENAY and CORONS D'AIX trench. Sent rations up at night. 1st R.M on our left in trenches. Dugout platoons which had been detached since June 29 and had been at BULLY attached to RNDE, rejoined Bn on 13th at 11 pm and went up to trenches today. Between 6 & 7 pm. our T.M's fired on enemy wire — Retaliation slight — Corons D'Aix Trench blown in at one or two places. Machine & Lewis Guns played on wire gaps during night. Large bodies of men employed clearing sand-bags from Tunnelling Coy — also repairing CORONS D'AIX Trench.	
	15th		No signs this morning of enemy having been able to repair his wire. At 1.30 pm. enemy hoisted a RED & WHITE flag at M26 c 16 — probably	[illegible] Ward Major Comdg Howe

T2134. Wt. W708—776. 500000. 4/15. Sir J. C. & S.

Instructions regarding War Diaries and Intelligence Summaries are contained in F. S. Regs., Part II. and the Staff Manual respectively. Title pages will be prepared in manuscript.

WAR DIARY
or
~~INTELLIGENCE SUMMARY.~~
(Erase heading not required.)

Army Form C. 2118.

JULY — HOWE BATT.

Place	Date	Hour	Summary of Events and Information	Remarks and references to Appendices
ANGRES I	15		artillery mark. Machine gun emplacement blown in by T.M. — dug out & repaired. New Trench boards laid in SPINNEY ALLEY. Patrol reported at 11.30 p.m. enemy working party opposite SAP 15. Lewis Guns fired — result not known. Situation quiet.	
	16th		New enemy field gun in action to-day — thought to be result of flag hoisted yesterday. Machine & Lewis Guns fired, as usual, during the night on enemy wire gaps. New Trench boards laid in MORROW. Sandbags cleared from Tunnelling Coy.	
	17th		Our wire strengthened & repaired last night. — 40 new trench boards laid in firing line. — CORONS D'AIX at junction of firing line deepened. 30 [illegible]. At 1.30 am a raid was made from SOUCHEZ II we lit smoke bombs & drew enemy attention to our sub. sector. Artillery barraged enemy. Result of raid not known. The Divisional & Brigade commanders visited the subsector this morning. They inspected nearly all of the front line, SPINNEY Trench & CORONS D'AIX Trench. The Divisional Commander commented most favourably on the generally cleanly condition of trenches, and [illegible] particularly	[illegible]

T2134. Wt. W708—776. 500000. 4/15. Sir J. C. & S.

Instructions regarding War Diaries and Intelligence Summaries are contained in F. S. Regs., Part II. and the Staff Manual respectively. Title pages will be prepared in manuscript.

WAR DIARY
or
~~INTELLIGENCE SUMMARY.~~
(~~Erase heading not required.~~)

Army Form C. 2118.

JULY — HOWE BATT

Place	Date	Hour	Summary of Events and Information	Remarks and references to Appendices
ANGRES I	17		Pleased with the way in which B & D Coys worked last night to repair the damage to the line. Situation somewhat unsettled during night.	
	18th		B & D Coys were relieved by A & C Coys. Patrols & work carried out as usual. Situation quiet.	
	19th		Lewis Guns relieved by Lewis Guns of ANSON Batt. Patrols & work carried on as usual last night. Situation quiet.	
	20th		Battalion relieved by ANSON Batt. Relief complete by NOON. Two companys moved into Reserve at BULLY & two companies to FOSSE 10. Men bathed.	(A & C)
FOSSE 10	21st		Fatigue parties supplied by Coys in BULLY. Companys at FOSSE 10 carried on Company training.	
	22nd		Major A.H. French D.S.O. R.M.L.I. relinquished command of the Battalion on appointment to Army Signals. Major L. Ward D.S.O. HAC assumed command. Companies at BULLY carried on fatigues. Companies at FOSSE 10 Company drill.	
	23rd		Church Parade at 10 a.m. Companies at FOSSE 10 took over fatigues. Commenced to carry up gas.	
	24th		Lewis Guns relieved ANSON Lewis Guns in ANGRES I — complete by 2 p.m.	

L. Ward Major
Comdg Howe

T2134. Wt. W708—776. 500000. 4/15. Sir J. C. & S.

Instructions regarding War Diaries and Intelligence Summaries are contained in F. S. Regs., Part II. and the Staff Manual respectively. Title pages will be prepared in manuscript.

WAR DIARY
or
~~INTELLIGENCE SUMMARY.~~
(*Erase heading not required.*)

Army Form C. 2118.

JULY — HOWE BATT

Place	Date	Hour	Summary of Events and Information	Remarks and references to Appendices
ANGRES I	25th		The Battalion relieved ANSON Batt. in ANGRES I. Relief complete by 11.30am. The H.T.M's carried on ~~intermittent~~ firing from 3pm. to 7pm. From 3pm to 6pm enemy searched for T.M's with shrapnel & T.M's. — Result — Trenches blown in in several places. Between 7.30pm & 8pm. enemy placed 8 - 5.9" round Batt. H.Q. — no apparent damage.	
	26th		Patrols report enemy wire apparently intact. No enemy working party or patrol seen or heard last night. Circulate Trench improved. Snipers barricade built at Bay 13. Lovers Lane improved & firing position & bombing post made there. Bombing post made at junction of PYRENEES & LINK. Trench boards & drains repaired in several places. Bays cleared from mines. A considerable amount of re-wiring was done during night	
	27th		M.T.M's fired from 3pm to 7pm. No retaliation. Wire examined & repaired at Solferino last night. Trench boards were taken up & drains ~~repaired~~ attended along nearly whole front. In places new boards were put down. Sandbags [illegible] from mines & used to build up in various parts of the line. Dug-out Platoons detached from battalion & attached to R.E's.	A Ramsay [illegible] Comdg. Howe

T2134. Wt. W708—776. 500000. 4/15. Sir J. C. & S.

Instructions regarding War Diaries and Intelligence Summaries are contained in F. S. Regs., Part II. and the Staff Manual respectively. Title pages will be prepared in manuscript.

WAR DIARY
or
~~INTELLIGENCE SUMMARY.~~
(*Erase heading not required.*)

Army Form C. 2118.

JULY — HOWE BATT

Place	Date	Hour	Summary of Events and Information	Remarks and references to Appendices
ANGRES I	28th		Our H&L artillery fired at 1.30 a.m. 2 am & 2.30 a.m. Observation was difficult. Wire was inspected along length of whole front. Several new sniper's posts were built & put into use, excellent results were obtained from them.	
	29th		The battalion was relieved by the ANSON & moved into RESERVE — two companies at BULLY & two at FOSSE 10. The junction of CORON D'AIX & FOREST was heavily shelled during the relief — resulting in CORON D'AIX being blown in and 3 men of the ANSON being wounded. Fatigue parties were supplied by B & D Coys from BULLY.	
FOSSE 10	30th		Church Parade at 9.30 a.m. Bathing & cleaning carried on. Night fatigues supplied by all companies.	
	31st		Parade 9 a.m. Company & Platoon drill carried on by A & C Companies. Afternoon & night fatigues carried on by all companies.	

A Lambert Ward
Major
Comdg. Howe

T2134. Wt. W708—776. 500000. 4/15. Sir J. C. & S.

Instructions regarding War Diaries and Intelligence Summaries are contained in F. S. Regs., Part II. and the Staff Manual respectively. Title pages will be prepared in manuscript.

WAR DIARY
or
INTELLIGENCE SUMMARY.
(*Erase heading not required.*)

Army Form C. 2118.

August 1916 — 188/63 — Vol 3 — Howe Bn 63rd (RN) D.

Place	Date	Hour	Summary of Events and Information	Remarks and references to Appendices
BULLY 1st Aug.			Bn moved into Support from Reserve changing places with 1/R.M. Two Companies and Hqrs to BULLY, one company in MECHANICS and one in CAP. DE PONT. Lewis Guns relieved those of Anson Bn	
ANGRES I	2.8.16		Relieved Anson Bn. Relief complete by 10 20 a.m. First companies left at 8 a.m. Patrol out from Sap 13 at night. Copy of report attached. Identifications were badly wanted. No casualties.	7/18 Report A
"	3.8.16		Usual work carried on, Hun quiet, very little shelling. Gas cylinders were carried up and installed on 24 to 27 July. Still there. More patrols at night but still no identification. HAWKE Bn on our right and 1/RM on our left. Two wounded.	
"	4.8.16		Same. one man wounded by rifle grenade in PAGE STREET. Bomb dumps set in order and complete stock taken.	
"	5.8.16		Usual work, relaying duck boards and revetting blown-in trench. Rifle grenade strafe at 6 p.m, which was more active in sector on our left where retaliation was drawn, 4.2 howitzer and minenwerfer apparently. Considerable visibility today [illegible]	

[illegible signature]

T2134. Wt. W708—776. 500000. 4/15. Sir J. C. & S.

Instructions regarding War Diaries and Intelligence Summaries are contained in F. S. Regs., Part II. and the Staff Manual respectively. Title pages will be prepared in manuscript.

WAR DIARY
or
~~INTELLIGENCE SUMMARY.~~
(Erase heading not required.)

Army Form C. 2118.

August 1916

HOWE Bn
188th Bde

Place	Date	Hour	Summary of Events and Information	Remarks and references to Appendices
ANGRES I	5.8.16		observation balloons up opposite us. The result was more shelling than we have had for the last 3 days – one man killed. Last night 3 hours' patrol by Sub Lt F.O. FORRESTER from sap 13 got information tending to show that hereabouts the Hun territory ends at his wire and that no saps come through it. Two patrols under different officers from left Company, B, brought in same information and could find no gaps in enemy wire. In No man's land there are several old trenches, not very deep and partly obscured by grass and weeds. Some of these should communicate with enemy trench, as system is a captured one, but they seem to have been blocked by him if this is the case.	
ANGRES I	6.8.16		Three officers' patrols out for 2½ hours each. None could find any gap in enemy wire or any enemy sap coming through his wire. Relieved by Anson Bn, relief complete by 7.50 am. Bn came back to support, A + B coys to BULLY and D in MECHANICS trench and C coy half in CAP DEPOT and half in ~~[illegible]~~ [illegible]	[illegible] Comdg Howe

T2134. Wt. W798–776. 500000. 4/15. Sir J. C. & S.

Army Form C. 2118.

WAR DIARY
or
~~INTELLIGENCE SUMMARY.~~
(*Erase heading not required.*)

Instructions regarding War Diaries and Intelligence Summaries are contained in F. S. Regs., Part II. and the Staff Manual respectively. Title pages will be prepared in manuscript.

August

HOWE Bn 63rd (RN) D
188 Bde

Place	Date	Hour	Summary of Events and Information	Remarks and references to Appendices
BULLY	6th		village. Enemy aeroplane brought down by gunfire. A quick relief, last being in BULLY by 9.30 am. A and most of B Coy bathed, 227 men in 3 hours. Sub Lt Edwards and 10 men went to Bde bomb School.	
	7th		At Bully, fatigues of 50 men per Company per day.	
	8th		Same. Lieut Comdr Edgar + Lieut Airey returned from First Army School La Condette at night. One slight casualty.	
	9th		Same	
ANGRES I	10th	6am	Proceeded to relieve ANSON Bn in ANGRES I. Last Company had left BULLY by 6.15 am and had passed Bn Hqrs in trenches by 7.30 am. All Companies in position and taken over by 8.3 am. A good deal of rifle grenade firing on right in consequence of our medium TMs starting to cut wire. They fired 4 60lb bombs and then ceased owing to Hun retaliation!! Result was many rifle grenades from the Hun, going on all day with very little interference. Two men wounded and some very narrow escapes. [illegible]	

T2134. Wt. W708–776. 500000. 4/15. Sir J. C. & S.

Instructions regarding War Diaries and Intelligence Summaries are contained in F. S. Regs., Part II. and the Staff Manual respectively. Title pages will be prepared in manuscript.

WAR DIARY
or
~~INTELLIGENCE SUMMARY.~~
(Erase heading not required.)

Army Form C. 2118.

August 1916 HOWE Bn 63rd (RN) Divn

Place	Date	Hour	Summary of Events and Information	Remarks and references to Appendices
ANGRES I	10th		west all preparations were made for discharging the gas, but the wind died down and the show was cancelled. Quiet night.	
	11th	9am	L.T.M's on right drew retaliation from enemy Minenwerfers and again got shut up!!	
		7.30pm.	TM's began near VASSEAU trench and drew retaliatory fire of enemy LTM onto PAGE St. ~~Some wounded by enemy LTM during day; all in right sector company.~~	
			NELSON Bn of 189 Bde are on our right.	
			At night 2 patrols out under Lieut CLAUDET and Lieut AIREY. The former went out 250 yards from end of sap 16 and heard a Hun wiring party and saw its covering party, but was not strong enough to interfere.	
			Casualties during the day, six wounded, caused by a new kind of light trench mortar, named a "pine apple", weighing about 3 lbs about 1 foot long, 4 wings.	
	12th		Enemy LTM began early but ~~we~~ were silenced by our artillery	

[signature] Lt Col

Instructions regarding War Diaries and Intelligence Summaries are contained in F. S. Regs., Part II. and the Staff Manual respectively. Title pages will be prepared in manuscript.

WAR DIARY
or
~~INTELLIGENCE SUMMARY~~
(Erase heading not required.)

Army Form C. 2118.

August 1916

HOWE Bn.

63rd (R.N.) Dn

Place	Date	Hour	Summary of Events and Information	Remarks and references to Appendices
ANGRES I	12th		Patrols at night under Lieut AIREY and Sub Lieut H. FRY. Latter went out 2. am (13th) & stayed out till dawn working along enemy wire. No casualties.	
"	13th		No casualties. Wind appeared favourable for gas discharge and all arrangements made but wind veered to S. and show was again put off. Hun did a strafe at 9. pm with his rifle grenades and LTM on our right for 15 minutes.	
	~~14th~~	3pm	~~Rel~~ Lewis Guns relieved by Anson L.G crews	
BULLY	14th	7am	Relieved by ANSON Bn. B Coy to MECHANICS. A Coy half to CAP DE PONT and half to CORONS D'AIX, C. D + Hqrs to BULLY GRENAY — the Bn being again in support. Relief complete by 8.2 am. All down in billet by 9.30 a.m. Rain later. Bathing 1.30 pm to 4.30 pm.	
"	15th		Fatigues. At night gas arrangements all on but had to be cancelled again.	
	16th		Fatigues	A Lambert Ward Lt Col HHL Cmdg Howe

T2134. Wt. W708—776. 500000. 4/15. Sir J. C. & S.

Instructions regarding War Diaries and Intelligence Summaries are contained in F. S. Regs., Part II. and the Staff Manual respectively. Title pages will be prepared in manuscript.

WAR DIARY
or
~~INTELLIGENCE SUMMARY.~~
(Erase heading not required.)

Army Form C. 2118.

August 1916

Howe Bn
63rd RND

Place	Date	Hour	Summary of Events and Information	Remarks and references to Appendices
Fosse 10	17th	7am	Bn moved into Reserve. C. D + Hq moving to Fosse 10 and A + B into BULLY. Lewis Guns went up the line. Yesterday had to hand over 170 steel helmets to 7th R.F.	
ANGRES I	18th		Relieved Anson Bn by 7.50 a.m. Left Fosse 10 at 5.30 a.m. Quiet day, one man wounded	
	19th		quiet. one wounded	
	20th		quiet, no casualties. A Coy of 7th R F which had been in for instruction was relieved today. One section had been attached to each platoon. On 18th the sections in front line had changed places with those in support and reserve. The new company, C, was similarly distributed today and was in place by 6.30 p.m. At 6.10 pm enemy began quite a brisk bombardment with L.T.M. doing very little harm to anything. At 6.20 pm asked for artillery at 6.30 got it, 64 rounds of 18 pounder in all were fired, with good effect. At 10.30 pm the gas we have had installed for a fortnight was liberated. The artillery began 5 minutes	

Instructions regarding War Diaries and Intelligence Summaries are contained in F. S. Regs., Part II. and the Staff Manual respectively. Title pages will be prepared in manuscript.

WAR DIARY
or
~~INTELLIGENCE SUMMARY.~~
(Erase heading not required.)

Army Form C. 2118.

August

Howe Bn.

Place	Date	Hour	Summary of Events and Information	Remarks and references to Appendices
ANGRES I	20		latter. Before the discharge enemy snipers were moderately active and this continued till 1035. There was then a lull of about 5 minutes and after that his mgs became active and his snipers developed about 10.50. Volume of rifle fire small, of mg fire intermittant but continuous. Star shells breaking into red and a green light were sent up at frequent intervals from 1037 onwards; occasionally a single red or a double red light went up. These seemed to be fired chiefly from support. Enemy artillery only began to open about 1050 p.m. He chiefly used field guns and light trench mortars, especially the latter. Heavy guns employed by him were estimated only at two 5.9's and four 4.2's. Some Minenwerfer projectiles came over on our left flank. Much of the field gun fire was directed on to COOKER ALLEY. Our casualties were one man wounded, slightly, and 3 slightly gassed.	
			Patrols went out afterwards, but the enemy were alert, his wire was intact, and there seemed no	

[illegible] Lt Col HAC
Commdg Howe

T2134. Wt. W708–776. 500000. 4/15. Sir J. C. & S.

Instructions regarding War Diaries and Intelligence Summaries are contained in F. S. Regs., Part II. and the Staff Manual respectively. Title pages will be prepared in manuscript.

WAR DIARY
or
~~INTELLIGENCE SUMMARY.~~
(Erase heading not required.)

Army Form C. 2118.

August — Howe Bn — 63rd (RN) Div

Place	Date	Hour	Summary of Events and Information	Remarks and references to Appendices
ANGRES I	20th		chance of a successful visit to his trenches. The wind was South of West and no part of enemy trenches South of ~~M~~ M.32.a.9.8. was affected by it, consequently patrol which left Sap 13 at 11.40 p.m. under Sub Lt FORRESTER had no chance. Other patrols left Sap 17 at 11.30 and returned 12.45 am (21st) and from Sap 18 at 11.30 and returned at 1.[illegible] am (21st) The latter was under Sub Lt MARLOW and reported no smell of gas and neither heard nor saw anything of the enemy.	
	21st		Some bombardment of LTM at about 10, but it did not last long. quiet day.	
	22nd		Relieved by ANSON. First Company in by 7.5 am but relief not complete till 8.40 am. Bn returned to Reserve billets, A.B and Hq in Fosse 10, C & D in BULLY. Draft of 114 divided up.	
	23rd		Fatigues and drill.	
	24th		Major Ward on a F.G.C.M. Fatigues cancelled. Special fatigue at night to carry out gas cylinders: 380 men.	[illegible]

T2134. Wt. W708—776. 500000. 4/15. Sir J. C. & S.

Instructions regarding War Diaries and Intelligence Summaries are contained in F. S. Regs., Part II. and the Staff Manual respectively. Title pages will be prepared in manuscript.

WAR DIARY
or
~~INTELLIGENCE SUMMARY.~~
(Erase heading not required.)

Army Form C. 2118.

August 1916 — HOWE Bn — 63rd (R.N.) Divn

Place	Date	Hour	Summary of Events and Information	Remarks and references to Appendices
Fosse 10 ~~ANGRES~~ I	25th		~~Relieved~~ Orderly room 10 am	
ANGRES I	26th		Relieved ANSON Bn in Angres I . Left Fosse 10 at 5 am relief complete at 8.15 am. 2" Trench Mortars are doing wire cutting. They fired from 1.30 to 2 pm and 6 to 6.30 p.m. without doing any harm to wire. All projectiles went too far.	
	27th		MTM's fired 7.15 to 7.45 am and 6.30 to 7 pm with same effect on wire – nil. Some 2's projectiles pitched on trench at M26c4.2 . Enemy replied vigorously with "Pine apples" (LTM) and six minenwerfers in right Coy area in reply to Evening 'strafe'. No casualties	
	28th		MTM's fired 6.15 to 6.45 am and 3 to 3.45 pm. Enemy sent over many pine apples and about half a dozen Minnies into our right Coy area. No casualties on our side but enemy seemed to have a premature in the pit at M 26c 5.4. from which white smoke emerged. "strafe" by heavies and all sorts of Mortars at 10.20 to 10.40 am on our right seemed very accurate and severe.	[signature] Lt Col HAL Comdg Howe

T2134. Wt. W708–776. 500000. 4/15. Sir J. C. & S.

Instructions regarding War Diaries and Intelligence Summaries are contained in F. S. Regs., Part II. and the Staff Manual respectively. Title pages will be prepared in manuscript.

WAR DIARY
or
~~INTELLIGENCE SUMMARY.~~
(Erase heading not required.)

Army Form C. 2118.

August 1916

Howe Bn
63rd (RN) Divn

Place	Date	Hour	Summary of Events and Information	Remarks and references to Appendices
ANGRES 2	29th		M.T.M. strafes 6 to 6.45 am and 2 to 2.45 pm. Usual retaliation from enemy. Later enemy did a surprize strafe with his "Pineapples" and caught a party, 2 killed 2 wounded and 2 ANSON men wounded. Lewis Gunners relieved by those of ANSON.	
Fosse 10	30th		Relieved by ANSON. Bn. Relief complete by 8.40 am. Back to Fosse 10 (C & D) and Bully (A & B). Two men wounded by enemy retaliation during "hate" of S.2 at 3.55 am. One of yesterday's wounded died. Gale.	
	31st		1 officer and 4 men went to Gas School. Two carpenters to CRE.	

A Lambert Ward
Lt Col HA
Comdg Howe

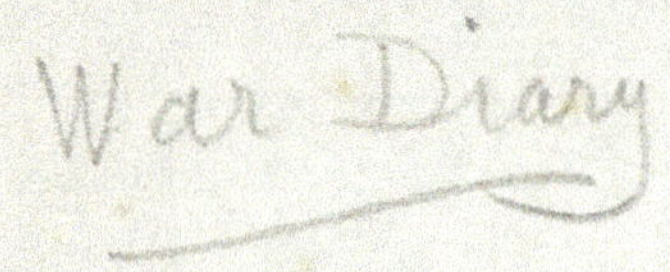

I/18.

REPORT "A".

Patrol of 1 officer and 10 men started out on a reconnaissance of Sap running towards enemies line from left to Sap 13 (A-A)

The patrol, in order to avoid thick barbed wire, got out of left sap, right hand side and then got into a little trench which rund from right Sap B in direction of sap patrol wished to proceed along. Trench ended in a "T" head Communication trench. This lead to a ridge X-X and leaving ridge to left, patrol proceeded to the sap required, A-A, hitting it about 20 or 25 yards from sap-head. Patrol proceeded, some in trench, some to right, some to left, and connecting files along trench for 126 paces. Trench was deep in places, but numerous shell holes. Where patrol stopped it got very much shallower and grass was shorter, (probably had been cut). When patrol tried to move beyond this point a wire was reported touched, (only a small piece of enemy's barbed wire on side of trench had prevously been encountered) and two blasts (officer only heard one) were sounded on a whistle. Three lights were shown in approximate positions D and E and F, and the sound of at least two men cocking rifles was heard and a word of command given. Patrol remained silent about 10 minutes and them another move was made. Immediately rifles were discharged, one shot being very close to sap, three of patrol were in, Poles of enemy's wire were seen about 20 yards ahead, but not the wire, nor was the enemy's sap-head identified. The lights went up quite close to one another and it seemed as if enemy's saps either side went further out than the one patrol was following. There being little possibility of surprising enemy, patrol returned.

It is believed that Sap E runs to very near Sap A-A, and probably commands it. It is suggested that a reconnaissance of the sap, directin of which is indicated by ridge might lead to useful results. It appeass that in all three cases that enemy's sap-heads are well hidden in high grass, no white appearance to show them up, whilst ours are plainly observable as big white double marks.

Sd. P.H.Edwards,
Lieut.Commander.

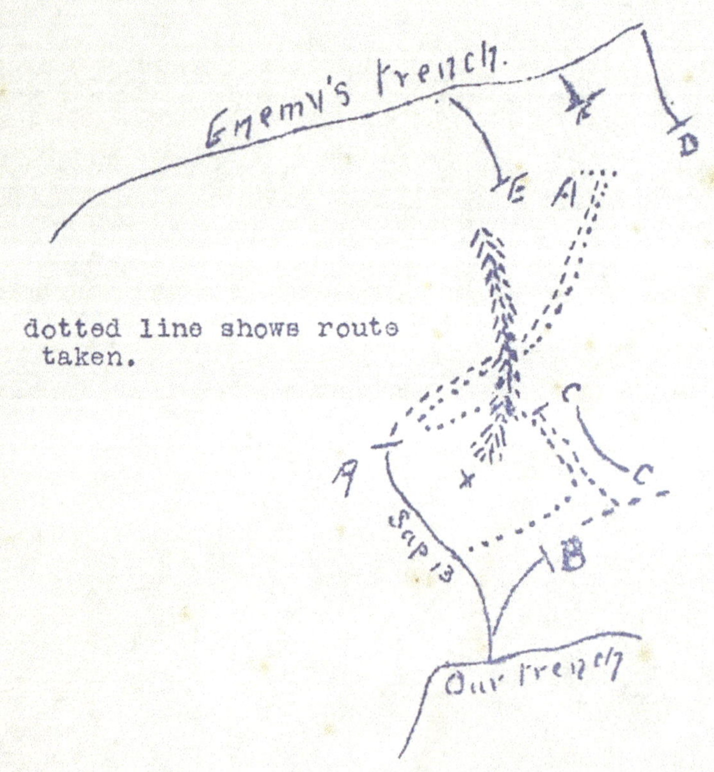

dotted line shows route taken.

I/18.

REPORT "E"

With 1 N.C.O. and 2 men I left the right sap of BULLY CRATER at 11-0 pm. and continued up the sap to a bombing post on the left of NEW CRATER over which we climbed. We then entered a short sandbagged Sap on the right tip of BULLY CRATER and got through our own obstacles there and cut through enemy's wire. Here we discovered a rope which we cut, it led from the right of shell hole in the Crater. We waited in the shell hole for some time and then worked back as we had been observed by a sniper. On our way back we heard a working party to the left of BULLY CRATER; we listened for a short time but shortly afterwards this party withdrew. We then went back and crawled through an opening in the wire starting from the right bombing post, and came across a single wire. We followed this single wire for about 15 yards and heard somebody kick a can and afterwards heard sound of digging, which appeared to come from the enemy's sap or front line, more probably the latter. After listening for about half an hour we returned to our own line at 12-40 am.

Sd. H.VAN PRAAGH
Lieut. R.H.

(1) Army Form C. 2118.

Vol 4

WAR DIARY
or
~~INTELLIGENCE SUMMARY~~.
(Erase heading not required.)

September 1916. Howe Bn.

Instructions regarding War Diaries and Intelligence Summaries are contained in F. S. Regs., Part II. and the Staff Manual respectively. Title pages will be prepared in manuscript.

Place	Date	Hour	Summary of Events and Information	Remarks and references to Appendices
SAINS en GOHELLE Fosse 10	1st		In Reserve in billets. A + B Companies at BULLY and C + D in FOSSE 10.	
"	2nd		Lewis Guns went to trenches, ANGRES I, to relieve those of ANSON Bn. "B" Coy 4th Bedfords came into Fosse 10 and under our orders.	
ANGRES I	3rd		Left at 5.45 am. Relieved ANSON by 8.5 a.m. A and B Coys in firing line, C in Support and B Coy 4th Bedfords in Reserve. Quiet day, some strafing of VIMY ridge above GIVENCHY wood.	
	4th		Quiet day. 8 Pineapples only in retaliation for MTM strafe, but one piece hit a man in neck and killed him T Z74 AB T Dixon. of A Coy. Court Martial at Bully, to try CZ 5240 AB D PATON of D Coy.	
	5th		B Coy 4th Bedfords went out and were relieved by D Coy Howe. Aeroplane at 8.25 am went over German lines at very low elevation and dropped something - message?	

T2134. Wt. W708—776. 500000. 4/15. Sir J. C. & S.

Instructions regarding War Diaries and Intelligence Summaries are contained in F. S. Regs., Part II. and the Staff Manual respectively. Title pages will be prepared in manuscript.

WAR DIARY
or
~~INTELLIGENCE SUMMARY.~~
(Erase heading not required.)

(2)

Army Form C. 2118.

September

HOWE Bn 188 Inf Bde R.N.D.

Place	Date	Hour	Summary of Events and Information	Remarks and references to Appendices
ANGRES I	6th		Not quite so quiet. Got a few "pineapples" sent over both in morning and evening.	
			At 6.35 an 'advertised' strafe of CALONNE on our left by heavies, but it brought no retaliation except 'whizz bangs' at suspected TM position on our left.	
BULLY	7th		Relieved by ANSON Bn by 8.15 am, but first Company was relieved by 6.55 am. A few 5.9's began to fall near Bn Hqrs just after we had left, no harm and most did not detonate very well. One fell among 1/RM & killed 8 as they were coming out a bit later.	
			Bn went D to MECHANICS, C ½ to CAP DU PONT and ½ to CORONS D'AIX, A, B and Hq to BULLY GRENAY.	
			Lieut K.E. PARKES, R.N.V.R. formerly Adjt of the Bn rejoined today, having been away since Nov 18th 1915.	
"	8th		In rest billets. Daily fatigues of 236. No shells into BULLY	
"	9th			
"	10th			

T2134. Wt. W708—776. 500000. 4/15. Sir J. C. & S.

(3)

Army Form C. 2118.

WAR DIARY
or
~~INTELLIGENCE SUMMARY.~~
(Erase heading not required.)

Instructions regarding War Diaries and Intelligence Summaries are contained in F. S. Regs., Part II. and the Staff Manual respectively. Title pages will be prepared in manuscript.

September

HOWE BN
188 Inf Bde

Place	Date	Hour	Summary of Events and Information	Remarks and references to Appendices
ANGRES I	11th		Relieved ANSON BN by 7.30 am. They had last night brought off a successful raid, 2 officers + 10 men fetching in a prisoner of the 103rd Regt (Saxon) from opposite sap 18 M26c 2.5.	
			Very quiet day. Fired 31 No 23 R.G. during night.	
"	12th		quiet day. Bombardment of Thompson's Crater at 3.33 pm. Enemy threw Minenwerfer at SOLFERINO and KELLET. At night a premature burst of a No 23 R.G. wounded 4 men two severely.	
	13th		C.O. went to view another sector. minnies at 7.15 pm on same place. Retaliation by Field Guns silenced them.	
	14th		Usual quiet day.	
BULLY	15th		Relieved by ANSON Bn by 7.20 am B Coy down to Mechanics A to CORONS D'AIX C, D, and Hqrs to BULLY GRENAY.	
	16th		One shell near BHQ, quiet day	
	17th		quiet day	

(4)

Army Form C. 2118.

Instructions regarding War Diaries and Intelligence Summaries are contained in F. S. Regs., Part II. and the Staff Manual respectively. Title pages will be prepared in manuscript.

WAR DIARY
or
INTELLIGENCE SUMMARY.
(Erase heading not required.)

September 1916

HOWE Bn

Place	Date	Hour	Summary of Events and Information	Remarks and references to Appendices
BULLY	18th		quiet, preparing for relief	
	19th		Were relieved by 11th. R. War. Regt who took over billet and trench stores, and some maps.	
HERSIN			On relief marched to HERSIN, where the Battalion arrived about 12.30 p.m.	
LA COMTÉ	20th		Bn set out at 9 am picked up transport and formed correct column at Fosse 5 and arrived at LA COMTÉ at 1 pm. No one fell out, and one man had to have his gear carried. Had halts at MAISNIL, cross roads just short of RANCHICOURT and ½ an hour short of LA COMTÉ. Here we passed 1/RM halted for food.	
	22nd		The Bn proceeded to training area South of MAGNICOURT and spent the day there. Many of the officers were attending a GCM at FRESNICOURT. Very fine weather after rain of the last 3 days	
	23rd		To training ground. Parade 8.30. Took cookers. Commander Ramsay-Fairfax R.N. assumed command of the Bn vice Lt Col A. L. WARD. D.S.O. who has been appointed to command 2/H.A.C.	

T2134. Wt. W708—773. 500000. 4/15. Sir J. C. & S.

(5)

Army Form C. 2118.

WAR DIARY
or
INTELLIGENCE SUMMARY.
(Erase heading not required.)

Instructions regarding War Diaries and Intelligence Summaries are contained in F. S. Regs., Part II. and the Staff Manual respectively. Title pages will be prepared in manuscript.

September

Howe Bn
63rd R.N.D.

Place	Date	Hour	Summary of Events and Information	Remarks and references to Appendices
LA THIEULOYE	24th		Bn went to training ground as usual, and meanwhile transport stores etc moved from LA COMTÉ to LA THIEULOYE where we took over billets from Worcesters. Moved at 2 p.m.	
	25th } 26th }		Battalion training	
	27th		Brigade training. Wave attack on a trench system.	
	28th		" " Open attack on a position.	
	29th		Divisional training, same operation as on 27th on bigger scale.	
	30th		" " a route march. Packed everything & all gear.	

W. J. [illegible] Commdr R.N.
O.C. Howe

T2134. Wt. W708—776. 500000. 4/15. Sir J. C. & S.

Army Form C. 2118.

Vol 5

Instructions regarding War Diaries and Intelligence Summaries are contained in F. S. Regs., Part II. and the Staff Manual respectively. Title pages will be prepared in manuscript.

WAR DIARY
or
~~INTELLIGENCE SUMMARY.~~
(Erase heading not required.)

October 1916

HOWE Bn
188 Inf B'de.

Place	Date	Hour	Summary of Events and Information	Remarks and references to Appendices
LA THIEULOYE	1st		Engaged in ~~B~~ Company training, Rainy day, came back midday.	
	2nd		Preparing to move. ~~From~~	
	3rd		Transport moved, to travel by road with rest of Bde transport. They spent the night at SIBIVILLE.	
	4th		Were to move at 11.30 am. marched as far as ORLENCOURT where we got news of delay – returned. Word to move at 9.45 pm. Fell in & moved off 10.30 pm.	
	5th		Reached LIGNY ST FLOCHEL at 12.30 am. Bn was entrained with blankets and rations issued by 2 ~~pm~~ am. The Lewis Gun handcarts took time and it was not easy to fit the 12 into one covered horse truck – handles were the difficulty. Train left 3.30 am arrived at FIENVILLERS-CANDAS at 8 am, halted 2 hours – reached VARENNES siding at 12.30 pm. marched via FORCEVILLE to wood at MAILLY MAILLET where camped in huts and tents. Balance of transport turned up during the night.	
MAILLY MAILLET	6th		Inspecting kit etc:	

T2134. Wt. W708–776 500000. 4/15. Sir J. C. & S.

Army Form C. 2118.

Instructions regarding War Diaries and Intelligence Summaries are contained in F. S. Regs., Part II. and the Staff Manual respectively. Title pages will be prepared in manuscript.

WAR DIARY
or
~~INTELLIGENCE SUMMARY.~~
(*Erase heading not required.*)

October 1916 Howe Bn R.N.D.

Place	Date	Hour	Summary of Events and Information	Remarks and references to Appendices
MAILLY MAILLET	7th		Training, Fatigue of 100 men at night.	
	8th		Moved to camp on outskirts of VARENNES. Rain all last night and a good deal this day. Left at 10.20 am. Accomodated in canvas huts with a few tarpaulins over them. No rations for 9th were sent.	
VARENNES	9th		After sending emergency wire got rations in the afternoon. Training.	
	10th		Training C.O M.O. and 4 other officers visited trenches of REDAN Sector	
	11th		Training 4 more officers visited trenches. & Fatigue party of 100 left at 6 am.	
	12th 13th 14th		Training and supplying fatigue parties. Officers and men visited trenches daily.	
	15th		same	
	16th		same	

T2134. Wt. W708—776. 500000. 4/15. Sir J. C. & S.

Instructions regarding War Diaries and Intelligence Summaries are contained in F. S. Regs., Part II. and the Staff Manual respectively. Title pages will be prepared in manuscript.

WAR DIARY
or
INTELLIGENCE SUMMARY.
(Erase heading not required.)

Army Form C. 2118.

October 1916

Howe Bn
RND

Place	Date	Hour	Summary of Events and Information	Remarks and references to Appendices
VARENNES	17th		Got word we were to go into trenches opposite ENGELBELMER. C.O. Adjt and 2 Coy commanders visited the sector.	
The line	18th		Relieved part of HOOD BN just North of HAMEL village. Left camp at 10:30 am. Went across country, met Field Kitchens in fields near ENGELBELMER. Entered GABION TRENCH just after 2 pm no guides, relief complete by 7 pm. C & D Coys in front line C on left, A & B in support, A on left. HOOD side slipped to right, 7th Royal Scots on our right (51st Div). Patrols out listening. Wet.	
	19th		Quiet day, at night patrolled enemy wire and found it much cut, resembling bushes in places. Cut own wire. Wet.	Frost.
	20th		Same, Shelled a bit in evening near GABION and QUEENS ST no one hurt. Sergt Major knocked out by a roll of barbed wire. Froze again, clear night. Artillery activity S of ANCRE at 8 – 9 pm and 5 am in morning of 21st.	
	21st		Cold and fine. At 12.6 pm. attack on Stuff and Regina trenches	

T2134. Wt. W708–776. 500000. 4/15. Sir J. C. & S.

Army Form C. 2118.

Instructions regarding War Diaries and Intelligence Summaries are contained in F. S. Regs., Part II. and the Staff Manual respectively. Title pages will be prepared in manuscript.

WAR DIARY
or
INTELLIGENCE SUMMARY.
(Erase heading not required.)

Place	Date	Hour	Summary of Events and Information	Remarks and references to Appendices
			away on our right. No retaliation our way, but work was held up in consequence in morning. Our MTM's fired short and damaged LONG SAP and BEDFORD ST and also caused 4 casualties, killing P.O. DURKIN and AB's RITCHIE & WIGMORE and wounding L.S. KENNEDY.	
ENGLEBELMER	22nd		Relieved by 1st/R.M. Out by 10 am and went into billets in Englebelmer, a village from which the inhabitants have been removed. Slept on floors but a roof over our heads. Got first news of operation.	
	~~23~~		Had to send 400 men out same night on working party.	
	23rd		Quiet day as regards work. Many Conferences.	
	24		Same	
Trenches	25		Relieved 1st/RM by 1.30 pm. All quiet but trenches very muddy. Same section of line ~~copies of operation orders attached~~ as	Pto/ [illegible]
	26th		Wind West at last. Has been E or SE since we were last in, and kept Gas alert on. Off at 9 am today.	
		5.30 pm	Raid on our left by 153 Bde.	
		10.5 pm.	Raid by us on enemy trench at Q 17 b 25.10. Zero was 10.5 pm	

Instructions regarding War Diaries and Intelligence Summaries are contained in F. S. Regs., Part II. and the Staff Manual respectively. Title pages will be prepared in manuscript.

WAR DIARY
or
~~INTELLIGENCE SUMMARY.~~
(*Erase heading not required.*)

Army Form C. 2118.

October 1916 HOWE Bn 63rd (RN) D

Place	Date	Hour	Summary of Events and Information	Remarks and references to Appendices
	26th/27th	10.5 pm	At zero the raiding party of 28 men under Lieut AIREY and Sub Lt CHANCE with P.O JAMES and TURNBULL 6. was lying at the enemy wire. When the barrage opened, which it did punctually, the party proceeded to enemy trench as prearranged and met no rifle, m.g or grenade fire The wire in front had been 50 ft thick and though much cut still presented some obstacle and it took 2' to get through it. A party was left to improve and mark the way back. On entering trench one party blocked to the left, another went right bombing traverse by traverse. At 10.20 a bomb thrown from the parados or support line killed one man and slightly wounded CHANCE The party carried on a bit further and blocked. No 3 party meanwhile followed and found a dugout (20 ft deep) with 2 entrances: a couple of 'P' bombs and a mills were put down either entrance and sentries posted at entrances. A light was seen in this dugout and No 2 party had thrown 2 mills bombs in at 2nd entrance, causing exclamations below. There was a gas blanket half way down the steps. The party (No 3) then looked for identifications but could only find 2 rifles, one set of	

T2134. Wt. W708–776. 500000. 4/15. Sir J. C. & S.

WAR DIARY
or
~~INTELLIGENCE SUMMARY.~~
(Erase heading not required.)

Army Form C. 2118.

Instructions regarding War Diaries and Intelligence Summaries are contained in F. S. Regs., Part II. and the Staff Manual respectively. Title pages will be prepared in manuscript.

October 1916

HOWE Bn
63rd RND.

Place	Date	Hour	Summary of Events and Information	Remarks and references to Appendices
Trenches near ENGLEBELMER.	26		equipment, some stick grenades, a respirator and a shrapnel helmet. There was a yellow and white sword knot on the bayonet. The party then withdrew 10.34pm with this loot, casualties 2 killed 3 wounded (2 still on duty). The dugout seemed to hold a sentry group. A fire step did not run all along the bays, but was short and more a single sentry's position, — two such places were seen in the trench visited. From zero plus seven, on, red Very lights were fired to guide party back.	
			The following points arise:— the barrage was excellent; the enemy took 20 minutes to get his guns on, and then fired behind our support line; the process of bombing up the trench is too slow if identifications are required, it frightens enemy away; a man or two along parados might have been useful; enemy trench being rather serpentine than square traversed, the traverses gave our bombing party poor protection from the back blast of own bombs: the red Very lights were fired at rather too frequent intervals and might have given away point of return, if enemy had understood them or had a disengaged m.g to turn that way.	

Instructions regarding War Diaries and Intelligence Summaries are contained in F. S. Regs., Part II. and the Staff Manual respectively. Title pages will be prepared in manuscript.

WAR DIARY
or
INTELLIGENCE SUMMARY.
(Erase heading not required.)

Army Form C. 2118.

October 1916 — HOWE Bn — 63rd (RN) Dn.

Place	Date	Hour	Summary of Events and Information	Remarks and references to Appendices
	26		Copy of G 2/45 - Bde Account - is attached	G 2/45.
ENGLEBELMER	27		Relieved in trenches by 1st/R.M. Went back to billets at ENGLEBELMER.	
	28		In Billets	
	29		In Billets Fatigues 160 men	
	30		" Fatigues 432 men	
	31		" Fatigue 460 men ; of these 60 worked both morning and afternoon. Transport and Q.M. stores moved from VARENNES to HEDAUVILLE yesterday amid torrents of rain.	

W. J. [illegible] Comdr R.N. OC HOWE 1/11/16.

Narrative of Events.

Raid night 26th/27th October 1916.

9.40 pm. Officer commanding Howe Battn notified line from KNIGHTSBRIDGE to Front line broken.

9.59 " Line still out of order.

10.05 " Barrage commenced

10 " Up to the present no enemy retaliation

12 " Our red lights (single) are beginning to go up.

13 " Machine gun fire heard, thought to be our own

20 " Reported by observation from KNIGHTSBRIDGE that enemy are putting up a number of Verys lights - but not so many as at first.

25 " Our red lights still going up.

25 " Appears to be some small retaliation on our Front Line.

27 " An enemy red light reported on the right.

29 " Our red lights still continuing

29 " Enemy beginning to put over shrapnel

31 " Report in by buzzer:-

ALL IN
3 CASUALTIES
NO PRISONERS
VERY LITTLE LOOT.

35 " Orders given to stop barrage.

Headquarters,
188th Inf Bde.

Report on Raid carried out on the night 26th/27th October 1916.

1. The raid was carried out in accordance with the attached Operation Order No 3 of today.

2 Prior to ZERO hour, the heads of the two columns were up to the enemy's wire.

3 Little difficulty was experienced in entering the enemy's trench, which was entered in accordance with programme.

4 No 2 party worked up the enemy's trench towards his left, the party bombing as they went.

Two dugout entrances were seen, in one of which lights were observed.

Into both entrances Mills and "P" bombs were thrown liberally by both No. 2 & 3 parties. "Muffled sounds" were heard within the blanket curtain, which was about halfway down the steps leading to the dugout.

5. At 10.15 pm the Officer i/c No 2 party was slightly wounded, and one man of this party was wounded (since died, probably killed outright); the remainder of No 2 party continued on to the next "bay". One other man was also killed, and one wounded.

The two former casualties, and probably all the casualties, were caused by bombs being thrown from behind the parados, or perhaps from bombing positions in rear of the enemy's front line, or even by some means e.g. catapult, from the Support line.

6. At 10.20 pm the Officer i/c of the raiding party gave the order to retire. All casualties were brought back, to our own lines.

7 The "loot" brought back, includes:-

2 rifles
Ammunition (2 kinds)
1 bayonet with belt and tassel.
helmet
gas helmet
bombs.

On the above there are various markings, but a complete inventory is attached.

8. The enemy trench was found to be from 9' to 10' deep, and some 4' wide

It is rivetted with hurdles.

The floor was duckboarded, and the trench was in very good condition.

It was of "serpentine" contour, the traverses thus affording little protection against our own bombs.

8 continued Fire step positions were only seen at intervals, and appeared to be positions only for sentries. The fire steps were about 6' long. The trench had little, if any, parapet, but a high parados.

There were no signs of gas cylinders.

9. The enemy's wire, while presenting no great difficulty in entering the trench, nevertheless forms a considerable obstruction as a whole by reason of its mass and depth which is 40' to 50'.

10. The signal for the hostile artillery support is reported to be a golden rain rocket.

His Artillery support appeared to be slow in its commencement and weak.

There was some slight, shrapnel H.E. and "Minnie" retaliation.

11. Our Artillery barrage was very good, and the Stokes Mortar barrage particularly so.

(Sig^d) W.J. Ramsay Fairfax
Commander R.N.
O.C. Howe Battalion.

26th Oct. 1916.

Operation Order
No. 3
by
Commander W. G. Ramsay Fairfax RN
Commanding Howe Bn

Map Ref:-

BEAUMONT HAMEL } Edition 2.
1/5000

1. The Battn will carry out a minor operation against the enemy's line on the night 26th/27th Oct. 1916 in order to obtain an identification

2) The objective of the raid will be that portion of the enemy's front line that lies between Q 17. b 2.1 and Q 17 b 3½. 1½

3. O.C. D Coy will detail 2 Officers and 25 O.R. to form the Raiding Party

4. This party will be sub-divided into 4 parties of which the composition and details will be:-

No 1 Party	{ 1 Leading Hand	{ Leading Hand & 2 men carry rifles & bayonets 2 men carry short handle picks. All men except L.H carry bombs in sand bags
No 2 Party	{ one Officer one Leading Hand 8 men	{ 2 Bayonet men, 2 bombers 2 Bomb carriers 2 bayonet men (one scaling ladder)
No 3 Party	{ 1 Officer i/c 1 Leading Hand 8 men	{ All carry rifles & 4 bombs each, 2 carry "P" bombs (if obtainable)
No 4 Party	{ 1 Leading Hand 2 men	{ All carry rifles & take a scaling ladder and coil of rope

A proportion of men in each of the above parties will carry wire cutters. A white band will be worn on the arm. Steel helmets will not be worn.

5 <u>Assembly</u> The parties will be disposed in GORDON ST in the following order from the left. No 4, No 1, No 2, No 3. The junction of parties Nos 1 & 2 will be opposite the point of entry (Q 17 b 2 1) to the enemy's line. OC D Coy will supervise generally and be responsible that the parties are in position one hour before ZERO hour.

6. The parties will form two columns {No 1 No 4 and {No 2 No 3, and commencing from 30 minutes before ZERO, will set out of

6 (contd) the trench in small numbers at a time, No 1 & 2 leading and creep towards the point of entry to the Enemy's line until the head of each column is within 50x of the enemy's wire.

7. At ZERO the artillery will open a "Box" barrage and while the STOKES MORTARS will engage the enemy's machine guns, this will be the signal to ADVANCE.

8 Action of the parties will be as under:-

On the artillery opening fire -

No 1 Party { Enters the enemy's trench, turns left, and blocks.

No 2 Party { Follows No 1 Party into the trench, turns right and proceeds down enemy trench for 50x and blocks. Waits 5 minutes and then retires back along the trench to point of entry which will be pt. of EXIT.

No 3 Party. { Follows No 2 party and carries out the purpose of the raid

No 4 Party { Remains outside Enemy's line and improves facilities of Exit

9. The order of exit from the enemy's trench will be as under:—

1st. No 3 Party less its Officer

2nd No 2 Party

3rd No 1 Party

4th. The Officer in charge

No 4 Party will make its way back to our lines when the other parties are clear of the enemy's line

10. No 2 Party will commence to retire at ZERO hour + 12 minutes and will pass the CODE WORD

11 The CODE WORD for RETIRE is "DANDY"

12. To guide the party back, red Verys lights will be fired continuously, commencing at ZERO + 7 from the neighbourhood of the junction of LONG SAP and GORDON and the junction of LOUVEROY St and GORDON trench OC D Coy is to detail the man to fire these lights and is to have two pistols at each point and a sufficiency of lights. When all the party are in he is to give the order to cease fire.

13. Watches will be synchronised at 6.30 PM by telephone, or by arrangement with the signalling Officer.

14 On return, the party in the absence of hostile shelling is immediately to report at Battn Hqrs at KNIGHTSBRIDGE moving via BEDFORD ST. OC D Coy will detail a PO to check the party and he will also arrange an advance checking post in the neighbourhood of ROBERT TRENCH

15. All results of the raid, loot, prisoners, identifications etc are to be sent to Battn Hqrs direct.

16 OC D Coy will select a suitable locality off GORDON trench for his stretcher bearers who are to be in position by 9 PM

17 The Sig Officer will establish telephone communication between Battn Hqrs and GORDON Rd by 8 pm.

18 OC C Coy will detail an Officer to report progress to Battn Hqrs by Telephone from GORDON Rd

19. The L. G. O will select suitable positions for B Coys L. Gs to operate over the flanks of the Raiding Party.

20 OC B Coy is responsible that those portions of his trench affected by the operation are cleared in sufficient time with their regard to safety of the line, of all but sentries. The garrison should be placed in the saps.

21. OC D Coy is responsible that all ranks taking part are warned that in the event of capture they are not bound to disclose anything beyond their rank and name. No other information is to be given. He is responsible that no letters, badges or identification of any description are to be carried.

22 The usual precautions are to be taken against hostile retaliation.

23. A table of Artillery Barrage + STOKES MORTAR targets is attached.

24. If trench (enemy) is full of wire it should not be entered – and the possibility of hostile bombing from the parados of the enemy trench is to be provided for.

25. ZERO HOUR is 10.5 PM tonight

26. The Corps HEAVIES will open fire at 9.50 PM tonight in order to create a diversion to the South and will cease at our ZERO hour. Care is to be taken that this opening of fire is not to be mistaken for our own BOX BARRAGE

27 The 153 HIGHLAND Bde on our left is undertaking a raid at 5.30 PM today. The usual precautions are to be

G 2/45.

Headquarters,

63rd (RN) Division

Reference 188th Inf. Bde Operations Order No. 48 dated 25th instant already forwarded to you, I now enclose the report of the Officer Commanding HOWE Battalion on the operation, together with a copy of his orders.

1. Though the object of the raid, viz., the obtaining an identification was not attained, I consider that useful information regarding the trench itself, and the state of the wire has been got. It is also probable that the occupants of the dug-outs which were bombed, have been killed.

2. As regards the use of "P" bombs in these raids.

When a "P" bomb is dropped into a dug-out, some time must elapse before it can be entered, and where time is of importance in a raid, an identification out of the dug-out cannot be obtained, and therefore the use of "P" bombs in future is not recommended.

3. Our barrage and covering fire with Stokes Mortars and Machine Guns was good and well carried out.

4. The arrangements made by the Officer Comdg. HOWE Battn., Commander Fairfax, were, I consider very satisfactory.

The party under the command of Lieut. G.R. Airey carried out their duties very gallantly and satisfactorily, and brought in all their casualties.

The breaking of the wire between Battn. Hqrs and the front line delayed the transmission of messages.

5. A narrative of events is attached.

Brigadier General
Commanding
188th Inf. Bde.

27th Oct. 1916.

188/63

Howe B
R N D
Vol 6

Novbr 1916

Instructions regarding War Diaries and Intelligence Summaries are contained in F. S. Regs., Part II. and the Staff Manual respectively. Title pages will be prepared in manuscript.

WAR DIARY
or
~~INTELLIGENCE SUMMARY~~.
(Erase heading not required.)

November 1916

Howe Bn R.N.D.

Army Form C. 2118.

Place	Date	Hour	Summary of Events and Information	Remarks and references to Appendices
ENGLEBELMER	1st		Fatigue parties of 360 away at 5 p.m.	
	2nd		Stood by to go up, but cancelled at 9.30 a.m. Fatigue of 360	
	3rd		} Providing fatigues	
	4th		}	
PUCHEVILLERS	5th		Left at 9 am for PUCHEVILLERS. Left all Special War Material under guard in billet No 28. Went across country by Companies to road at U 6.a. where the Field Kitchens were met. Thence by road through HARPONVILLE and TOUTENCOURT. Arrived at 3 pm. Billets poor, nearly all officers sleeping on floor. Men's billets fair, dry, some straw.	
	6th		Cleaning up, Coy drill and bathing and scabies inspection in afternoon.	
HEDAUVILLE	7th		Set off at 11.15 am for ENGLEBELMER, by same route but while Bn was halted for dinner just outside HARPONVILLE a Staff officer brought change of orders, giving our destination as HEDAUVILLE. On arrival at 3.30 pm found billetting party just back from ENGLEBELMER. Blankets had all been dumped there and last were not back till 9.30 p.m. Rain and strong	

T2134. Wt. W708—776. 500000. 4/15. Sir J. C. & S.

Instructions regarding War Diaries and Intelligence Summaries are contained in F. S. Regs., Part II. and the Staff Manual respectively. Title pages will be prepared in manuscript.

WAR DIARY
or
INTELLIGENCE SUMMARY.
(Erase heading not required.)

Army Form C. 2118.

Nov. 1916.

Howe Bn
RND

Place	Date	Hour	Summary of Events and Information	Remarks and references to Appendices
HEDAU-VILLE			wind till midday, roads very muddy. Everyone arrived wet through but cheerful.	
	7th - 8th		Cleaning up and paying - company parades. 80 on fatigue party plus 20 to Varennes dump.	
	9th 10th			
ENGLEBELMER	11th		Moved to shelters near ENGLEBELMER. Issued war material such as red flares, rockets, wire cutters, hedging gloves, Very pistols and lights	
	12th	11am	Moved for the line to take up battle position and were in place by 2:30pm according to program. Had our headquarters in a mine tunnel that was narrow and draughty. Place of assembly for first and second waves was GORDON trench, for 3rd and 4th, ROBERTS trench. Enemy did some shelling and some firework display in the afternoon and we had 10 casualties, 4 killed including P.O. Townsend. The rest of the night was quite peaceful and quiet.	
	13th	5.45 am	This was ZERO hour for the attack. Brigade operation Order Nos 56 and 57 are attached. also barrage table and maps. Also own operation Order and its amendments, except for the last two.	

T2134. Wt. W708—776. 500000. 4/15. Sir J. C. & S.

Army Form C. 2118

Instructions regarding War Diaries and Intelligence Summaries are contained in F. S. Regs., Part II. and the Staff Manual respectively. Title pages will be prepared in manuscript.

WAR DIARY
or
INTELLIGENCE SUMMARY.
(Erase heading not required.)

November 1916 — Howe Bn RND.

Place	Date	Hour	Summary of Events and Information	Remarks and references to Appendices
	13th		The original Operation Order had been dated 23.10.16 and since then there had been postponements. The wire cutting had been very thorough and spread over a long period. At ZERO hour it was fairly dark and there was a thick mist which prevented the enemy's light signals from being seen. The Artillery barrage opened punctually and the 4 waves went over. The waves were not very regular, and if anything rather close together. ANSON passed over and then 4th BEDFORDS. No reports came back but a lot of m.g. fire could be heard on left and bombing in front line on our right front. The Signal Officer, Sub Lt Fletcher then went forward to select new Bn Hqrs, but was shot on parapet of first line. Three messengers in succession sent reported bombing in front line, and then at 7.20 am Bn Hqrs moved forward and established itself at Q17b2.3 which subsequently became Report Centre No 2. Here a dugout was found with a sentry on it, and an NCO and 15 men came out and were made to carry down our wounded. In the trench there was a mixed force of 2/RM, Howe and Anson, perhaps 100 in all. It soon became evident that enemy still held his third line from Q17b66 southwards, his second from Q17b43 and it was not clear whether he was properly cleared out of his front line either.	

T2134. Wt. W708–776. 500000. 4/15. Sir J. C. & S.

Instructions regarding War Diaries and Intelligence Summaries are contained in F. S. Regs., Part II. and the Staff Manual respectively. Title pages will be prepared in manuscript.

WAR DIARY
or
INTELLIGENCE SUMMARY.
(Erase heading not required.)

Army Form C. 2118.

Nov 1916

Howe Bn
RND.

Place	Date	Hour	Summary of Events and Information	Remarks and references to Appendices
	13th		A bombing attack led by ~~the~~ Commander Ramsay-Fairfax drove the enemy back a short distance along his second line and secured 20 prisoners from a dugout, but owing to being outthrown nothing else could be done but a 'stop' was made. From this dugout P.O WEEDON of the Anson was rescued wounded, and an AB of the NELSON. Both had been taken prisoner. A similar post was established in the front line at Q17 b 4.1. At about 3 p.m. having heard and gathered that the attack had swept on on both sides of this strong point, it was decided to advance Hqrs, if possible to the Yellow line (BEAUCOURT ROAD) which was said to be held. Hqrs proceeded accordingly over the open slightly to the left of where CIRCUS trench had been but when level with German 3rd line, it came under fire of snipers at Q 17 b 6.6. and had to retire, being quite in the open. Here Lieut SEWELL RFA was killed, he being F.O.O. There was also a machine gun, No 2503, in the enemy 3rd line about this point, but it could not fire into the depression. Hqrs got back safely except for one messenger killed and another wounded, and returned to Q.17 b 2 3. where the night was passed. During the afternoon snipers from the 3rd line had been active and Lieut ASTON, L.G.O had been shot dead. The night passed quietly.	

T2134. Wt. W708—776. 500000. 4/15. Sir J. C. & S.

Instructions regarding War Diaries and Intelligence Summaries are contained in F. S. Regs., Part II. and the Staff Manual respectively. Title pages will be prepared in manuscript.

WAR DIARY
or
INTELLIGENCE SUMMARY.
(Erase heading not required.)

Army Form C. 2118.

Nov 1916 HOWE BN RND.

Place	Date	Hour	Summary of Events and Information	Remarks and references to Appendices
	14th		Early in the morning a "Tank" arrived, well over to the South, guided by Lieut A. CAMPBELL of the 188 LTM BY, and some 400 Germans gave in to it, the whole of the 1st & 2nd lines and part of the 3rd line being cleared. White flags were shown on the parapet of the 3rd line. Sub Lieut FORRESTER, who had just come up with 30 reinforcements then took a party of 20 of these and entering the 3rd line at Q17 b 66 cleared it and the big Coy Hqrs dugout at Q18 a 2.5½, bringing back 5 officers and 129 other prisoners.	
			At 4 pm Hqrs moved to this dugout, and almost at once moved on to the GREEN LINE (trench just East of Station Road) where touch was obtained with ANSON on the left at a gully about Q12c 2.3, whence we extended 100x to the right. There were then about 70 men with Hqrs. Shortly after received orders we could make ourselves comfortable for the night, so returned to Company Commander's dugout at Q18 a 2.5½ where our telephone had been installed. This dugout had belonged to 10th Coy, 3rd Bn 55 R.I.R, II Gd Res. Div. All the Company books were found & sent in. and a quiet night passed.	

T2134. Wt. W708—776. 500000. 4/15. Sir J. C. & S.

Instructions regarding War Diaries and Intelligence Summaries are contained in F. S. Regs., Part II. and the Staff Manual respectively. Title pages will be prepared in manuscript.

WAR DIARY
or
INTELLIGENCE SUMMARY.
(Erase heading not required.)

Army Form C. 2118.

Howe Bn

RND.

Place	Date	Hour	Summary of Events and Information	Remarks and references to Appendices
			Nov 1916	
	15th		At dawn parties of 4 under N.C.O.s proceeded to bury dead and to search dugouts. The row of big dugouts at Q 18 a 6 6 had been dealt with by 'P' bombs and were still burning.	
			At noon moved back by small parties, having been relieved by 37th Div. Cleared NO MANS LAND by 1 pm, returned to ENGLEBELMER where tea was ready - thence to HEDAUVILLE where went in to billets. Were cinematographed leaving ENGLEBELMER. Left HEDAUVILLE by lorries at 11 pm for PUCHEVILLERS	
[P]UCHEVILLERS	16th		Halted. Casualties amount to 19 officers, (6 dead) and 368 O.R. Lieut MAYNARD + ASTON, dead Sub Lieuts FLETCHER, WAGNER, HAKEN and HOWARD killed. Lieut Comdr P.H. EDWARDS, Lieuts K.E. PARKES, G. R. AIREY Sub Lieuts B. W. WEBB, R. V. IRELAND, W. MARLOW, R. GRAY H. FRY, H. REDDICK wounded Lieut C. D. F. de la MOTHE, and Sub Lieuts G. N. STRANG and AEN CHANCE missing.	
GÉZAINCOURT	17th		Marched to GÉZAINCOURT. Adjutant went with GSO3 to visit battlefield and take notes of booty. Found 2 m.g. 3 large wooden minenwerfer (one destroyed by a shell)	

T2134. Wt. W708—773. 500000. 4/15. Sir J. C. & S.

Army Form C. 2118.

Instructions regarding War Diaries and Intelligence Summaries are contained in F. S. Regs., Part II. and the Staff Manual respectively. Title pages will be prepared in manuscript.

WAR DIARY
or
INTELLIGENCE SUMMARY.
(Erase heading not required.)

HOWE Bn

Place	Date	Hour	Summary of Events and Information	Remarks and references to Appendices
			Nov 1916 RND.	
			Three iron heavy Minenwerfer, and some 6 or 8 machines for firing 'Pineapple' bombs. The 190th Bde was engaged in clearing the battlefield and was collecting all material. The ground was frozen and mud hard.	
BERNAVILLE	18th		Snow on the ground, very cold Marched to BERNAVILLE	
	19		Halted	
	20		Inspected by G.O.C RND who said a few complimentary words.	
CRAMONT	21		marched to CRAMONT, a short march, only one halt.	
MARCHEVILLE	22		TO MARCHEVILLE	
	23		TO SAILLY BRAY Bad billetting	
	24		TO FAVIÈRES A very straggling village and very wet surroundings'	
FAVIERES	25		Cleaning up	
	26		Draft of 150 OR from 3rd Entrenching Bn	
	27		Began training.	
	28		Training on fields near FAVIÈRES	Charles [illegible] Lieut Col. Comdt HOWE
	29 30		Training on area East of ROMAINE.	

T2134. Wt. W708–776. 500000. 4/15. Sir J. C. & S.

S E C R E T.   Copy No...6......

188th. INFANTRY BRIGADE ORDER No. 56.

Brigade Headquarters,
9th. November, 1916.

Reference 1/20,000 sheet
and attached maps.

188th. Infantry Brigade Operation Order No. 44, dated 23rd. October, 1916, is cancelled.

Plan ✓ 1. (a) The Reserve Army is to attack the Enemy on both sides of the river ANCRE.

(b) The Vth. Corps is to capture ~~BEAUREGARD DOVECOTE~~ BROWN LINE., and form a defensive flank from that place Westward along the high ground to SERRE and JOHN COPSE.

(c) The II Corps, on the South of the ANCRE, is to attack Northwards, and, after capturing ST. PIERRE DIVION, and GRANDCOURT, will seize MIRAUMONT and all crossings over the river between that place and BRIDGE ROAD (Q.18.b.8.7.)(both inclusive). The line of the MIRAUMONT -BEAUCOURT-sur-ANCRE ROAD, between L.35.c.9.3. and a point South of BOIS d'HOLLANDE will also be captured by II Corps.

(d) The date of attack, to be referred to as "Z" day, and the hour "ZERO" will be notified later.

Preliminary Bombardment. ✓ 2. The attack will be preceded by an intense bombardment on "X" and "Y" days, beginning at 5-0a.m. and becoming intense at 6-0a.m.

Objectives. ✓ 3. (a) The objectives allotted to the Battalions of this Brigade are shewn on the attached map"A". Also the dividing line between Brigades and Right and Left Battalions of 188th. Infantry Brigade. ✓

(b) The Front of attack of the 63rd. Division will be from Railway Road to about Q.17.a.4.5. ✓ The final objective of the Division will be PUIXIEUX RIVER TRENCH from the MIRAUMONT - BEAUCOURT ROAD to about R.2.b.2.9.(BROWN LINE).

Tasks of Brigades. ✓ 4. The GREEN, YELLOW, and BLUE LINES will be captured by the 188th. and 189th. Infantry Brigades; the BROWN LINE by the 190th. Infantry Brigade.

Assembly Areas. ✓ 5. The Assembly Areas for Infantry Brigades are shown in map "B", which is attached.

Advanced Brigade Headquarters. ✓ 6. The advanced Brigade Headquarters will be at -

KNIGHTSBRIDGE BARRACKS about Q.16.d.3.8½.

(map b) and will be occupied by 5-0p.m. on "Y" night.

"UP" and "DOWN" Trenches. ✓ 7. Communication Trenches will be allocated for "UP" and "DOWN" traffic as follows, from "ZERO" onwards:-
"UP" - GABION AVENUE, LONG SAP.
"DOWN" - LONG ACRE, CONSTITUTION HILL, KNIGHTSBRIDGE, RAILWAY.

"Jumping off" Trenchos.

8. The "Jumping off" trenchos are as follows:-

1st. and 2nd. Wavos - GORDON TRENCH, and extension thoreof to the North.

3rd. Wave - ROBERTS TRENCH and continu- -ation into CHARING CROSS.

4th. Wave - In "T" heads, which have boon constructed leading off Parados of ROBERTS TRENCH, and CHARING CROSS.

Time Tablo of Attack.

9. The attack will be carried out in accordance with the attached table of Barragos. It must be clearly understood, however, that the times are published merely as a guide to the Infantry, and are not orders for the exact time of assaults.

It is of paramount and vital importance that the Infantry keeps close up to the Artillery Barrago and advances whonever it lifts.

Artillery.

10. The 63rd. Division will be supported by the Artillery of two Divisions and by a large number of heavy guns.

There will be a barrago of howitzers in advance of the 18 pounder barrage mentioned in the Time Table, while Corps artillery will bombard the Enemy's positions still further inside the German linos.

Scheme of Attack.

11. The Brigade will assault with two Battalions in Front Line. Each Battalion will have four Companies in Line, in column of platoons, the platoons forming the first, second, third and fourth waves respectively. Platoons will be in single rank with ten yards distance between first and second waves, and about 50 yards between the remainder.

The two Supporting Battalions will be in 2nd. Line in similar formation, the leading lines 150 yards distance from fourth wave position of leading Battalion, and will advance over the top from their Assembly Areas.

The dividing line between Battalions is LONG SAP and GABION AVENUE.

ORDER OF BATTALIONS.

Left Front, 1st. Royal Marines.
Right Front, Howe Battalion.
Left Support, 2nd. Royal Marines.
Right Support, Anson Battalion.

Capture of DOTTED GREEN LINE.

12. (a) 1st. Royal Marines and Howe Battalion will be responsible for the capture of the first objective, i.e, RESERVE TRENCH in the Enemy Front Line system (DOTTED GREEN LINE), and the cleaning up of all three lines. The first and second waves will advance straight through to this DOTTED LINE, the third wave will clean up the Enemy's SUPPORT LINE and the fourth wave, the Enemy's FRONT LINE

(b) /

12 (contd)

(b) LEFT FLANK. Officers Commanding Left Battalions will pay particular attention to the protection of the Left Flank of the Brigade. To ensure this, the frontage allotted to the Left Company should be less than that allotted to other Companies, and the proportion of Lewis and Vickers guns increased.

It should be explained to those Companies that in the event of the attack on our left being held up, our Advance must not be delayed, but that provision must be made for forming a defensive flank, should circumstances render it necessary, by formation of Strong Points, defended by Machine Guns.

Capture of GREEN LINE.

13. The DOTTED GREEN LINE will be captured at "0" hour, 18 minutes. At "0" hour, 23 minutes, 2nd. Royal Marines and Anson Battalion will pass through 1st. Royal Marines and Howe Battalion and capture GREEN LINE.

The first and second waves will advance straight through to this line and consolidate it.

The third wave will clean up dug-outs in the STATION ROAD.

The fourth will clean up DOTTED BLUE LINE, and the many dug-outs on reverse slope of the hill.

Bombers from the 2nd. Royal Marines will block STATION ALLEY.

There will be a halt of one hour on the GREEN LINE. During this halt there will be four pauses of five minutes in the 18 pounder Barrage. Commanders should take advantage of these pauses to obtain a view of the ground over which they are to advance, and to check their bearings.

The rate of fire of the Artillery Barrage during this halt will be reduced.

At the end of the fourth pause, i.e, at 1. 40' an intense barrage will re-open and this will be the signal to the Infantry to advance.

Capture of YELLOW LINE.

14. The advance on the YELLOW LINE will be carried out by 1st. Royal Marines and Howe Battalion. These Battalions will have re-organized in the German Front system and move forward to the GREEN LINE at 1. 10'.

Bombers and Lewis Guns will be sent up STATION ALLEY by 1st. Royal Marines. There will be a halt of ~~about~~ 1 hour on the Yellow Line. During this halt, 2nd. Royal Marines and Anson Battalion will close up to the YELLOW LINE.

There will be four pauses of five minutes in the Artillery barrage during this halt. At the end of the fourth pause, i.e, at 3. 20' an intense barrage will re-open, and this will be the signal for the Infantry to advance.

Capture of DOTTED YELLOW LINE.

15. The advance against the DOTTED YELLOW LINE will be by 2nd. Royal Marines and Anson Battalion, with 1st. Royal Marines and Howe Battalion in Support.

Capture of DOTTED BROWN LINE.

16. A halt of about four minutes will be made on the DOTTED YELLOW LINE. During this halt, 1st. Royal Marines and Howe Battalion will pass through 2nd. Royal Marines and Anson Battalion, and close right up to the Artillery barrage, which will be halted 100 yards in front of the DOTTED YELLOW LINE.

At 3.38' the barrage will again commence lifting and 1st. Royal Marines and Howe Battalion, supported by 2nd. Royal Marines and Anson Battalion will advance on and capture the DOTTED BROWN LINE.

Capture of BLUE LINE. 17. Immediately the DOTTED BROWN LINE is captured, the whole of the Brigade will advance to and consolidate the BLUE LINE, keeping close up to the Artillery Barrage. Battle patrols will be sent forward from this line along the entire front and especially towards the BOIS D'HOLLANDE, and ARTILLERY AVENUE will be blocked.

A halt of one hour will be made on the BLUE LINE. During this halt there will be four pauses of five minutes each in the Artillery Barrage. Meanwhile the 190th. Infantry Brigade will advance to the BLUE LINE.

Capture of BROWN LINE. 18. The opening of an intense barrage at the end of the fourth pause, i.e, 5.20', will be the signal for the advance of the 190th. Infantry Brigade on the BROWN LINE, passing through the 188th. and 189th. Infantry Brigades.

The Brigade will advance will all four Battalions in Front line.

The first and second waves will advance straight through to the Support line and consoli-date it.

The third and fourth waves will halt on and clean up the PUISIEUX TRENCH.

The 188th. and 189th. Infantry Brigades will meanwhile re-organize on the BLUE LINE.

It is absolutely essential that the BROWN LINE should be consolidated as strongly as possible. Counter-attacks are certain, and in no circumstances whatever must ground once gained by the Royal Naval Division be re-occupied by the Enemy.

Advance of 37th. Division. 19. After the capture of the BROWN LINE, it is probable that the 37th. Division will pass through the 63rd. Division and advance on BEAUREGARD DOVECOTE.

Strong Points. 20. Strong Points will be formed in all objectives as under:-

DOTTED GREEN LINE -	1st. Royal Marines,	Q.11.d.1.0.
	Howe Battalion,	Q.17.b.8.7.
DOTTED BLUE LINE -	Anson Battalion,	Q.12.c.0.0.
GREEN LINE -	1st. Royal Marines,	Q.12.c.2.5.
YELLOW LINE-	1st. Royal Marines,	Q.12.b.0.9.
DOTTED YELLOW LINE-	Anson Battalion,	R.7.a.3.8.

The ½ Company, Divisional Engineers together with ½ "C" Company of the Worcester Regiment will concentrate in our Front Line Trench, moving from their place of Assembly in rear of the Left Support Battalion as soon as the fourth Wave of this Battalion has left our Trenches. These two Units have been allotted special tasks in construction of Strong Points under separate orders, namely at Q.11d.6.8. and Q.6.c.9.3.

The remaining Strong Points enumerated above will therefore be constructed solely by Infantry Battalions concerned without R.E. help.

These Units will not leave our Front Line Trenches until the DOTTED BLUE LINE has been taken.

Machine Guns.

21. Four Machine Guns will be allotted to the close support of each Front Battalion. These will advance with the Battalion, moving to each objective as soon as it is gained.

Officers Commanding each group of guns will maintain touch with Battalion Headquarters concerned.

Four Machine Guns will cover the advance of the attack on the first objective from the vicinity of SHOOTERS HILL. Detailed instructions are being issued direct to Officer Commanding 188th. M.G. Company.

The remaining four guns will be kept in Brigade Reserve and brought into action at the dis--cretion of Officer Commanding Machine Gun Company in accordance with instructions previously issued to him by the Brigade Commander.

The principle to be observed in the use of Machine and Lewis guns is that they should be pushed boldly forward into each objective gained, and by their fire secure it against counter-attacks, as the Infantry will be busy digging.

A Machine Gun is not a gun until it is in action.

Stokes' Mortars.

22. Officer Commanding 188th. Light Trench Mortar Battery will arrange for two guns to accompany the Front Line Battalions and two to accompany the Support Battalions. These should be used on the Left flank of the advance and also against any Strong Points met with. The remaining guns will be brought into forward positions available to replace guns destroyed.

Headquarters and Advanced Depots in the Hostile Line.

23. Position of Battalion, Brigade Headquarters, and Dumps within our own lines are shewn in sketch map attached. The probable positions of the former in Enemy's lines will be as under when Brigade has occupied BLUE LINE. Brigade and Battalion Head--quarters will be established in the following vicinities, at the most suitable sights available:-

(a) Brigade Headquarters, Q.12.c.2.4.
Battalion Headquarters, ~~R.1.d.3.8.~~ Q12b.4.6.

(b) Telephone and Signal Stations, in the neighbourhood of Brigade and Battalion Headquarters.

Advance of Headquarters.

24. (a) The forward movements of Battalion Headquarters will be by successive bounds. Battalion Commanders will not advance until the objective of their attack has been gained.

Representative of Battalion Headquarters should follow the last wave of Battalion and select a sight for the Headquarters near locality previously decided on. This will be notified to the Battalion Commander who will proceed direct to his new Head--quarters as soon as the objective is gained, information being immediately sent back to Brigade Headquarters as to his new position.

(b) When the Brigade is established on the BLUE LINE, Brigade Headquarters will be moved forward to the GREEN LINE.

Aeroplane Co-operation. 25. Contact Aeroplanes will be employed to fix the positions gained by the Infantry in accordance with the principles lately practised by the Division.

Flares will be lighted:-

(a) On attaining each objective.
(b) Whenever hung up.
(c) When an aeroplane sounds its Klaxon horn.
(d) Just before dark and in the early morning if an aeroplane is above.

Communications. 26. Communications from Battalion to Brigade Headquarters at "ZERO" hour will be as follows:-

From each Battalion Headquarters, a telephone will be laid direct to Brigade together with Lateral lines between Battalions.

A Visual Station in telephonic communication with Brigade Headquarters will be established in RIDGE TRENCH, Q.22.d.7.9.

At least two pigeons per Battalion will be at Battalion Headquarters, and they should be used singly and sparingly. The pigeons will be replaced if possible later in the day, at MESNIL, Q.28.c.7.8.

An Advanced Report Centre (No.1.) will be established at POND STREET, Q.17.c.5.8. to which all communications should be directed after Battalions have left their first Headquarters

As soon as the DOTTED GREEN LINE is taken Report Centre No.2. will be established at Q.17.b.4.4.

As soon as GREEN LINE has been occupied and the attack has advanced against the YELLOW LINE, Report Centre No.3. will be established at Q.11.d.9.0.

Re-lay Posts for runners will be established at Report Centres Nos. 1 and 2. by one runner per Battalion from those allotted to Brigade Headquarters and at Report Centre No.3, by one runner from Batt-alion Headquarters when Battalions move forward.

It is to be understood that the Re-lay system will only be brought into use if telephonic communi-cation has broken down between Advanced Report Centres and Brigade Headquarters. Officer Commanding 188th. Machine Gun Company will establish his Headquarters with those of Anson Battalion and Officer Commanding Light Trench Mortar Battery with those of 2nd. Royal Marines.

Messages to and from these Units will be passed through the affiliated Battalion.

The following runners additional to the three Battalion runners, already detailed per Battalion for duty at Brigade Headquarters, are to be told off:-

2 per Battalion for duty at Brigade Headquarters
2 per Battalion for duty at Battalion H.Q.

Thus/

Para. 26 contd.

Thus there will be in each Battalion:-

5 runners for duty at Brigade Headquarters.
5 runners for duty at Battalion Headquarters.

Over and above those Battalion and Brigade runners, the following are to be detailed for duty at Brigade Headquarters for Divisional-Brigade Communication:-

1st. Royal Marines,	3.
2nd. Royal Marines,	2.
Anson Battalion,	2.
Howe Battalion,	3.

All the above runners for duty at Brigade Headquarters are to report at Signal Office, KNIGHTSBRIDGE HEADQUARTERS, at 5-0p.m. "Y" day.

All runners and mounted dispatch riders will carry dispatches in left hand breast pocket. Anyone seeing a killed or wounded runner or dispatch rider will search him for dispatches and hand them in with as little delay as possible to the nearest runner post or Signal Office.

One Surplus Officer from each Battalion will be told off for duty at Battalion Headquarters as Brigade Liaison Officer. His duties will be to report in person to Brigade Headquarters as each objective is taken and the situation clear. He should also be used for very important messages from Battalion to Brigade in the event of other communications failing. Pitcairn

Tunnels.

27. Communication across NO MAN'S LAND must be opened as soon as the GREEN LINE has been captured. The pair of Tunnels near LONG SAP will be available for the Brigade. These tunnels will be blown up by the Officer Commanding Tunnelling Company as soon as GREEN LINE is captured, orders to blow up being given direct to the TUNNELLERS by Brigadier.

These Tunnels should, therefore, not be used for the accommodation of large numbers of men previous to ZERO.

Tanks. ✓

28. The 63rd. Division attack will be assisted by six Tanks, which will act in accordance with the principles already issued to all concerned.

During night "Y/Z" the noise of the Tanks moving to their positions of Assembly between the hours of 7-0p.m. and 10-0p.m. must be drowned by noise demonstrations.

Officer Commanding Machine Gun Company will arrange for bursts of Machine Gun Fire throughout this period.

Tanks have been ordered to keep as close to the barrage as possible. Infantry must, however, be specially warned <u>not</u> to wait for the Tanks.

The ultimate objective of all Tanks has been given as PUISIOUX TRENCH. A map with the route to be taken by each Tank has been issued.

Infantry escorts will not be required for the Tanks.

Gas. ✓ 29. Early on night "Y/Z" gas shells will be fired into valley South of SERRE and into BEAUMONT HAMEL.

Isolation of Area of Attack. ✓ 30. From now onwards, between the hours of 6-0p.m. and 5-0a.m. daily, the area of attack will be isolated as much as possible, by bursts of Machine Gun fire and Artillery fire being directed on all approaches known to be used by the Enemy.

~~Synchronization of Watches.~~ 31. ~~Watches will be synchronized at 9-0p.m. on "Y" day and at one hour before ZERO.~~ Cancelled

Equipment. ✓ 32. All troops will be in Battle order and will carry 220 rounds S.A.A.

4 Sandbags.(passed through the belt two on each side).
At least one Iron Ration.
Unexpended portion of day's ration.
Gas Helmets.
1 Flare.
1 Very's Light cartridge.

Special men will be detailed to carry buckets, Grenades. In addition to the above, 80% of the third and fourth waves of the attacking troops in the Front and Support Battalions will carry pick or shovel.

As many wire-cutters as possible will be issued beforehand by Divisional Headquarters.

Men carrying wire-cutters will wear a yellow armlet. Runners will be lightly equipped and will not carry rifles.

They will wear a blue armlet with a white stripe.

✓ 33. The following enclosures to Order have been issued as under:-

Maps of the German Trenches with objectives marked, 30 copies per Battalion, 7 copies per 188th. M.G. Company and L.T.M. Battery.

Map E. shewing Assembly areas of Brigades, one copy per each Brigade Unit.

Tank maps, one copy per Battalion.

Administrative Orders, one copy per each Brigade Unit.

S. O. S. 34. The S.O.S. rocket signal is WHITE,GREEN,WHITE. These have been issued to Battalions, and each Company will carry forward at least three GREEN and six WHITE rockets.

Medical. 35. Three Bearer Sub-divisions, 63rd.(R.N.) Division Medical Unit have been allotted to the Brigade Attack Area.

Orders have been issued to them direct by A.D.M.S.

These/

35 (contd)

These Units will take their places in in the Line on "Y" day according to Assembly Orders which have been issued.

H. St. Lecker-Smollett?
Captain,
Brigade Major,

Issued to Signals at

Copies to:-

No. 1 File.
2. War Diary.
3. 1st. Royal Marines.
4. 2nd. Royal Marines.
5. Anson Battalion.
6. Howe Battalion.
7. 188th. M.G. Company.
8. 188th. L.T.M. Battery.
9. No. 2 Field Coy, D.E.
10. No. 2 Signal Section.
11. 63rd. Division(3 copies)
12. 189th. Inf. Brigade.
13. 190th. Inf. Brigade.
14. 153rd. Highland Brigade.
15. ½ "C" Coy. 14th. Worcesters.
16. "C" Group, R.F.A.
17. Brigade Major.
18. Staff Captain,
19. Captain Sherman.
20. Intelligence Officer.
21. C.R.A, 63rd. Division.

APPENDIX "A"

NOTES ON OPERATION ORDERS.

Hot Drink. 1. Arrangements will be made by Battalions for the distribution of a hot drink during "Y/Z" night. This must be completed during darkness.

Movement. 2. It cannot be too clearly impressed upon all ranks that no movement whatever must take place between the first streak of dawn and "ZERO hour. Striking of matches is to be carefully screened.

Great coats will be rolled in bundles before dawn, and no man will be permitted to leave the ranks after 5-0a.m. # Qr. Lyons.

Synchroni--zation of Watches. 3. Watches will be synchronized with Brigade Headquarters by telephone as follows:-

"Y" day - 6-30p.m. and 7-15p.m. 9-30p.m. an Officer from each Battalion will report to Advanced Brigade Headquarters. What officer Fletcher

"Z" day - 5-15a.m. by telephone.

The code word "SLIP" will be used in each case to denote the hour. Thus - 7-15p.m. will be described as "SLIP FIFTEEN".

Compass Bearings. 4. Bearings must be taken on the map of the line of advance of each Battalion, and communi--cated to all Officers.

Flares. 5. Red flares only will be used by attacking Infantry of 63rd.(R.N.)Division.

Listening Patrols. 6. Listening Patrols will be established as usual on "Y/Z" night.

Liaison Officers. 7. Officer Commanding Anson Battalion will detail a surplus Officer for Liaison duty with 153rd. Highland Brigade, which is operating on our Left. This Officer is to report to 188th. Infantry Brigade Headquarters at 10-0a.m. on "Y" day.

The Brigade Intelligence Officer will act as Liaison Officer with 189th. Infantry Brigade on Right.

Assembly Move Orders. 8. Assembly Move orders will be issued shortly.

Checks. 9. It must be impressed on all concerned that they are on no account to halt because Units on their flanks happen to be held up. The best way of assisting their neighbours on such occasions will be to continue their own advance.

Direction. 10. All Company Commanders must be impressed with the necessity of maintaining their direction and marching straight on to their objective. With this object, the ground must be carefully studied beforehand, land-marks noted wherever possible, and compas bearings taken.

APPENDIX "A" (contd.)

Wire. 11. Officers Commanding Front Line Battalions will ensure that where necessary, diagonal strips be cut in our wire on "Y/Z" night; cut wire will be loosely thrown over the gaps.

Trench Bridges. 12. Officer Commanding No. 2 Field Company, Divisional Engineers will arrange that all trenches are prepared with ladders or steps for rapid exit and with bridges for the passage of troops coming up in Support, to be in position by "Y" night.

Secret Papers. 13. No papers likely to be of value to the Enemy will be taken over the parapet.

Surplus Personnel. 14. Not more than 20 Officers per Battalion must take part in an assault and a proportion of reliable N.C.O's must also be left behind.

A.D. [illegible]

Captain,
Brigade Major,
188th. Infantry Brigade.

2-11-16.

APPENDIX "B"

ORDERS FOR

½ Company No. 2. Field Company, Divisional Engineers,
And. ½ "C" Company, 14th. Worcestershire Regiment.

Assembly Points — 1. The ½ Company Divisional Engineers and ½ "C" Company 14th. Worcesters will report as stated in Assembly Orders.

Tasks. — 2. They will advance from the British Front Line Trench as soon as GREEN LINE has been captured, and will construct a Strong Point at Q.11.d.6.8.

As soon as YELLOW LINE has been taken a further Strong Point will be constructed at Q.6.c.9.3.

Construction. — 3. The ½ Company Worcester Regiment will work under the orders of the Officer Commanding ½ Field Company Divisional Engineers. Material to be carried will be arranged for by the latter Officer, who will also be responsible for the type of Strong Points to be constructed according to the locality and contours of the ground, paying particular attention to the protection of the Left flank.

Communications. — 4. With reference to para. 2, Officer Commanding ½ Company Divisional Engineers will maintain communi--cation by runners with Headquarters of Left Support Battalion, viz, 2nd. Royal Marines in ST. JAMES' STREET.

After Divisional Engineers and ½ Company Worcester Regiment leave the Front British Line, the Officer Commanding ½ Field Company Divisional Engineers will ensure that full information as regards progress of work is transmitted to Brigade Head--quarters through the Advanced Report Centres.

A.D. Telfer-Smollett

Captain,
Brigade Major,
188th. Infantry Brigade.

9-11-16.

APPENDIX "C"

ORDERS FOR

188th. Machine Gun Company.

Distribution. 1. Four guns will advance with each Front Line Battalion. Six guns will cover the advance to the first objective with indirect fire from the line CARNALEA-SHOOTERS HILL-OLD FRENCH TRENCH.
On the first objective being gained these six guns and the remaining two guns will follow the Support Battalions to the second objective.

Object. 2. All guns must be pushed boldly forward, and come into action in close support of the Battalions with which they advance.
The Left flank of the Brigade must be carefully protected. Section Officers in the Left Sub-section on reaching their objective should endeavour to obtain position from which the Left flank of each successive advance may be covered.
On arriving at the final objective all guns available must cover all approaches and the flanks of the Brigade, should the advance on the flanks be held up.

Hostile Strong Points. 3. Should these be encountered, Machine Guns should be detailed to cover them.

Assembly. 4. On "Y" day four guns in support of the Howe Battalion will be close to the junction of ROBERTS TRENCH and BEDFORD STREET, four guns in support of 1st. Royal Marines near the junction of ROBERTS TRENCH and LONG SAP, two guns near the junction of BEDFORD STREET and VICTORIA STREET.
Officer Commanding Machine Gun Company to arrange with Officer Commanding Battalions concerned.

Headquarters. 5. Headquarters will be attached to Anson Battalion.

Personnel. 6. 32 men will be attached as Ammunition carriers (two per gun). These will report on the evening of "X" day as laid down in Assembly Orders.

8 per Bn

A.D. Tupper-Carey (?)

Captain,
Brigade Major,
188th. Infantry Brigade.

9-11-16.

LTM ?
10 men to carry bombs.

SECRET

NOTES ON TANKS.

****

1. Concealment from view and hearing is of utmost importance. There should be no movement by day forward or at detraining station except for the actual detraining. Tanks must be kept under tarpaulins by day as they are easily distinguished by aircraft and kite balloons.

2. Tanks should move off to positions of assembly on night X/Y, not more than 1 mile in rear of starting points. Where cover does not exist pits must be dug - tank personnel cannot do this. Pits should be 16 feet wide, 6 feet deep and 32 feet long exclusive of ramps. During construction of pits earth must be scattered and the pits should not be left uncovered by day.

3. Tracks should be prepared for the approach march on night Y/Z. Communication trenches, 1st,2nd and 3rd line trenches should be filled in when necessary. Tanks move with great difficulty by night if any obstacles are encountered. As far as possible regular routes and tracks should be followed and rough ground avoided. Movement should be during hours of moonlight.

4. PACE.

By night allow 15 yards a minute for movement.
By day allow 15 yards a minute over very heavily shelled ground.
30 yards a minute over lightly shelled ground or trenches.
Woods and heavily shelled ground should be avoided as objectives.

5. SIGNALS.

Signal communication will be required between A.H.Q. and central Tankerdromo, and between Corps H.Q. and the Tank Company Commander (the latter requires an instrument to himself and not merely the use of some existing office).
The following signals have been used with success:-

Tanks to infantry	-	RED FLAG	- Broken down.
		GREEN FLAG	- Am on objective.
Infantry to tank	-	"Enemy in sight" signal	- Tanks required.
Tanks to aircraft	-	Lamp succession of T	- Broken down.
		succession of H	- Am on objective.

6. PIGEONS.

Two pigeons por tank required from Corps.
Officers have been instructed in using pigeons.

7. DUMPS.

Forward dumps for companies are required of ammunition, water, petrol stores.

8. PETROL.

Aeroplane petrol is required.

9. MECHANICAL ASSISTANCE.

Assistance is required in fitters, as establishment is quite inadequate.

10/

10. TRANSPORT.

Assistance will probably be required in transport for heavy stores from Railhead to Tankordrome and thence to companies. From Compabies to broken down tanks, pack animals would be invaluable if forthcoming, at the rate of 2 per tank in action.

11. OFFICERS.

Officers are short of experience and will require very careful instruction. It should be made very clear whether tanks are to have their starting points at zero, or cross our front line at zero, when these cases occur.

12. BREAKDOWNS.

Tanks will not continue to function once they have broken down. Patching up is no real use and only leads to disappointment and failure. Junior officers are often very sanguine as to the possibilities of a patched up tank.

13. REPORTS.

It will be of he greatest assistance if formations to which tanks are attached will repeat to the next higher tank unit all reports affecting tanks which they send to their own next higher formation. This refers both to G. and A. Branches.

14. SUCCESS OF TANKS depends :-

(a) On mechanical fitness.

(b) On concealment and preparation of approaches.

(c) On every tank officer knowing exactly what he has to do.

15. In should be impressed on Infantry that they should on no account wait for tanks.

C.O.

NOTES BY THE DIVISIONAL COMMANDER.

1. ENEMY STRONG POINTS.

When some strong point holds up an attack it should not be assaulted by the line with the aid of reinforcements. This causes unnecessary loss. It should be masked by rifle or Lewis gun fire and troops should push round the flanks and surround it.

Its surrender is then only a matter of time and the attack is not delayed.

2. CLEARING ENEMY DUGOUTS.

Troops should not enter dug-outs until they are cleared, nor should surrenders be accepted until the Boches in the dug-outs come outside.

All the exits of each dug-out should be found and a sentry put in each before it is attacked by "P" bombs. If this is not done our own men may go in at one entrance whilst a "P" bomb is thrown down another and also Boches may escape by an unguarded exit.

3. GUARDING FLANKS.

(a) Whatever may be the original plan it seldom works out entirely successfully. Hence flanks must always be most carefully watched in case the troops which ought to be there have been held up and the flanks become uncovered.

(b) The flank companies of battalions and brigades and the flank battalions of the Division must always obtain touch with the neighbouring troops and fix the exact position in which these neighbouring troops are, reporting at once to higher authority either where they are or that they have failed to find them.

4. SENDING IN INFORMATION.

It is absolutely essential that all units should continually send in every possible information, both positive and negative.

In the heat of the fight this is often forgotten, yet the timely receipt of some apparently trivial information may make the difference between success and failure.

5. CONSOLIDATION.

All objectives should be consolidated, i.e. trenches reversed and cleared. This is done to provide a line of defence in case of counter-attack.

It follows that the final objective is the most important and must be made as strong as it possibly can be, and as quickly as possible however exhausted the men may be.

A considerable number of machine and Lewis guns must be got up in each objective as soon as it is gained.

In the last objective every single machine and Lewis gun there is must be got into position at once.

6. BATTLE PATROLS.

When the final objective is gained Battle patrols of 10 or 12 men with a proportion of tools must be immediately pushed forward, as far as possible, and until close touch with the enemy is gained.

These parties should be about 75 yards apart and should dig themselves in strongly.

When this is complete, some Lewis Guns should be sent forward, to, at any rate, alternate posts.

Under the protection of these posts, further working parties must be sent forward to connect the posts by a continuous trench.

The object being to gain every possible inch of ground, with a view to a future renewal of the attack.

The line thus made eventually becomes the front line and the original objective, the support line.

1000 50 boxes. 120 12 250 1000 250 12 500 240 80 P. 3 boxes

7. HELPING NEIGHBOURING TROOPS.

The fact that one portion of our attack is checked is no reason for neighbouring portions to halt. On the contrary the best way to help those who are held up is for the troops on the flanks to push on and so turn the flanks of the enemy and bring an enfilade fire to bear on him.

8. SUPPORT LINE.

When the first objective is reached, and, in a less degree, in all objectives, a support line must always be dug.

It frequently happens that the front line is heavily shelled and that casualties are saved by holding it almost entirely with machine and Lewis guns whilst the bulk of the infantry occupy the support line behind.

Machine and Lewis guns thus used should be laid so as to bring a cross fire on all approaches likely to be used by the enemy.

9. REFORMING.

Every commander must lose no opportunity of reforming the troops under his command.

Troops extended should be closed whenever the ground and the enemy's fire permits and no troops should be extended unnecessarily.

By this means only can the men be steadied and the power of command retained.

10. CONCLUSION.

I hope that these notes may be of some assistance to junior commanders and help them to maintain, and to add to, the already splendid traditions of the Royal Naval Division and to obtain the maximum result from the enormous superiority which the men of the Division possess over their treacherous and cowardly enemy.

C.D.SHUTE. Major General,
Comdg. 63rd (Royal Naval) Division.

23rd October, 1916.

1 runner to Report Centre
No.
1 guide to rations

Order 56.

ASSEMBLY MOVE ORDERS.

1. With reference to 188th. Infantry Brigade Order No. 56 dated 9th. instant, the following procedure will be adopted by Units moving into the Assembly Areas on "Y" day:-

1st. Royal Marines and Howe Battalion will be in Assembly positions by 2-30p.m. under arrangements to be made between Commanding Officers concerned.

2nd. Royal Marines will move via GABION TRENCH and clear KNIGHTSBRIDGE by 3-30p.m.

Anson Battalion will move via GABION TRENCH and clear KNIGHTSBRIDGE by 5-30p.m.

188th. Light Trench Mortar Battery will clear KNIGHTSBRIDGE by 6-0p.m. moving in rear of Anson Battalion.

188th. Machine Gun Company will be in position by 11-0a.m.

½ 2nd. Field Company 63rd. Divisional Engineers and ½ "C" Company, 14th. Worcesters will report at Headquarters 2nd. Royal Marines at ENGLEBELMER Bivouacs not later than 12-30p.m. on "Y" day. These Units will follow that Battalion to the Trenches and will be allotted their Assembly positions by Officer Commanding 2nd. Royal Marines. Officer Commanding ½ 2nd. Field Company and ½ "C" Company Worcester Regiment will arrange for a supply of water to be taken up for use on "Y/Z" night, and they will also arrange for a hot drink to be issued during the night.

2 Bearer Sub-divisions of 63rd.(R.N.) Division Medical Unit. The Bearer Sub-division from No. 1 Field Ambulance will report to Headquarters, 2nd. Royal Marines in Bivouacs at ENGLEBELMER, and that from No. 3 Field Ambulance to Headquarters, Anson Battalion in Billets at ENGLEBELMER, all at NOON on "Y" day. They will then follow these Battalions into the Assembly Area where Officers Commanding Battalions concerned will make provision for their accommodation during "Y/Z" night.

CARRYING PARTIES.

(a) For 188th. Machine Gun Company.

8 men per Battalion (except the Battalion in the Line, whose men will report at the Machine Gun Company Headquarters in VICTORIA STREET at 6-0p.m. on "X" day) will report at 6-0p.m. on "X" day at Headquarters, 188th. Machine Gun Company at ENGLEBELMER, and will be attached to that Unit.

ASSEMBLY ORDERS (Contd.)

CARRYING PARTIES (Contd.)

(b) For 188th. Light Trench Mortar Battery.

Ten men per Battalion will report at Headquarters, Anson Battalion, in Billets ENGLEBELMER, at 1-30p.m. on "Y" day, where a guide from 188th. Light Trench Mortar Battery will meet them and conduct them to their Assembly position, moving in rear of Anson Battalion.
Carrying Parties will not carry any war materials extra to equipment except four sand bags per man.

2. Brigade Headquarters will be established at Battle Headquarters by 5-0p.m. on "Y" day.

3. As soon as each Brigade Unit has taken up its position, the following code messages will be despatched to Brigade Headquarters by the Unit concerned:-

CASTLE)
KNIGHT)
QUEEN)
PAWN) "FISH" = Move completed.
CHECK)
MATE)

4. Attention is called to the undesirability of frequent use being made of the telephone during "Y/Z" night, since an increase of messages imply a concentration of troops.

5. The programme and time table recently issued to Battalions with the sketch map at the foot is not to be taken into the attack, but is to be destroyed on "Y" night.

Captain,
Brigade Major,
188th. Infantry Brigade.

?-11-16.

Issued to Signals at

S E C R E T.

MEMORANDUM ISSUED WITH 188th. INFANTRY BRIGADE ORDER No. 57.

With reference to Brigade Order No. 57 attached, the following points are to be noted:-

1. 1st. Royal Marines and Howe Battalion must so arrange their advance that they are in position behind GREEN LINE ready to follow Barrage to YELLOW LINE in successive waves at 1.43'.

Similarly 2nd. Royal Marines and Anson Battalion must arrange to be in position behind YELLOW LINE to advance on RED LINE at 3.20'.

2. In the advance from YELLOW to RED the Right flank of the Right Battalion should advance on the Line of the North edge of the BOIS D'HOLLANDE.

In para 14 as amended, the importance of the Signal for the advance to the RED LINE must be impressed on all ranks, namely, the above barrage which re-opens at 3.20' at the end of the fourth pause.

3. The following must be impressed on all:-

(a) The importance of always keeping up to our barrage.

(b) The constant passing back of information, both positive and negative, and also of the sketch maps which have been issued marking the positions of the Units concerned together with the hour of despatch. This latter is most important.

4. Battle patrols when sent out must dig in and stay out, and keep contact with the Enemy. Strength of patrol 12 to 15 men, with an Officer, if in an important position.

Captain,
Brigade Major.
188th. Infantry Brigade.

11-11-16.

APPENDIX "D"

ORDERS FOR

188th. Light Trench Mortar Battery.

1. The Battery will be divided into ADVANCED Half Battery and RESERVE Half Battery.

Advanced guns. 2. The ADVANCED Half Battery with guns will assemble on "Y" night in the Stokes' gun position, viz, Ammunition Dump and Tunnel in ROBERTS TRENCH.

3. The ADVANCED Half Battery will follow the fourth wave on the 1st, Royal Marines and Howe Battalion and will at once make for positions selected and come into action, ie,

LEFT SECTION.

Gun Positions.	Targets.	Approximate Ranges.
Near junction of German Second Line and LEEK WAY.	Enfilade SUNKEN ROAD and COMMUNI--CATION TRENCH in vicinity of Q.11.d.4.4.	380 to 420yds.

RIGHT SECTION.

Gun Positions.	Targets.	Approximate Ranges.
Near junction of German Second Line and CIRCUS TRENCH.	QUARRY at Q.11.d.5.2. and enfilade LEEK WAY and dug-outs in CIRCUS TRENCH.	400 yards.

umps. 4. When advanced guns have come into action, which must be as quickly as possible, the two men allotted as pioneers per Section will make Ammunition Dump near each Section as secure as possible from Enemy fire, using ammunition sand-bags.

Plates. 5. Each gun of Advanced Half Battery will have a second Base Plate dug in to face the Left flank, so that if necessary the guns can be brought into action immediately on the flank of the Brigade.

unition. 6. Each Battalion is providing ten men as an Ammunition carrying party making 40 in all. They will report at Headquarters, Anson Battalion, ENGLEBELMER AT 1-30p.m. "Y" day and will be met by a guide from Stokes' Battery.

These men will immediately follow up behind Anson Battalion on "Y" night and will be met by an Officer detailed from Stokes' Battery at junction of VICTORIA STREET and BEDFORD STREET. They will come immediately under the orders of this Officer.

SECRET

O.C. 1st. Royal Marines.
O.C. 2nd. Royal Marines.
O.C. Anson Battalion.
O.C. Howe Battalion.
O.C. 188th. M.G. Company.
O.C. No. 2 Field Company.
O.C. "C" Company, 14th. Worcesters.
Transport Officer,
1st. Royal Marines.
2nd. Royal Marines.
Anson Battalion.
Howe Battalion.
188th. M.G. Company.
Brigade Transport Officer.

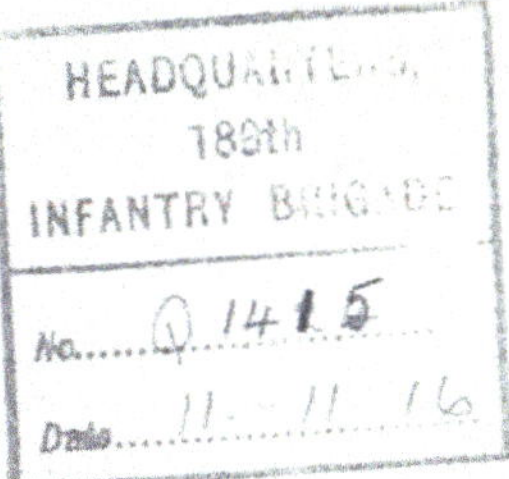

The attached notes on Pack Transport are intended to consolidate all orders previously issued on the subject. Copies are being sent direct to Transport Officers

[signature]
Captain,
Staff Captain,
188th. Infantry Brigade.

11-11-16.

APPENDIX "D" (contd.)

Reserve Guns.	7. RESERVE guns will come under the immediate orders of the Officer Commanding Battery and will, in the ordinary course of events, follow the fourth wave of the 2nd. Royal Marines and Anson Battalion, and wait in the Enemy third line until the GREEN LINE has been taken, when the whole Battery will move forward, and leaving two guns in each of the two Strong Points, the remaining four guns will come into action in positions to be selected by Officer Commanding Section near GREEN LINE and enfilade STATION ALLEY and take on any other targets that may be holding up the troops in the immediate vicinity.
COMMUNICATIONS.	8. One runner will be attached to Left Company of 1st. and 2nd. Royal Marines for information regarding Left flank. One runner at Anson Battalion Headquarters, Two runners at Brigade Headquarters.

[signature]

Captain,
Brigade Major,
188th. Infantry Brigade.

10-11-16.

Copy No. 24

AMENDED TIME TABLE OF 63rd (RN) DIVISION ATTACK

(to accompany Order No. 68, dated 10th November, 1916).

Time	Artillery (18-Pdrs).	Infantry
ZERO	All guns open intense barrage, 75% on enemy front line, 25% on No Man's Land, 50 yards in front of it.	Leave trenches and advance.
0.2'	Barrage on No Man's Land lifts to front line.	
0.6'	All guns lift from front line, and move back to DOTTED GREEN LINE at average rate of 100 yards in five minutes; stay there five minutes, and then lifts 100 yards beyond it, where barrage dwells till 0.26'.	Assault enemy front trench.
0.21'		Capture of DOTTED GREEN LINE completed. Troops for advance on GREEN LINE pass straight through and move close up to the barrage.
0.26'	Barrage lifts 100 yards and continues to lift 100 yards every five minutes till it reaches GREEN LINE. It stays on GREEN LINE five minutes and then lifts to 150 yards beyond it, where it dwells (with exception of four pauses of five minutes, see below) till 1.58').	
0.46'		Capture of GREEN LINE completed. Halt 1 hour 10 minutes on GREEN LINE. During this halt infantry for attack of YELLOW LINE move up from enemy front system to GREEN LINE and reserve brigade moves forward to enemy front system.
0.55'.1.0') 1.15'.1.20') 1.30'.1.35') 1.31'.1.56')	Pauses in Barrage.	
1.56'	Intense barrage re-opens 150 yards beyond GREEN LINE.	Advance towards YELLOW LINE.
1.58'	Barrage lifts 100 yards, and continues to lift 100 yards every five minutes till it reaches YELLOW LINE. It stays on YELLOW LINE five minutes and then	

lifts

Time	Artillery (18-Pdrs).	Infantry.
	lifts to 150 yards beyond it, where it dwells (with the exception of four pauses of five minutes, see below) till 3.45'.	
2.43'		Capture of YELLOW LINE completed. Halt one hour on YELLOW LINE. During this halt troops for capture of RED LINE move up from GREEN LINE to YELLOW LINE, and reserve brigade moves to GREEN LINE.
2.50'.2.55') 3.5' .3.10') 3.20'.3.25')) 3.41'.3.46')	Pauses in Barrage.	
3.46'	Intense barrage re-opens 150 yards beyond YELLOW LINE.	Advance towards RED LINE.
3.48'	Barrage lifts 100 yards, and continues lifting 100 yards every five minutes till RED LINE is reached. On the left and left centre, whene RED LINE consists of a trench, the barrage will stay on the trench for five minutes and will then lift 150 yards beyond it, where it will dwell for 15 minutes. It will then lift back to a line joining R.1.a.5.0. and R.8.a.8.5, (to be called the DOTTED RED LINE) where it will eventually die down. On the right and right centre, where the RED LINE is not defined by a trench the barrage will move straight through from the YELLOW to the DOTTED RED LINE by lifts of 100 yards every five minutes, and there will be no pause of 15 minutes in front of the RED LINE. N.B. After the barrage has died down, in the event of a new protective barrage being called for by the infantry, it will, in the absence of more definite orders, be put down on the DOTTED RED LINE.	
4.18'	the artillery will put down a barrage if their assistance is called for without further particulars being given.	Capture of RED LINE completed. As soon as this line is captured, small patrols will be pushed forward, close under the barrage, towards the line R.1.a.5.0. - R.8.a.8.5. They will not establish themselves within 100 yards on either side of this line, which is the line on which

SUPPLEMENTARY.

SECRET.

Operation Order
SOO 1/1

Disposition 1/ For battle on Z day the battalion will be disposed between its LEFT and RIGHT boundaries in the following order from the LEFT.
C Coy, A Coy, B Coy, D Coy spacing being pro rata according to strength inclusive of attachments.

Machine Guns. 2/ The 4 M.Gs. attached to the Battn. will move 2 with the D Coy's 3rd Wave and 2 with D Coy's 4th Wave.
These guns will be placed on the left, but not on the extreme left of their respective waves. Until ZERO these guns will be under the orders of O.C. D Coy and after ZERO they will be under the orders of the senior M.G.O. attached.

~~Bombs~~
RND.E. 3/ The ½ Section of the 2nd Field Coy RNDE will be equally distributed among Coys and will move with the 4th Wave. They will be under the orders of the O.C. their respective Companies and should be employed, so far as possible, as specialists.

Bombs 4/ Each Coy will carry as a MINIMUM, its full complement of bombs viz:- 240 which are to be distributed among those specially selected.

"P" Bombs 5/ Each Coy will carry its allotment of 60 'P' bombs which likewise are to be distributed among those specially selected of whom a proportion are to be in each wave.

"C" Coy 6/ O.C. C Coy in advancing will include within his left boundary the CIRCUS communication trench and take the necessary steps to deal with it.

Strong Points 7. O.C C. Coy will detail from his 1st + 2nd Waves 10 men to work under the direction of his party of RNDE in the formation of Strong Points at Q.17.b.6.7. And Q.12.C.2.4. on arrival at the Dotted GREEN, and GREEN LINES respectively

Lewis Guns 8. The Coy L. Gs will move with their respective Coys in the 1st + 2nd Waves in the positions selected by their respective Coy Comdrs, who, in their dispositions, are to provide for the close proximity of the spare L.G. detachments.

The Hqrs L Gs. will move with Battn Hqrs and are to be prepared at all times to move to be in support of any Coy at a moments notice.

The Battle position of these guns will be at the GORDON end of Battn Hqrs tunnell.

Signals. 9 The Signalling Officer will act as the Representative of Battn Hqrs and will move with eight signallers and 2 pioneers immediately in rear of the 4th Wave.

His first function is to report the gain of the dotted green line to Battn Hqrs.

On arrival in the captured Enemy's line he will act, so far as circumstances permit, as an advanced report centre until Battn Hqrs moves forward but Coy runners must be prepared to continue on to Battn Hqrs should the S.O. be unable to forward their message.

The same procedure as above will be followed in the capture of succeeding objectives.

The S.O. will detail special signalling personnel as under:-

Aeroplane signallers -- 3

Visual " -- 2

The former will carry the aeroplane shutters and the latter Flappers. Their position will be with Battn Hqrs.

Guide Cards 10. These are in course of preparation and will be issued on Y day. Officers are to take every possible step to ensure that not only non-commissioned officers but men clearly understand the principle of the attack and the system of Barrages.

Barrage 150x beyond GREEN LINE 11. It is of great importance that after reaching the GREEN LINE and before ZERO + 1 hr. 10 minutes the HOWE Battn should advance 100x but not more beyond the GREEN LINE.

If this is not done the Barrage may not be over taken for after its second pause it dwells for only 2 minutes before jumping forward a further 100x.

On the other hand, if the distance to which the Bn advances on this occasion is beyond 100x men will run the risk of being caught by our own Barrage.

M.O. 12. The MO will move with Battn Hqrs.

Blue Line 13. On arrival at the BLUE LINE the Bde will re-organize as under (from left to right)

1st R.M., 2nd RM, HOWE, ANSON

[illegible]

Commander R.N.

O.C.

Howe Battn

Secret.

With reference to Barrage table issued with Operation Order No 44 of [illegible] inst.

Please note that in future the Barrage moves back 100 yds in 4 mins i.e. it moves 100 yds at a time and not 25 yards in a minute.

[illegible]

4-11-16

Lieut & Adjt.

(1)

Operation Orders No 19.

1. Plan.

The date of attack, to be referred to as "Z" day and the hour of "ZERO" will be notified later.

2. Preliminary Bombardment — The attack will be preceded by an intense bombardment on X and Y days, beginning at 5 A.M. and becoming intense at 6 A.M.

3 Objectives (a) The objectives allotted to the Battns of this Bde are shewn on the attached map "A". Also the dividing line between Brigades and Right and Left Battns of 188th Inf Bde

(b) The Front of attack of the 63rd RN Divn. will be from RAILWAY ROAD to about Q.17.a.4.5. The final objective of the Division will be PUISIEUX RIVER TRENCH from MIRAUMONT - BEAUCOURT ROAD to about R.2 to 2.9

4 Tasks of Brigades — The GREEN, YELLOW and BLUE lines will be captured by the 188th + 189th Inf Bdes; the BROWN LINE by 190th Inf Bde.

6. Advanced Brigade Headquarters — Advanced Bde Hqrs will be at KNIGHTSBRIDGE BARRACKS about Q.16.d.3.8½. and will be occupied by 6 p.m. 5 a.m. on Y night.

7. "UP" and "DOWN" Trenches — Communication trenches will be allocated for "UP" and "DOWN" traffic as follows from ZERO onwards:—

"UP" GABION AVENUE, LONG SAP

"Down" LONGACRE, CONSTITUTION HILL, KNIGHTSBRIDGE, RAILWAY.

8. "Jumping up off" trenches — The Jumping off trenches are as follows:—

1st + 2nd Waves — GORDON TRENCH and extention thereof to the north

3rd Wave — ROBERTS TRENCH and continuation into CHARING CROSS

4th Wave — In "T" heads, which have been constructed leading off Parades of ROBERTS TRENCH and CHARING CROSS

9 Time table of attack. — The attack will be carried out in accordance with the attached table of barrages. It must be clearly understood, however, that the times are published merely as a guide to the Infantry and are not orders for the exact time of Assaults.

It is of paramount and vital importance that the Infantry keeps close up to the Artillery barrage and advances whenever it lifts.

10 Artillery — The 63rd Divn. will be supported by the Artillery of two Divns and by a large number of heavy guns. There will be a barrage of howitzers in advance of the 18 pounder barrage mentioned in the Time table, while Corps Artillery will bombard the Enemy positions still further inside the German lines.

A visual station close to Brigade Hqrs. will ~~be laid direct~~ also be established, the exact locality of which will be notified to Bn. Signal Officers later. At least 2 pigeons per Bn. will be at Bn. Hqrs., and they should be used singly and sparingly. The pigeons will be replaced if possible later in the day.

An advanced Report Centre (No 1) will be established at POINT STREET Q.17.c.5.8., to which all communication should be directed after Bns. have left their first Hqrs.

As soon as GREEN LINE has been occupied and the attack has advanced against the YELLOW LINE, Report Centre No 2. will be established at Q.11.d.9.0

Re-lay posts for runners will be established at Report Centre No 1 by one runner per Bn. from those allotted to Bde. Hqrs. and at Report Centre No 2 by one runner from Bn. Hqrs. when Bns. move forward.

It is to be understood that the re-lay system will only be brought into use if telephonic communication has broken down between Advanced Report Centres and Bde. Hqrs.

O.C. 188th M.G. Coy. will establish his Hqrs. with those of Anson Bn. and O.C. L.T.M. Battery with those of 2nd R.M.

Messages to and from these Units will be passed through the affiliated Bn.

TUNNELS. 27. Communication across NO MAN'S LAND MUST BE OPENED as soon as the GREEN LINE has been captured. The pair of Tunnels near LONG SAP will be available for the Brigade. These Tunnels will be blown up by the O.C. Tunnelling as soon as GREEN LINE is captured, orders to blow up being given direct to Tunnellers by Brigadier.

The Tunnels will then be connected to the German Front Line by trenches, to be dug by half a company 14th Worcester Regiment. These Tunnels should, therefore, not be used for the accomodation of large numbers of men previous to ZERO.

TANKS. 28. The 63rd. Division attack will be assisted by six Tanks, which will act in accordance with the principles already issued to all concerned.

During night Y/Z the noise of the Tanks moving

STRONG POINTS. 20. Strong Points will be formed in all objectives as under:-

DOTTED GREEN LINE.... 1st. Royal Marines, Q.11. d.1.0.
Howe Battalion, Q.17. b. 6.7.
DOTTED BLUE LINE..... ~~2nd. Royal Marines, Q.11. d.4.5.~~ &
Anson Battalion, Q.12. C 0.0.
GREEN LINE...... ~~Howe Battalion~~ Q.12. C 2.5. 1st R.M.
YELLOW LINE...... 1st Royal Marines Q.12. b.0.9
~~1st Royal Marines Q.12. b.4.6~~ +
DOTTED YELLOW LINE...... ~~2nd Royal Marines Q.6. d.8.4.~~ &
ANSON Battalion R 7. a.3.8.

MACHINE GUNS. 21. Four M.G.s. will be allotted to each Front Bn.

STOKES MORTARS. 22. O.C. 188th. L.T.M. Battery will arrange for two guns to accompany the Front line Bns. and two to accompany the Support Battalions.

HEADQUARTERS and ADVANCED DEPOTS in the HOSTILE LINE. 23. Position of Bn., Bde. Hqrs. and Dumps within our own lines are shewn in sketch map attached. The probable positions of the former in Enemy's lines will be as under:-

When Bde. has occupied Blue Line. Bde. and Bn. Hqrs. will be established in the following vicinities, at the most suitable sights available:-

(a) Bde. Hqrs., Q.12. c.2.4.
Bn. Hqrs., R.1. d.3.3.

(b) Telephone and Signal Stations. In the neighbourhood of Bde. Hqrs. and Bn. Hqrs.

ADVANCE of HEADQUARTERS. 24. (a) The forward movements of Bn. Hqrs. will be by successive bounds. Bn. Commanders will not advance until the objective of their attack has been gained.

(b) When the Bde. is established on the Blue Line Bde. Hqrs. will be moved forward to GREEN LINE.

AEROPLANE CO-OPERATION. 25. Contact aeroplanes will be employed to fix the positions gained by the infantry in accordance with the principles lately practiced by the Division. Flares will be lighted:-

(a) On attaining each objective.
(b.) whenever hung up.
(C.) when an aeroplane sounds its Klaxon Horn.
(d.) Just before dark and in the early morning if an aeroplane is above.

Communications. 26. Communications from Bn. to Bde. Hqrs. at ZERO hour will be as follows:-

From each Bn. Hqrs. a telephone will be laid direct to Bde., together with lateral lines between Battalions.

(4)

18 "Continued" It is absolutely essential that the BROWN LINE should be consolidated, as strongly as possible. Counter-attacks are certain, and under no circumstances whatever must ground once gained by the R.N.D. be re-occupied by the Enemy.

19 After the capture of the BROWN LINE it is probable that - - - - - - - will pass through the 63rd Division and advance on BEAUREGARD DOVECOTE.

14. Capture of YELLOW LINE — The advance on the YELLOW LINE will be carried out by 1st RM. and Howe Battns

These Battns will have re-organized in the German Front system and move forward to the GREEN LINE at O hour 50 minutes. Bombers and Lewis guns will be sent up STATION ALLEY, by 1st R.M.

There will be a halt of about half an hour on the YELLOW LINE. During this halt, 2nd R.M. and Anson Battns will close-up to the YELLOW LINE

At 2 hours 15 minutes, the 18 pounder barrage will pause for one period of five minutes. The re-opening of an intense barrage at 2 hours 20 minutes will be the signal for the advance on the dotted YELLOW LINE

15 Capture of dotted YELLOW LINE — The advance against the dotted YELLOW LINE will be by 2nd RM and Anson Battns, with 1st RM and Howe Battns in Support.

16. Capture of dotted BROWN LINE — A halt of five minutes will be made on the dotted YELLOW LINE. During this halt 1st R.M. and Howe Battns will pass through 2nd RM and Anson Battns, and will advance on the dotted BROWN LINE directly the barrage lifts.

17 Capture of ~~BROWN LINE~~ BLUE — Immediately the dotted BROWN LINE is captured, the whole of the Bde will advance to and consolidate the BLUE LINE. Battle patrols will be sent forward from this line along the entire front and especially towards the BOIS d'HOLLANDE and ARTILLERY AVENUE will be blocked.

A halt of about 15 minutes will be made on the BLUE LINE.

Meanwhile the 190th Inf. Bde. will have advanced through the YELLOW LINE to the BLUE LINE

At 3 hours 35 minutes, the 18 pounder barrage will pause for one period of five minutes. The re-opening of an intense barrage at 3 hours 40 minutes will be the signal for the advance of the 190th Inf. Bde on the BROWN LINE, passing through the 188th & 189th Inf Bdes.

18 Capture of BROWN LINE — The 190th Inf. Bde will then advance on the BROWN LINE with all four Battns in Front line.

The 188th Inf. Bde will meanwhile re-organize on the Blue Line.

11. Scheme of attack. The Brigade will assault with two Battalions in Front line. Each Battn. will have four Companies in line, in column of Platoons, the platoons forming the first second, third and fourth waves respectively. Platoons will be in single rank with ten yards distance between first and second waves, and about 50 yards between the remainder.

The two Supporting Battns. will be in 2nd line in similar formation, the leading lines 150 yards distance from fourth wave position of the leading Battn. and will advance over the top from their Assembly Areas.

The dividing line between Battns. is LONG SAP and GABION AVENUE.

ORDER of BATTALIONS — LEFT FRONT, 1st R. Marines
RIGHT " HOWE Battn.
LEFT SUPPORT 2nd R Marines
RIGHT " Anson Battn.

12 Capture of dotted GREEN LINE (a) 1st R.M. and Howe Battn. will be responsible for the capture of the first objective, i.e., RESERVE TRENCH in the Enemy Front line system (DOTTED GREEN LINE), and the cleaning up of all three lines. The first and second waves will advance straight through to this dotted line, the third wave will clean up enemy's SUPPORT Line and the fourth wave the Enemy's frontline.

(b.) LEFT FLANK. Officers Commanding left Battns. will pay particular attention to the protection of the left Flank of the Bde. To ensure this, the frontage allotted to the left Company should be less than that allotted to the other Companies, and the proportion of Lewis and Vickers guns increased.

It should be explained to these Companies that in the event of the attack on our Left being held up; our advance must not be delayed, but that provision must be made for forming a Defensive flank, should circumstances render it necessary, by formation of Strong Points, defended by machine guns.

13. Capture of GREEN LINE The dotted GREEN LINE will be captured at O hour 18 minutes. At O hour 23 minutes 2nd R.M. and Anson Battns. will pass through 1st R.M. and Howe Battns. and capture GREEN LINE.
The first and second waves will advance straight through to this line and consolidate it.
The third wave will clean up dug-outs in STATION ROAD.
The fourth will clean up dotted BLUE LINE and the many dug-outs on reverse slope of the hill.
Bombers from 2nd R.M. will block STATION ALLEY.

SECRET.

HOWE BATTALION TIME TABLE.

TIME	
ZERO.	Advance from our trenches, follow the barrage.
0-18.........	Complete capture of DOTTED GREEN (German third line 500 yards ahead) CONSOLIDATE.
	ANSON PASSES THROUGH HOWE.
0-50'.........	Advance from DOTTED GREEN to GREEN (a trench just beyond STATION ROAD, 500 yds. ahead of DOTTED GREEN).
	HOWE PASSES THROUGH ANSON.
1-10'.........	When barrage resumes after 2nd pause follow it to YELLOW (trenches on the BEAUCOURT ROAD 900 yds. from GREEN).
1-50'.........	Complete capture of YELLOW. HALF AN HOUR'S HALT and CONSOLIDATE.
	ANSON PASSES THROUGH HOWE
	CHANGE DIRECTION ABOUT 25° RIGHT
2-20'.........	Advance in support of ANSON
2-34'.........	On arrival at YELLOW DOTTED (RAILWAY TRENCH 350 yds. ahead) There is a 5 minutes BREATHER during which HOWE passes through ANSON, follows the barrage and at:—
2-55.........	captures DOTTED BROWN (ARTILLERY LANE 250 yards ahead) IMMEDIATELY advance with WHOLE BRIGADE and at
3-25.........	HALT at BLUE (an imaginary line a third of the way up the slope 700 yards ahead). CONSOLIDATE and send out battle patrols.

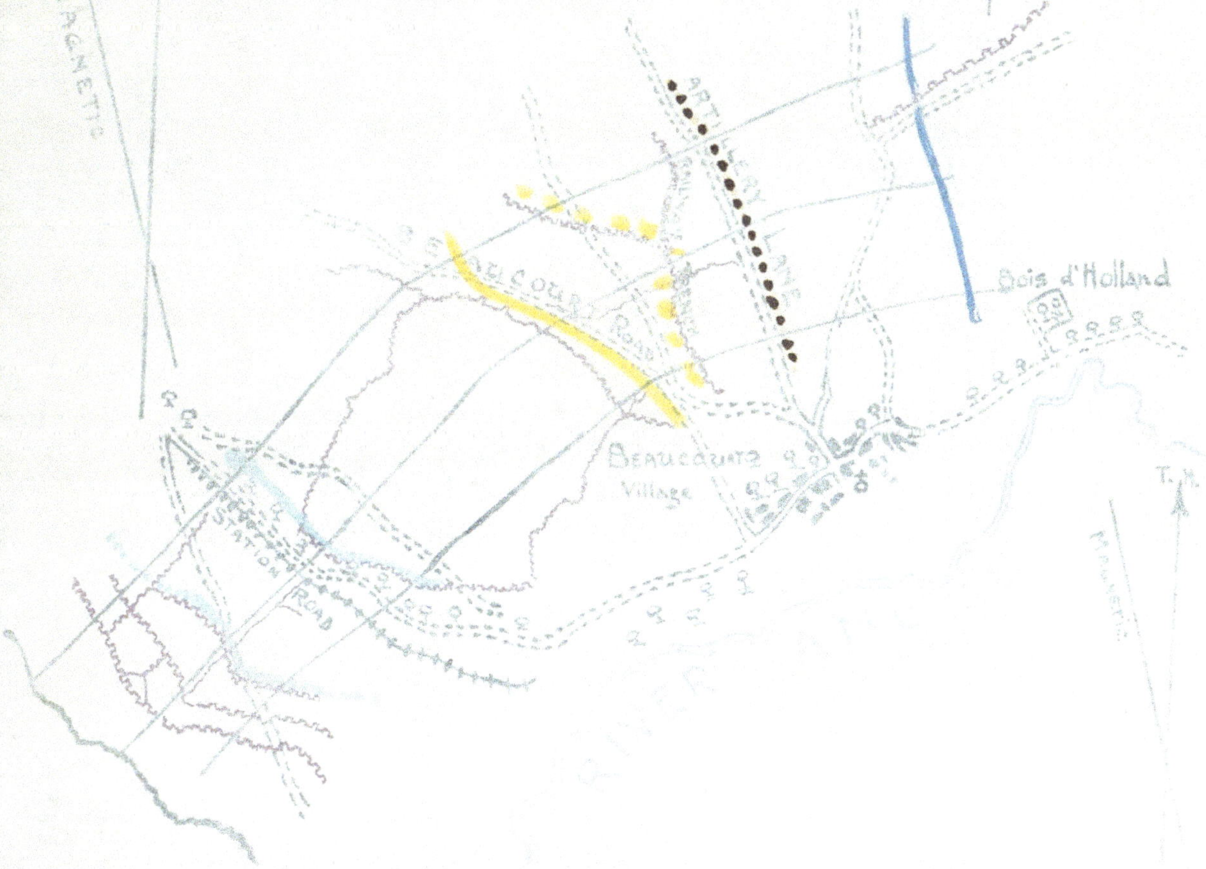

to the position of assembly between the hours of 7-0 p.m. and 10-0 p.m. must be drowned by noise demonstrations. O.C. M.G. Coy. will arrange for bursts of M.G. fire throughout this period. Tanks have been ordered to keep as close to the barrage as possible. Infantry must, however, be specially warned not to wait for the Tanks.

The ultimate objective of all Tanks has been given as PUISIEUX TRENCH. A map with the route to be taken by each Tank is issued herewith. Infantry escorts will not be required for the Tanks.

GAS. 29. Early on night Y/Z Gas shells will be fired into valley South of SERRE and into BEAUMONT HAMEL.

Isolation of AREA of ATTACK 30. From now onwards between the hours of 6-0 p.m. and 5-0 a.m. daily, the area of attack will be isolated as much as possible, by bursts of M.G. fire and Artillery fire being directed on all approaches known to be used by Enemy.

SYNCHRONIZATION of WATCHES. 31. Watches will be synchronized at 9-0 p.m. on 'Y' day and at one hour before ZERO.

EQUIPMENT. 32. All troops will be in Battle Order and will carry

120 rds. S.A.A., 4 Sand Bags (2 passed through the belt on each side), at least one Iron Ration. Unexpended portion of days ration. Gas Helmet. 1 Flare and 1 Very's Light Cartridge.

Special men will be detailed to carry buckets, grenades. In addition to the above 50% of third and fourth waves of the attacking troops in the Front and Support Bns. will carry pick or shovel. As many wire-cutters as possible will be issued. Men carrying wire-cutters will wear a yellow armlet. Runners will be lightly equipped and will not carry rifles, and will wear a blue armlet with a white stripe.

NOTES. 34. (a) It must be impressed on all ranks concerned that they are on no account to halt because Units on their flanks happen to be held up. The best way of assisting their neighbours on such occasions will be to continue their advance.

(b) All ranks must be impressed with the necessity of maintaining their direction and marching straight on to their objective. With this object, the ground must be carefully studied beforehand, land marks noted wherever possible and compass bearings taken.

(e) No papers likely to be of value to the Enemy will be taken over the parapet.

(f). Not more than 20 Officers of Battalion will take part in an assault, and a proportion of reliable N.C.O's. is also to be left behind.

Helder

64 . 64
128
256
8
2048.
128
77

S E C R E T.

P A C K T R A N S P O R T.

ECHELON "A".

This consists of 18 animals per Battalion as follows:-

8 Pack Animals.
8 Riding Horses.
1 Spare Pack Animal.
1 Spare Light Draught.

TOTAL 18

These animals will be loaded as follows:-

14 animals carrying rations for Battalion.
1 animal carrying rations for detachments of M.G. Company, and L.T.M. Battery attached to the Battalion.
3 animals carrying water.

No rations will be sent up to Units on "Y" day, so that at the beginning of "Z" day, all men will be in possession of the extra day's ration and the ordinary Emergency Ration.

Rations drawn on "Y" day will be kept inhand by Q.M.S. and packed in sand-bags by NOON "Z" day ready to be loaded on to Pack animals of ECHELON "A".

Battalion convoys will be started off by the Brigade Transport Officer P.M. on "Z" day, guides being sent by Units to the point selected Q.17.b.9½ by 3-0p.m. This point should be easily recognisable as it is where an old track crosses the Front German Line, and very close to the site of a proposed new road, which, if completed in time, can be used by these convoys.

A plan of this proposed new road has been issued to each Transport Officer.

The convoys of ECHELON "A" will be under the command of the Transport Officer of the Unit concerned, who when once he has picked up his guide will use his discretion as to how near the rations can be taken to the point where his Unit may be.

All Transport Officers will reconnoitre the site of the proposed new road, and the alternative route through MESNIL and HAMEL and study the map with a view to possible Dumping Grounds beyond the present German Front Line.

When rations have been dumped they will be left under the charge of Company Q.M.S, the guides returning to their Units to report the position of the Dump.

Q.M.S. of Machine Gun Company and Light Trench Mortar Battery are responsible that the rations of each detachment of their Unit are handed over to the Q.M. of the Unit to which they are attached by 10-0a.m. on "Z" day and the following days for dispatch with the Battalion convoy, and should keep in touch with the Q.M's concerned by reporting to them at "Q" office, HEDAUVILLE, at 9-0a.m. each morning commencing "Z" day.

Officers Commanding detachments of 2nd. Field Company and 14th. Worcesters will make arrangements with Officer Commanding 2nd. Field Company for rationing their parties.

Each convoy will carry two shovels.

ECHELON "B".

This ECHELON of all Brigades is under the Command of Major C.E.C. Eagles, 2nd. Royal Marines, and will receive its orders from "Q" branch, 63rd. Division, commencing "Z" day.

The distribution, so far as this Brigade is concerned, of personnel and animals for the purposes of organization and training is shewn on attached table.

P A C K   T R A N S P O R T.

TABLE SHEWING
DISTRIBUTION OF ECHELON "B".

HOW COMPOSED.

SUB-SECTION I.	SUB-SECTION II.	SUB-SECTION III.	SUB-SECTION IV.	SUB-SECTION V.
Machine Gun Company and 14th. Worcesters.	1st. Royal Marines.	2nd. Royal Marines.	Howe Battalion	Anson Battalion.
Officers - 1. Sub-Lt. Dean, Howe Bn	Officers - 1 2nd. Lieutenant Pipe	Officers - 1. Sub-Lt. M. Ofield.	Officers - 1. Sub-Lt. F.O.Forrester	Officers - 1 Sub-Lt.D.S.Allison,Anson.
N.C.O's - Ser.Major M.G. Company. - 2 from 2/RM	N.C.O's - 2	N.C.O's. - 2.	N.C.O's. - 2.	N.C.O's - 2.
Men - 20	Men - 18. (9 from 1st. Line Tpt. 9 from Battalion).	Men - 18. (9 from 1st. Line Tpt. 9 from Battalion).	Men - 18. (9 from 1st. Line Tpt. 9 from Battalion).	Men - 18. (9 from 1st. Line Tpt. 9 from Battalion).
Animals - 20. Made up of 14th. Wor. 5. 188th. M.G. Coy. 15.	Animals - 18.	Animals - 18.	Animals - 18.	Animals - 18.

S.O.O 1/6

The following amendments to Operation Order No 19. are circulated.

Para: 20 STRONG POINTS

Delete following strong points Q.12.b.4.6., Q.11.d.4.5. Q.6.d.8.4.

Add:- "The 1/2 Coy R.N.D.E. and 1/2 "C" Coy of the Worcester Regt: have been allotted special tasks, under separate orders; construction of Strong Points at Q.11.d.6.8 and Q.6.c.9.3.

The remaining Strong Points enumerated will therefore be constructed by Infantry Bns without R.E. help.

The Strong point at Q.12.c.2.5. will be constructed by 1st R.M. not by Howe Battn:

Para 27

Delete last para:

Para 32

For 50% read 80%

Para 35

Add this para:- "The S.O.S. rocket signal in WHITE, GREEN, WHITE. These will be issued and each Company will carry forward three GREEN and six white (WHITE) rockets and sticks."

Para 26

Add:- "All runners will carry dispatches in left hand breast pocket.

Anyone seeing a killed or wounded runner will search him for dispatches, and forward them with as little delay as possible"

[signature]
Lieut and Adjt
Howe Battn:

S.O.O. 1/5.

Rations on 'Z' day.

1. Rations will be brought up by convoys of pack animals. Convoy will be in charge of our own Transport officer.
Rations will be in sandbags..
Company Q.M.S. will accompany the daily convoy.

2. Route. The convoys will come up a track which runs close to LOUVERCY STREET on its North side.

3. Guides. One guide from each Company and one from Hqrs will meet this convoy at 3pm on Z day at Q17b 90.05. which is a point where our old trench crosses the present German front line.

4. Guides will wait till the convoy arrives, will show the officer in charge convoy where their unit is, will go with convoy till the officer decides to dump and will then return to their unit to report position of the dump.

5. Dump. The provisions will be taken as near up as possible, and when dumped the Coy QMS will remain in charge of dump till parties are sent back to fetch rations. When rations have been taken up to Companies, Q.M.S will return to

Battalion Q.M. store.

6. This procedure will hold as long as it is necessary after "Z" day

Copy No. 1 Filed
2 OC A
3 " B
4 " C
5 " D
6. Q.M.
7. TO
8 QMS A
9 " B
10 " C
11 " D
12 " HQ

Operation Order.

S.O.O. 1/4
[illegible]

The following instructions about prisoners should be observed.

i. Prisoners will be searched for weapons as soon as captured. Nothing else is to be taken from them.

ii Escorts will watch that they do not drop or destroy any papers.

iii Officers and N.C.O.s should be kept apart from the men.

iv Prisoners should not be allowed to smoke or be given food or drink, – nor may casual passers by speak to them.

v They should be made to carry back ~~the~~ wounded.

vi Escorts must be cut down absolutely to a minimum, but should be found from unit making capture.

[illegible signature]

Officer Commanding,
~~1st Royal Marines~~
~~2nd Royal Marines~~
Howe Battalion
~~Anson Battalion~~
~~188th L.T.M. Battery~~
~~188th M.G. Company~~

188th Inf. Brigade No.G. /63

1. From ZERO on 'Z' day the use of Vth Corps Code Calls and Code Names will be discontinued, all messages being sent in clear.

2. Code Calls will, however, continue to be used in communicating with aeroplanes, Heavy Artillery, and in all wireless messages.

188th Inf. Brigade
29th October 1916.

Major.
Brigade Major.

Secret

Signal officer.

3 copies

Supplementary O.O. ~~4 ...~~ 1/3

1. The Visual Station mentioned in para 26 of the Order already issued will be established in the first instance in RIDGE TRENCH at Q 25 d. 8.8. Subsequent positions will be notified at the time

2. Watches will be synchronized with B.H.Q. by telephone as follows:-

'Y' day. 6.30 pm and 7.15 pm.
At 9.30 pm you will report yourself at advanced BHQ (This will be in Knightsbridge)

'Z' day 5.15 a.m. by phone.

Companies will send representatives with good watches at these times.
The code word 'SLIP' will be used in each case to denote the hour. Thus 7.15 pm will be described as 'SLIP FIFTEEN'.

E Allen
25.10.16 Adjt

To Sigs

Eight

Secret Supplementary Operation ~~S.O.~~

S.O.O. 1/2

(1). **Movement**:
It cannot be too clearly impressed upon all ranks that no movement whatever must ~~to~~ take place between the first streak of dawn and ZERO hour.
The striking of matches is to be carefully screened.
Great coats are to be rolled **before** dawn, and no man will be permitted to leave the ranks after 5 am.

(2) Watches will be synchronized with B.de Hqrs by telephone as follows:-
"Y" day - 6.30 p.m. and 7.15 p.m.
"Z" day 5.15 am ~~by teleph~~.
This will be done by telephone. Each Coy should send a representative with a good watch to Battalion Hqrs at these hours, to set his watch.
All watches should be set from this.

(3). Bearings must be taken on the map of the line of advance, and communicated to all officers.

13.36
12 20
1.16

It should be noted that on the 1/10000 Beaumont map the vertical lines are not true N. and S. but are 1° 16' West of North
Explanation is on 1st margin of 1/20000 map
57 D.S.E.

(4). Red flares only will be used by attacking Infantry of 63rd (R.N.) Divn.

(5). Listening patrols will be established as usual on Y/Z night.

(6) Reference para 13 of Operation Order R.N.1 issued to you, for "13 minutes" read "18 minutes" in the ~~first~~ second line.

7. The following in continuation of para 13.
There will be a halt of about 30' on the GREEN Line. During this halt there will be TWO pauses of 5' in the 18 pdr barrage, the first between 0.50' and 0.55', the second between 1.5' and 1.10'.
Commanders should take advantage of these pauses to obtain a view of the ground over which they are to advance, and check their bearings.
At the end of the SECOND pause, an intense barrage will reopen, and this will be the signal to the Infantry to advance.

8. The following correction should be made to para 14:-
Sub para 4, beginning. "At 2 hours 15 minutes .... to YELLOW LINE" is cancelled, and the following substituted
"As in the case of the halt on the GREEN LINE, there will be two pauses of 5' in the 18 pounder barrage during the halt on the YELLOW LINE, the first between 2. and 2.5' and the second between 2.15 and 2.20.
The reopening of an intense barrage at 2.20 at the end of the SECOND pause, will be the signal for the Infantry to advance on the DOTTED YELLOW LINE.
Great care must be taken both on the GREEN and the YELLOW LINE that the Infantry advance is not resumed at the end of the first pause, or our men would be caught by the fire of our own barrage

9. In the barrage Time table add in the Infantry Column, opposite ZERO, "Leave trenches and advance".

EM

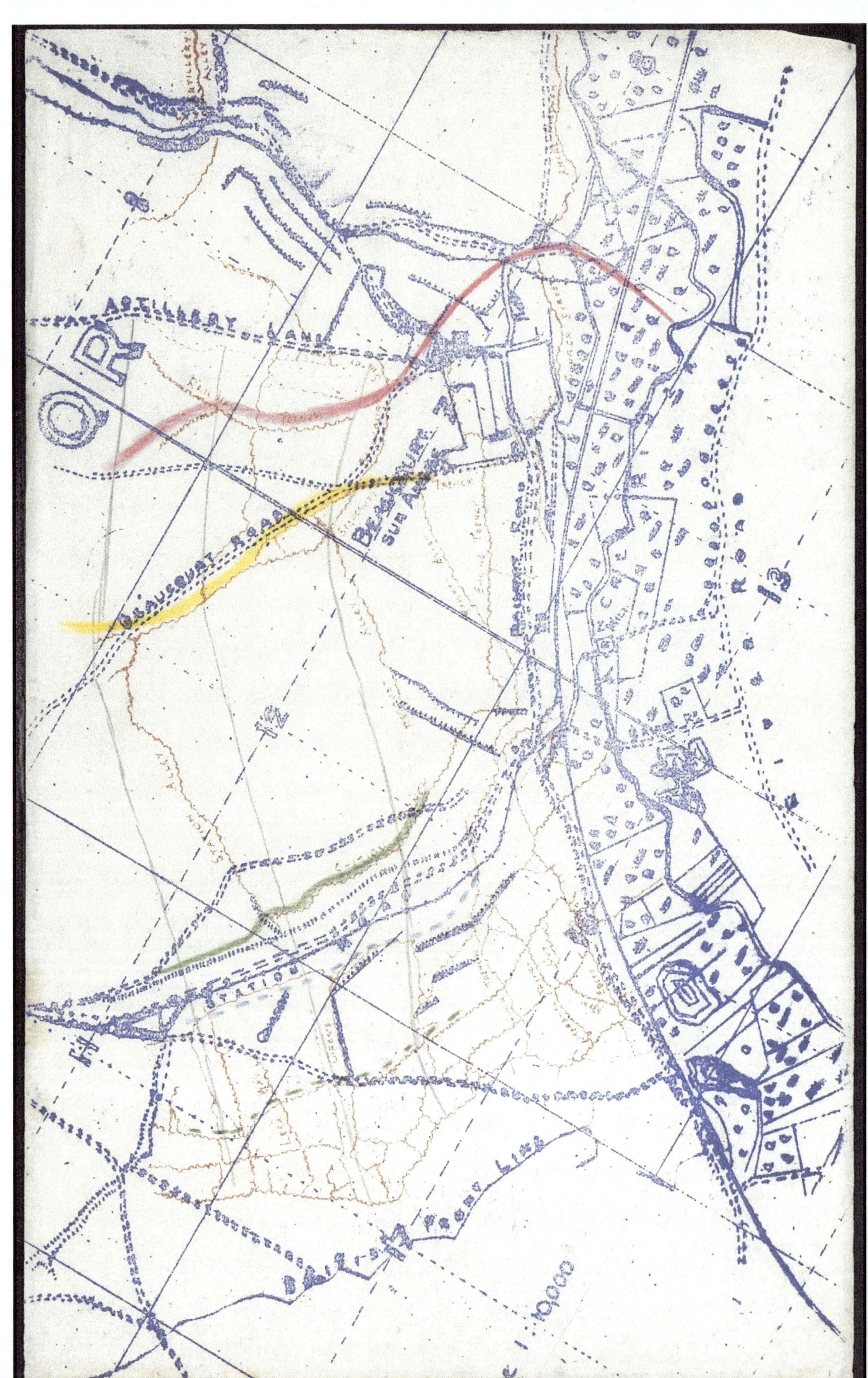

ARTILLERY LANE
BEAUCOURT ROAD
BEAUCOURT SUR ANCRE
STATION
FRONT LINE
1:10,000

5. The following paras. have to be deleted:-

15, 16, 17, and 18.

In para 20 delete "Strong Point of DOTTED YELLOW LINE."

In para 23 and para 24 (b) for the word "BLUE LINE" read "YELLOW LINE".

6. With reference to para 28, the Tanks will co-operate in the attack if, in the opinion of the Officer Commanding Heavy Machine Gun Corps they have a reasonable chance of reaching the German Lines.

ACKNOWLEDGE.

Captain,
Brigade Major.

Issued to Signals at 16-30 11/11/16

Copies to:-

No. 1 File.
2 War Diary.
3 1st. Royal Marines.
4 2nd. Royal Marines.
5 Anson Battalion.
6 Howe Battalion.
7 188th. M.G. Company.
8 188th. L.T.M. Battery.
9 No.2 Field Co. D.E.
10 No.2 Signal Section.
11 63rd. Division(2copies)
12 189th. Inf. Brigade.
13 190th. Inf. Brigade.
14 153rd.Highland Brigade.
15 ½ "C" Coy. 14th. Worcesters.
16 "G" Group, R.F.A.
17 Brigade Major.
18 Staff Captain.
19 Captain Sherman.
20 Intelligence Officer.
21 C.R.A, 63rd. Division.

6

S E C R E T.

188th. INFANTRY BRIGADE ORDER No. 57.

Brigade Headquarters,
11th. November, 1916.

1. Following orders are modification of Brigade Order No. 56, dated 9th. November, 1916.

2. The final objective of the Brigade on "Z" day will be the RED LINE shown on attached map.
Final objectives of other Divisions of Vth. Corps and of the 39th. Division on our Right will be the YELLOW LINE.
Para 1 (b) and (c) and para 3 (b) and para 4 to be amended accordingly.

3. All orders regarding DOTTED YELLOW LINE, DOTTED BROWN LINE, the BLUE LINE and the BROWN LINE are cancelled.
The attack on all objectives up to and including the YELLOW LINE will be precisely in accordance with Brigade Order No. 56, except for a very slight modification in the Barrage Table which will be issued separately and does not affect those orders.

4. The following amendment will be made to para 14:-

Delete at the end of this para "And this will be the signal for Infantry to advance" and substitute " And this will be the signal for the advance on the RED LINE. The RED LINE will be captured by 2nd. Royal Marines and Anson Battalion, 1st. Royal Marines and Howe Battalion remaining in the first instance to consolidate the YELLOW LINE. Portions of these Battalions may be pushed forward if required as re-inforcements, but the YELLOW LINE is not to be left without a garrison, in strength of at least ½ Battalion of each of the Battalions consolidating the Line, with the proportion of Vickers and Lewis guns supporting these Battalions.
2nd. Royal Marines and Anson Battalion will advance straight through to the RED LINE and consolidate the best tactical position available in this line.
When the final objective is reached it should be consolidated and made as strong as possible by reversing the trenches or building new ones. Every available machine and Lewis gun will be brought up, but the line should be held lightly and as many troops withdrawn to a Support Line in rear, as is possible. To hold the Front line with a large mass of men only increases casualties from shell fire.
Battle patrols will be pushed forward with a view to gaining as much ground as possible to the East and North East of the RED LINE. Special attention is directed to the Trench junction in R.1.c.2.8.
The 190th. Infantry Brigade meanwhile has advanced to the GREEN LINE and, remains in readiness to support the leading Brigades if required."

27 (contd) taken against hostile retaliation.

28 C Coy Officer will receive a telephone code to encypher his reports.

(Sigd) W.G. Ramsay-Fairfax
Comdr RN
O.C. Howe Battn

Instructions regarding War Diaries and Intelligence Summaries are contained in F. S. Regs., Part II. and the Staff Manual respectively. Title pages will be prepared in manuscript.

Vol 7

Army Form C. 2118.

WAR DIARY

or

~~INTELLIGENCE SUMMARY.~~

(*Erase heading not required.*)

December 1916 HOWE Bn RND.

Place	Date	Hour	Summary of Events and Information	Remarks and references to Appendices
FAVIÈRES	1st		In training. Lecture on PT1 by Major Campbell at CROTOY	
			D Coy fired two platoons on 30x range, 10 rounds each.	
	3rd		Rest of D Coy fired on 30 yards range. Leave party away.	
	4th			
	5th		C Coy began firing on a second 30 yards range. T/Sub Lt T H RYAN joined the Bn with 69 O.R.	
	6th		C Coy continued.	
	7th		Route march.	
	8th		The military salute was introduced. A Coy fired on Range.	
	9th		A Coy on range.	
VERCOURT	12th		The Battalion moved to VERCOURT. Training ground much closer.	
	13th		Training resumed. T/Sub Lieut P.D. CLEGG joined the Bn on 11.12.16. with 86 OR	
	14th		T/Sub Lieut L.C. COWARD joined the Bn with 48 O.R.	
	15th		Band formed.	
	16th		Two N.C.O.s awarded the military medal for Services during the operations N. of the ANCRE:- namely. M2194 P.O. T.B. WALL C Z1292 P.O. J. KERR.	

1577 Wt. W10791/1773 500,000 1/15 D. D. & L. A.D.S.S./Forms/C. 2118.

Army Form C. 2118.

WAR DIARY

or

~~INTELLIGENCE SUMMARY.~~

(*Erase heading not required.*)

Instructions regarding War Diaries and Intelligence Summaries are contained in F. S. Regs., Part II. and the Staff Manual respectively. Title pages will be prepared in manuscript.

December 1916 HOWE Bn RND

Place	Date	Hour	Summary of Events and Information	Remarks and references to Appendices
VERCOURT	17th		Sunday	
	18th		Bayonet Fighting and Bombing trenches taken in hand and completed by 23rd. 30 yards range made in a chalk pit with a trench at the firing point. Bath house set in order	
	19		Training of 1st spare L G crews for each Company taken in hand and carried on during the week, ending with range firing. Brigade Boxing competition held at VILLERS, the following men won championships of their weights. KW 114 AB L. CRAVEN (Light Wt) and L2173 AB P. GRANGE (Welter Wt)	
	20		Brigade route march via VRON, ARRY, CANTEREME. One man fell out.	
	21		L.G Instruction and company training carried on.	
	22		Same work.	
	23			
	24			W. J. [illegible] Comdg. Howe Bn

1577 Wt. W1079/1773 500,000 1/15 D. D. & L. A.D.S.S./Forms/C. 2118.

Instructions regarding War Diaries and Intelligence Summaries are contained in F. S. Regs., Part II. and the Staff Manual respectively. Title pages will be prepared in manuscript.

WAR DIARY
or
~~INTELLIGENCE SUMMARY~~
(Erase heading not required.)

Army Form C. 2118.

December 1916 Howe Bn R N D

Place	Date	Hour	Summary of Events and Information	Remarks and references to Appendices
VERCOURT	25th		Christmas Day. Service 9.30 am Range competitions in morning, sport in afternoon, concert in evening.	
	26			
	27		Training continued, chiefly as a Battalion. Companies began	
	28		firing 3rd and 4th practices at the range.	
	29			
	30			
	31st		Sunday. Service 9.30 am. Inspection of billets.	[illegible] OC Howe

1577 Wt. W10791/1773 500,000 1/15 D. D. & L. A.D.S.S./Forms/C. 2118.

Instructions regarding War Diaries and Intelligence Summaries are contained in F. S. Regs., Part II. and the Staff Manual respectively. Title pages will be prepared in manuscript.

WAR DIARY
or
~~INTELLIGENCE SUMMARY.~~
(Erase heading not required.)

Army Form C. 2118.

Vol 8

January 1917

Howe Bn 63rd (RN) Dn

Place	Date	Hour	Summary of Events and Information	Remarks and references to Appendices
VERCOURT	1st		Training. Bombers, Scouts, Snipers under their own officers.	
	2nd		All available officers went to meet the Corps Commander	
	3rd		3 NCOs. & 8 men went for bomb course at Brigade Hqrs.	
	4th } 5th }		Fitted small box respirators to 665 men Six reinforcements arrived from the base, including C Z 6228 AB J. Steel.	
	6th		Brigade attack was planned but postponed through bad weather	
	7th		~~Brigade attc~~ mentioned in despatches of C in C dated 13.11.1916 T. Sub Lieut J. H. Bennett and C Z 4899 L Shg J. KIRKLAND.	
	8th		Brigade attack in morning. T Lieut A. I. HUMPHREYS rejoined from leave.	
	9th		Lewis Gun handcarts abolished. L. Gs and their SAA in future to be carried in Limbers made available by rearrangement of loads of SAA in Mobile Reserve. Major H. J. de C. WYMER. DSO Hampshire Regt joined as 2nd in Command	

1577 Wt. W10791/1773 500,000 1/15 D. D. & L. A.D.S.S./Forms/C. 2118.

Instructions regarding War Diaries and Intelligence Summaries are contained in F. S. Regs., Part II. and the Staff Manual respectively. Title pages will be prepared in manuscript.

WAR DIARY
or
~~INTELLIGENCE SUMMARY~~.
(Erase heading not required.)

Army Form C. 2118.

January 1917 — Howe Bn RND

Place	Date	Hour	Summary of Events and Information	Remarks and references to Appendices
VERCOURT	10th		Filled in own bayonet fighting and bombing trenches. dismantled gallows and sent timber to Town major RUE.	
	11th		Filled in attack trenches and returned tools to Town Major.	
	12th		Preparing for move, returned billet stores.	
			In Battalion orders of 5.1.1917, extract from D.R.O. 1331 T Sub Lieut W.C. HAKEN, awarded M.C (Supplement to London Gazette of Jan 1st 1917)	
			D.R.O. 1310. The following have been awarded decorations in connection with recent operations N of the ANCRE. T. Lieut E.V. ELLIS T Lieut J.F.A. PITCAIRN T Sub Lt F.O. FORRESTER. The Military Cross.	
			DRO 1357. Commander W.G.A RAMSAY FAIRFAX R.N (Emergency List) awarded D.S.O in connection with the same operations.	
			In Connection with the raid carried out by the Howe Bn on 26.10.16 the following awards were made:— L. Lieut G.R. AIREY, the Military Cross	

1577 Wt. W10791/1773 500,000 1/15 D. D. & L. A.D.S.S./Forms/C. 2118.

Instructions regarding War Diaries and Intelligence Summaries are contained in F. S. Regs., Part II. and the Staff Manual respectively. Title pages will be prepared in manuscript.

WAR DIARY
or
~~INTELLIGENCE SUMMARY.~~
(Erase heading not required.)

Army Form C. 2118.

January 1917 — Howe Bn R.N.D.

Place	Date	Hour	Summary of Events and Information	Remarks and references to Appendices
			and TZ2146 L.S. T. BROWN and TZ4712 AB. R. SMITH were awarded the Military Medal. (Supplement to London Gazette dated 6.1.1917).	
			In connection with the operations N. of the ANCRE the following were awarded the Military Medal by DRO 1182. M2194 P.O T. B. WALL and CZ1292 P.O J. KERR.	
NOUVION	13th		Marched to NOUVION EN PONTHIEU. 8 miles. A good many fell out on the way, though all were brought in by the rear party - chiefly they were new draft men.	
MARCHEVILLE	14th		Marched to MARCHEVILLE, 8 miles. Six fell out. Billetting crowded not proper room for two Battalions in this village. Sub Lt Meadmore rejoined from leave	
LE MEILLARD	15th		Marched to Le Meillard, 16 1/8 miles. As far as AGENVILLE marched opened out; had halt of over 1 hour and closed up: thence marched as a Brigade, closed and at once had aggravating halts. Reached LE MEILLARD at 4.30 pm, having left MARCHEVILLE at 7.~~40~~ 50 am. Six fell out only, marching much better.	

1577 Wt. W10791/1773 500,000 1/15 D. D. & L. A.D.S.S./Forms/C. 2118.

Army Form C. 2118.

Instructions regarding War Diaries and Intelligence Summaries are contained in F. S. Regs., Part II. and the Staff Manual respectively. Title pages will be prepared in manuscript.

WAR DIARY
or
~~INTELLIGENCE SUMMARY.~~
(Erase heading not required.)

January 1917 HOWE Bn R.N.D.

Place	Date	Hour	Summary of Events and Information	Remarks and references to Appendices
LE MEILLARD	16		Rested, cleaned up and inspected. Leave party of 10 left yesterday, of 14 today. The following new officers joined in the evening: Sub Lieuts HAMBLEY GRACE SHEA TAYLOR	
RAINCHEVAL	17		Marched to RAINCHEVAL, 15 miles, leaving at 10.50 a.m. going by way of MEZEROLLES and right bank of AUTHIE river to HEM, BRETEL, DOULLENS Citadel, LE BON AIR, HULEUX, TERRAMESNIL, BEAUQUESNE. Got in after dark. Snowed.	
ENGLEBELMER	18		Marched at 10 am to ENGLEBELMER, 9 miles, in by 2 pm billets crowded. Snowed.	
Trenches	19		Relieved 6th Lincs above THIEPVAL. Two reserve Coys are situated in lowest part of Thiepval which no longer exists except as a very shell tumbled area. Ground covered with snow, shell holes all full of water frozen over 1/2 an inch thick. Front line is held by half a company in eleven posts, the other half Coy having to live in a dugout both entrances of which face the enemy and are under observation. Support and reserve line are	

1577 Wt. W10791/1773 500,000 1/15 D. D. & L. A.D.S.S./Forms/C. 2118.

Instructions regarding War Diaries and Intelligence Summaries are contained in F. S. Regs., Part II. and the Staff Manual respectively. Title pages will be prepared in manuscript.

WAR DIARY

or

~~INTELLIGENCE SUMMARY~~. HOWE Bn

(*Erase heading not required.*)

January 1917

Army Form C. 2118.

R.N.D.

Place	Date	Hour	Summary of Events and Information	Remarks and references to Appendices
Trenches	19th		also held by posts, the other half of the same Coy being in dugouts in BULGAR and RANSOME trenches. The latter can be visited by day, but not so any of the posts. Relief complete by 7.20 pm. Night relief parties left cookers at 4.45 p.m. The night passed quietly except that the duck board tracks were shelled by whizz-bangs about 10 pm. The enemy seemed to have the situations of these tracks very certainly and in the snow they are probably more conspicuous than trenches.	
"	20th		Work on clearing up dugouts and opening out new ones. In the front line at night the work of connecting up posts continued: party of Worcester pioneer Bn at work on PEEL trench. A little shelling, chiefly drawn by careless exposure of individuals near O.P.'s on sky line.	
	21st		Carried on same work. Enemy sent up "Golden rain" rockets at 4.30 pm and shelling followed directed to our right.	
	22nd		Same work. 3 men wounded by a Mills bomb which went off while an old dump was being cleared up.	

1577 Wt. W10791/1773 500,000 1/15 D. D. & L. A.D.S.S./Forms/C. 2118.

Instructions regarding War Diaries and Intelligence Summaries are contained in F. S. Regs., Part II. and the Staff Manual respectively. Title pages will be prepared in manuscript.

WAR DIARY
or
~~INTELLIGENCE SUMMARY.~~
(Erase heading not required.)

Army Form C. 2118.

January 1917 — Howe Bn R.N.D.

Place	Date	Hour	Summary of Events and Information	Remarks and references to Appendices
Trenches	22nd		At night relieved front line Coys B & D by A and C respectively. Relief complete by 8.48 pm. 2nd R.M on our left down to the ANCRE, a Bn of Middlesex Regt, 18th Dn on our right. Sub Lieut E.C. CATT joined from England, yesterday – and on the day before Sub Lieut W.R. HAINES, both RNVR.	
"	23rd		Day quiet but at night ration party going to front Coy got shelled on the duckboards at 6.45 pm. Doubtful whether this shelling was meant for the party or for PEEL trench near by which is under construction. Shelling went on for some time with 77 mm guns. CPO's H. CARDUS and S.W. ELLIOTT both hit, neither badly, and a man of D coy, also slight.	
"	24th		Quiet day and not much shelling in the evening.	
"	25th		Relief. Daylight portion, 2½ Companies, relieved by noon night parties were late. Front Coy complete by 8 40 pm and Support Coy by 10.40 pm. Front coy Hqrs heavily shelled 6.30-645 pm so it was as well that the relief was late. Relieved by Anson.	

1577 Wt. W10791/1773 500,000 1/15 D. D. & L. A.D.S.S./Forms/C. 2118.

Instructions regarding War Diaries and Intelligence Summaries are contained in F. S. Regs., Part II. and the Staff Manual respectively. Title pages will be prepared in manuscript.

WAR DIARY
or
~~INTELLIGENCE SUMMARY.~~
(*Erase heading not required.*)

Army Form C. 2118.

January 1917

HOWE Bn
R N. D.

Place	Date	Hour	Summary of Events and Information	Remarks and references to Appendices
			Cookers and watercarts exchanged. Coys marched back independantly by companies.	
ENGLEBELMER	26		Fatigue of 150 to W16b by 10.15, 25 to Town Major and 9 to DHQ. A.B. ELLIOT for Cookery to NOUVION.	
	27		Fatigues 150 to W16b by 8 am, 25 to Town Major, 9 to DHQ, 1 NCO + 9 to 175th Tunnelling Coy for attachment. Sub Lt HAMBLEY and AB TOZER to LETOUQUET for LG Course, AB MOXON and PESTER to NOUVION for same course.	
	28		Train cancelled – above men could not go. 50 men to W16b for fatigue, 9 to DHQ and 25 to Town major. Still very cold and freezing hard.	
	29		Fatigues easier, 12 to DHQ, 25 to Town Major.	
	30		Above fatigues, plus 50 to LANCASHIRE DUMP.	
	31		12 to DHQ. Relieved ANSON in trenches, Relief complete by 8 pm. Relief passed off quietly but an SOS signal seen at 10.12 pm on our left, believed N. of ANCRE. General flap till 10.50 p.m. when "stand down" was sent round. Freezing since 19th every day, more snow last night. Shell holes must be frozen nearly solid, 6" thick anyhow.	[signature] Commdr RN Howe 1/2/17

1577 Wt. W10791/1773 500,000 1/15 D. D. & L. A.D.S.S./Forms/C. 2118.

Army Form C. 2118.

WAR DIARY
or
~~INTELLIGENCE SUMMARY~~.
(Erase heading not required.)

Instructions regarding War Diaries and Intelligence Summaries are contained in F. S. Regs., Part II. and the Staff Manual respectively. Title pages will be prepared in manuscript.

February 1917

Howe Bn
RND

Vol

Place	Date	Hour	Summary of Events and Information	Remarks and references to Appendices
Trenches	31st Jan		In the line, section 14.S. The Bn holds from R 14 d 1 9 to R 20 b 9 3. At night the enemy fired on a fixed system bursts of intense fire on Battery valley and front line posts. These bursts were at 10 pm, midnight, 4 am and 6 am and each burst had 2 parts with a silent period between of 2 minutes.	
	1st		Night firing similar, bursts at 9 pm 11 pm and 5 am. MG in left entrance of front Coy HQ dugout knocked out. Two men wounded	
	2nd		Relieved 2 front Coys by 2 Reserve Coys which did not move till 6 pm. Relief complete by 10 pm. Night bursts of fire as usual from enemy, 9.45 pm and 3.45 am. Telephone line cut 3 times. A party of enemy, 12, out in front of their trench at 9.30 pm at R 14 d 5.8, working; they were plainly visible at 200 yards from No 9 post working in valley near bank. Snow still lying makes patrolling impossible and any work in the open dangerous. Wind still easterly and 18th Dn on our right captured a prisoner in an unsuccessful enemy raid who says gas apparatus is up and is being dug in	

1577 Wt. W10791/1773 500,000 1/15 D. D. & L. A.D.S.S./Forms/C. 2118.

Instructions regarding War Diaries and Intelligence Summaries are contained in F. S. Regs., Part II. and the Staff Manual respectively. Title pages will be prepared in manuscript.

Army Form C. 2118.

WAR DIARY
or
~~INTELLIGENCE SUMMARY~~
(Erase heading not required.)

February 1917

Howe Bn
RND.

Place	Date	Hour	Summary of Events and Information	Remarks and references to Appendices
Trenches			on their front.	
3.2.17			quiet day, but at night at 11 pm the 189 Inf Bde attacked PUISIEUX TRENCH and RIVER TRENCH N. of the ANCRE from that stream to ARTILLERY ALLEY: took both except for one strong point in center in which 30 enemy held out till next Day – over 200 prisoners. Enemy retaliation began at 11.15 pm and from 11.20 till 11.40 pm they shelled OG1, their own front line S of the ANCRE – Then a golden rain rocket was fired and the shelling stopped, being resumed on Battery valley.	
4.2.17			Early enemy counter attacked, and at 11 am again, once from the North and once along the Railway. Both times they were caught by barrage fire. from 10.40 am to 1.30 pm during one of these counters enemy maintained heavy fire on our front company dugout entrances which face him, and on the front posts. Owing to the snow the enemy is probably able to see our visiting patrols and ration parties at night and has thus located the posts.	

Army Form C. 2118.

Instructions regarding War Diaries and Intelligence Summaries are contained in F. S. Regs., Part II. and the Staff Manual respectively. Title pages will be prepared in manuscript.

WAR DIARY
or
INTELLIGENCE SUMMARY.
(Erase heading not required.)

FEB 1917 HOWE Bn RND

Place	Date	Hour	Summary of Events and Information	Remarks and references to Appendices
Trenches	5.2.17	[illegible]	A raid carried out on our right in R16 on Folly Trench. One prisoner taken. Last night our artillery fired on OG1 at 11.20p, 2.30 am 4.30 am + 5.45 am. Retaliation weak. At 9pm enemy shelled forward post + obtained direct hit on No 33. Lieut A.I. HUMPHREYS RNVR O/c C Coy was killed while attending to a wounded man in an exposed spot. 3 O.R. killed - 1 wounded. About 6pm a patrol consisting of Sub Lt J.F. BUNCE + LS (HG) C. McLUCKIE went out from No 1 post and entered OG1 - the German front line - They then went North for 150 yards finding no trace of the enemy. This was the first definite information procured of the enemy retirement - a movement which later assumed great proportions and was of far reaching importance. At 7.45pm the same patrol accompanied by Sub Lt H.M. GRAHAM and P.O. S. STIRLAND went out again and proceeded as far as R14d 9.9. again finding no trace of the enemy. They entered 2 dugouts and discovered signs of recent occupation. They found the wrappings of a parcel addressed to a Landsturm man of the 85th I.R 1st Bn 36th Bde 18th Inf Divn 9th Army Corps. Attempts had been made to destroy dugout entrances and one was found on fire. Very little in the way of equipment had been left behind - a few rifles - a large number of stick bombs etc Patrol returned	[signature]

1577 Wt. W10791/1773 500,000 1/15 D. D. & L. A.D.S.S./Forms/C. 2118.

Instructions regarding War Diaries and Intelligence Summaries are contained in F. S. Regs., Part II. and the Staff Manual respectively. Title pages will be prepared in manuscript.

WAR DIARY
or
~~INTELLIGENCE~~ SUMMARY.
(Erase heading not required.)

Army Form C. 2118.

FEB 1917 HOWE Bn RND

Place	Date	Hour	Summary of Events and Information	Remarks and references to Appendices
			at 9.5 pm. At 9.30 pm this news was passed to left Bn who sent out a patrol with similar results.	
Trenches	6th		2 pm established a post in OG1. 3 pm moved 1 platoon into it, move complete at 3.30 pm. Moved second platoon in at 4.30 pm and also relieved 1st platoon. 4.35 pm a post was established at R15 a 48. Other posts along OG1. OG2 non existent. Internal relief. D coy holds OG1 (2 platoons) and has 2 platoons and Hq in dugout at R14 c 9.2. B coy holds Posts 1 to 11 and 30 to 37, with one platoon in dugout at R20 c 27 and Hq at R20 c 71 in BULGAR, C coy remains in RAMSOME, BAINBRIDGE and BULGAR, one platoon in THIEPVAL R25 b 7.2 and coy Hq as for B, A coy returns to OLD German 1st line R25 b 3.6.	
Trenches	7th		Day spent in consolidation of O.G.1. The forenoon was quiet. In the afternoon the enemy shelled Battery VALLEY; during the shelling the Adjutant Lt E V ELLIS MC RNVR was hit. He died soon after reaching the A.D.S THIEPVAL. Further internal relief C. Coy relieved B Coy.	
Trenches	8th		Consolidation of O.G.1. during the day. B Coy were relieved at 1.0 pm & proceeded	

1577 Wt. W10791/1773 500,000 1/15 D. D. & L. A.D.S.S./Forms/C. 2118.

Instructions regarding War Diaries and Intelligence Summaries are contained in F. S. Regs., Part II. and the Staff Manual respectively. Title pages will be prepared in manuscript.

WAR DIARY
or
~~INTELLIGENCE~~ SUMMARY.
(Erase heading not required.)

Army Form C. 2118.

HOWE Bn
RND

FEB 1917

Place	Date	Hour	Summary of Events and Information	Remarks and references to Appendices
Trenches	8th		to ENGLEBELMER. The remainder of the Battalion was relieved by the ANSON BN after dark & proceeded to dug outs at THIEPVAL.	
THIEPVAL	9th		B & A Coys bathed at ENGLEBELMER in morning. The Bn provided during the day 250 men for working parties taken from the three companies at THIEPVAL. Orders received to move to ~~other~~ N of ANCRE. These orders cancelled & orders received by wire at 11.40 p.m. that the Bn. would move to FORCEVILLE on 10th leaving THIEPVAL at 10.15 a.m. Men of skilled trades interviewed at ENGLEBELMER.	
FORCEVILLE	10th		Bn. moved to FORCEVILLE arriving at destination at 3.50 p.m., ~~[illegible] remain~~	
"	11th		Employed the day in a general clean up, bathing etc	
"	12th		Drill under Company arrangements. An officer & sergeant of the North'd Fusiliers who are attached for musketry instruction, took classes including all the NCOs and most of the rifle sections.	
ENGLEBELMER	13th		Battn. less D Coy moved during forenoon & billetted at ENGLEBELMER. C.O. & 2nd i/c went early in the morning to visit our new sector.	
	14th		In the afternoon the G.O.C. RND came to inspect billets & spoke to company commanders. At 5.30pm the battn. proceeded via MESNIL, HAMEL & BEAUCOURT to relieve the 7th R.Fus. as right support battalion. Disposition as follows:–	

1577 Wt. W10791/1773 500,000 1/15 D. D. & L. A.D.S.S./Forms/C. 2118.

Instructions regarding War Diaries and Intelligence Summaries are contained in F. S. Regs., Part II. and the Staff Manual respectively. Title pages will be prepared in manuscript.

WAR DIARY
or
~~INTELLIGENCE SUMMARY.~~
(Erase heading not required.)

Army Form C. 2118.

FEB 1917

HOWE Bn
RND

Place	Date	Hour	Summary of Events and Information	Remarks and references to Appendices
	Feb			
TRENCHES	14th		Front Coy in shell holes N.W of BOIS d'HOLLAND	
			Second " SUVLA trench 400 yards in rear The quarry S of BEAUCOURT MIRAUMONT Road	
			Third " Shell slit in PUISIEUX Valley Road	
			Fourth " dugouts in BEAUCOURT Trench.	
			Battn HQ at BEAUCOURT at R7c 95 Relief passed off without incident and was completed at 11.55 pm. Enemy fire much less than of late.	
	15th		Disposition of battn remained the same except that front Coy was relieved. Hostile artillery pretty active especially during the night. Counter battery firing was asked for more than once and proved effective. Various stores etc were drawn in view of the forthcoming operation	
	16th		The battn is to move up tonight & occupy a frontage of 400 yards in PUISIEUX and RIVER trenches. The attack will take place about dawn, the HOWE objective being the SUNKEN ROAD from R3c 35 to R3a 25. The 1st R.M. will cooperate on the left & the 18th + 2nd Divns on the right, South of the ANCRE.	
		7pm.	Battn moved up. On account of the darkness + difficulty of moving it was decided to take up battle positions at once. This was marked by a tape laid out by the R.E. running from R2b 30 – R2d 85 – a 400 yard front	[illegible initials/signature]

1577 Wt. W10791/1773 500,000 1/15 D. D. & L. A.D.S.S./Forms/C. 2118.

Instructions regarding War Diaries and Intelligence Summaries are contained in F. S. Regs., Part II. and the Staff Manual respectively. Title pages will be prepared in manuscript.

WAR DIARY
or
~~INTELLIGENCE~~ SUMMARY.
(Erase heading not required.)

Army Form C. 2118.

FEB 1917 HOWE Bn RND

Place	Date	Hour	Summary of Events and Information	Remarks and references to Appendices
Trenches Ht	16th		On the way up D Coy lost an officer and about 17 men from shell fire which was heavy & persistent. Battn HQ was established at R 2d H5 in a dugout in PUISIEUX Trench. Battle positions were taken up by 2.30 am	
Trenches	17th		Zero was at 5.45 am when the barrage opened and battn advanced on the SUNKEN ROAD the 1st R.M. advancing on the left. The objective was taken without much difficulty. Hostile barrage was considerable. We captured a M.G. & a number of prisoners - probably about 40. Consolidation was immediately begun & proceeded very satisfactorily - a line of posts being established 50-100 yards E of the Sunken Road. During the day enemy artillery maintained a heavy fire, PUISIEUX & RIVER trenches receiving special attention. Our casualties during the day were about 180 including 2 Officers killed (Sub Lts SHEA and HAINES.) and 7 wounded.	
"	18th		At 11.30 am the 1/RM. on our left sent the S.O.S. A barrage was immediately opened. The S.O.S. was cancelled ½ hour later. Enemy forces estimated at 2 battns had attempted to counter-attack advancing on a ¾ mile front under cover of the mist. Heavy casualties by shell fire & M.G. were inflicted on them & they never reached our lines. Enemy shelling persistent throughout the day but not so heavy as yesterday. In the evening 2 companies of the Anson relieved our front. The relief was very slow owing to the dark and the muddy conditions. A & B Coys went to dugouts	[illegible] Commdg Howe Battn

1577 Wt. W10791/1773 500,000 1/15 D. D. & L. A.D.S.S./Forms/C. 2118.

Instructions regarding War Diaries and Intelligence Summaries are contained in F. S. Regs., Part II. and the Staff Manual respectively. Title pages will be prepared in manuscript.

WAR DIARY

or

~~INTELLIGENCE SUMMARY.~~

(Erase heading not required.)

Army Form C. 2118.

FEB 1917

HOWE Bn
RND

Place	Date	Hour	Summary of Events and Information	Remarks and references to Appendices
	Feb			
France	18		in Beaumont Trench, C + D in PUISIEUX VALLEY and the QUARRY. Battn H.Q. as before.	
	19		Major General Lawrie assumed command of the Division. Day spent resting, cleaning up and refitting as far as conditions would permit. All ranks are much exhausted. Sub Lieut BUNCE died of wounds received on 17th.	
	20		As yesterday.	
	21		In the afternoon the Battn was relieved by the 1/H.A.C. and proceeded to HEDAUVILLE in G.S. Wagons. Relief was reported complete at 5.30 p.m.	
HEDAUVILLE	22nd		Time employed in cleaning up, reorganizing and getting into a fighting state. Several	
	23rd		new officers joined – companies now brought up to a strength of 4 each. Several small fatigues.	
	24th		In the afternoon the Corps Commander inspected and spoke to the Officers + N.C.O.s of the Battn, G.O.C. RND also being present. His remarks were highly complimentary.	
	25th		Divine service celebrated at 10.30 a.m.	
	26th		A party was sent to the scene of the recent operations to bury dead. They buried 13 bodies. Carried out company training	
	27.		Sent bomber to be attached to Casualty Clearing Stations at CONTAY and VARENNES	
	28		C + D Coys went to VARENNES for work on the railway at ACHEUX. A Coy firing on the range.	[signature illegible]

1577 Wt. W10791/1773 500,000 1/15 D. D. & L. A.D.S.S./Forms/C. 2118.

TRENCHES CORRECTED FROM LATEST AIR PHOTOS - FEB 13 - 1917.
— TRENCH MAP —
SCALE - 1:5,000.
Old Battery Position probably occupied.
Dugouts
Three small Belgian Guns here 29/1/17
Susp^d MG
MG
Old Batt^y Positions probably occupied
Dugout
H.Q.
Puisieux Alley (Strongly held)
Sentry Post
Post
Trench lightly held or Patrolled.
Patrol reports this post well wired and very strongly held.
Posts
Much used.
In good condition
Strong Point
Wired strong Point
Old Battery Positions probably occupied
Swan Trench
Susp^d M.G.
Sunken road from R 3 b 40·75 to 133 c 7·2 has been worked on a great deal recently
Large Hole
6' deep
Susp^d Dugouts
O.P. and MG
TM
Old O.P.
PRESENT BRITISH FRONT LINE
NOT USED
Artillery Alley
River Trench
Puisieux Trench
PUISIEUX ROAD
Old B^n HQ
Susp^d MG
Miraumont Alley Strongly Held In good condition
Strong Point
Barricade
Susp^d Dugout
Baillescourt Farm
32
33
2
3
L
R
- NOTE -
ALTHOUGH NO WIRE IS SHOWN THERE IS PROBABLY SOME IN FRONT OF ENEMY POSITIONS.
— REFERENCE —
DUGOUTS
OLD BTY POSITIONS
TRENCHES IN GOOD CONDITION
MACHINE GUN
POST. (HOSTILE)
TRENCH MORTAR
OBSERVATION POST
OBLITERATED TRENCHES

1089

Stuns

Oct 17th 1917

APPENDIX "A".

ACTION BY 188th. and 190th. MACHINE GUN COMPANIES.

190th. M.G.Company. 1. 12 guns of the 190th. Machine Gun Company will be employed, under instructions issued by the Corps Machine Gun Officer, to place a barrage round the Northern and North Eastern flanks of the advance, from positions in the vicinity of GRANDCOURT and PUISIEUX ROAD.

The remaining four guns will be maintained in their present positions in R.2.a., and will be used for the defence of the present Northern flank held by the Brigade

188th. M.G.Company 2. (a) 8 guns of the 188th. M.G.Company will be employed under instructions from Corps Machine Gun Officer, to bring a barrage fire on to the Eastern front of the objective from the vicinity of PUISIEUX ROAD, and OLD POST LINE.

The remaining 8 guns will be used as under :-

3 guns will take over the positions now held by guns of 190th. Machine Gun Company at R.2.b.05.4., R.2.b.3.0., and R.3.c.0.05., and will remain in these positions in defence, or for repelling counter-attacks.

(b) 2 guns will advance in rear of second wave of Left Company of 1st ROYAL MARINES and occupy positions in the vicinity of L.32.d.8.1., and R.2.b.9.9., the former position to enfilade the SUNKEN ROAD to the North, the latter to fire East and North-East.

(c) The 6th.gun will move up with the second Company of HAWKE Battalion (reference para.9 of Brigade Order No.82.), and take up a position in the vicinity of R.2.b.3.7.

(d) The 7th gun will advance in rear of the second wave of the 1st ROYAL MARINES and take up a position at Point R.3.a.3.7., which is being consolidated as a Strong Point. This gun will be accomodated until ZERO hour beside the gun at R.2.b.05.4.

(e) The remaining gun will be accomodated until ZERO hour beside the gun now at R.2.b.3.0., and will advance in rear of the second wave of the Left Company of the HOWE Battalion and take up a position just East of SUNKEN ROAD in vicinity of R.3.a.2.5.

These guns, enumerated in sub-paras. (b),(c),(d), and (e), will cover the consolidation of the Northern and Eastern flanks.

3. A party of 10 men has been detailed by Officer Commanding HOWE Battalion as carrying party for the 5 guns taking part in the advance.

A.D. Tedford Smollett

Captain.
Brigade Major.
188th. Infantry Brigade.

15th. February, 1917.

S E C R E T   B.O. 82/3.

M E M O R A N D U M

Brigade Headquarters,
16th. February, 1917.

With reference to 188th. Infantry Brigade Order No.82 of 15th. February, 1917.:-

Zero hour will be 5·45 AM 17th inst.

~~"[illegible]"~~ - n.

A C K N O W L E D G E

A D Tedder-Smalle CP

Captain.
Brigade Major.
188th. Inf. Brigade.

Copies to :-.

1st Royal Marines
2nd Royal Marines
Anson Battalion
Howe Battalion
188th. M.G.Company
2nd Field Ambulance
1st Field Ambulance
14th. Worcesters
2nd Field Company R.E.
189th. M.G.Company
189th. L.T.M.Battery
"G" Group, R.A.
Hawke Battalion
Hood Battalion
190th. M.G.Company

SECRET

RATION SUPPLY.

With reference to O.O.82

1. The supply will be normal for the night preceding operations.

2. Rations for night following operations will be pooled - packed in sandbags containing 10 rations each - 6 bags to each animal.

Units will be divided into groups for the purposes of pack transport. The rations of the first three groups beimg sent to R1.d.7.7., (Left forward dump), and of the fourth to R7.b.8.1. (Right forward dump).

Groups will be loaded at ENGLEBELMER as follows :-

(A) Those for R1.d.7.7.

	RATIONS	ANIMALS
1/R.M.BN. Q.M.Stores.		
1/Royal Marines	840	14
Hood Battalion	300	5
Water Tins	80	10
2/R.M.BN. Q.M.Stores.		
2/Royal Marines	840	14
Hawke Bn. (2 Coys.)	180	3
No.2 Coy., R.E.	120	2
Water Tins.	80	10
Howe Battn. Q.M.Stores.		
Howe Battalion	720	12
14/ Worcesters	120	2
Water Tins.	56	7

(B) Those for R7.b.8.1.

	RATIONS	ANIMALS
Anson Battn. Q.M.Stores.		
Anson Battalion	660	11
189th.L.T.M.Bty.	60	1
Water Tins	48	6

The groups will be divided into sections of 5 or 6 animals each by Brigade Transport Officer.

Units other than Battalions of this Brigade will send their rations packed in tens as above, to the Q.M.Stores of their Group by 3 p.m.

Convoys will be loaded and started off under the direction of the Brigade Transport Officer.

All rations on arrival at R1.d.7.7. will be handed over to an Officer who will take charge of them until ca rying parties arrive. All parties should be given authority signed by an Officer stating number of rations to be drawn.

3. Arrangements for rationing on subsequent nights will be notified later.

A.P. Tomes
Captain.
Staff Captain.
188th. Infy. Brigade.

16/2/17

B.C. 82.

A P P E N D I X "B".

ACTION BY 189th. LIGHT TRENCH MORTAR BATTERY.

Northern Guns. 1. The 189th. Light Trench Mortar Battery will assist the attack by establishing 2 guns at about R.2.a.6.7., and R.2.a.9.6., to bombard the RIVER and PUISIEUX Trench Systems North of ARTILLERY ALLEY. 2 guns will also be retained in their present positions in about R.2.a.0.5. and R.2.a.5.6., for the purpose of guarding the Northern flank.

When the attack has reached the objective, one of the Right hand guns will move to a position in the vicinity of R.2.b.3.7., in order to bring fire on North Eastern flank of our new line in SUNKEN ROAD.

Southern Guns. 2. The 2 guns now established at R.3.c.5.4. and R.3.c.4.6. will bring enfilading fire to bear on the SUNKEN ROAD in the vicinity of R.3.c.3.8., and R.3.a.2.5.

These guns will cease firing at ZERO + 10 and after the objective is captured the Southern gun will be moved up the SUNKEN ROAD to the vicinity of R.3.a.2.5., whence it can deal with SWAN TRENCH East of the SUNKEN ROAD. The other gun will block MIRAUMONT ALLEY 300 yards East of the SUNKEN ROAD.

A.D. Tupper-Carey [signature]

Captain.
Brigade Major.
188th. Infantry Brigade.

15th. February, 1917.

SECRET

Copy No 6.

RATION SUPPLY.

With reference to O.O.82

1. The supply will be normal for the night preceding operations.

2. Rations for night following operations will be pooled - packed in sandbags containing 10 rations each - 6 bags to each animal.

Units will be divided into groups for the purposes of pack transport. The rations of the first three groups beimg sent to R1.d.7.7., (Left forward dump), and of the fourth to R7.b.8.1. (Right forward dump).

Groups will be loaded at ENGLEBELMER as follows :-

(A) Those for R1.d.7.7.

1/R.M.BN. Q.M.Stores.	RATIONS	ANIMALS
1/Royal Marines	840	14
Hood Battalion	300	5
Water Tins	80	10

2/R.M.BN. Q.M.Stores.	RATIONS	ANIMALS
2/Royal Marines	840	14
Hawke Bn. (2 Coys.)	180	3
No.2 Coy., R.E.	120	2
Water Tins.	80	10

Howe Battn. Q.M.Stores.	RATIONS	ANIMALS
Howe Battalion	720	12
14/ Worcesters	120	2
Water Tins.	56	7

(B) Those for R7.b.8.1.

Anson Battn. Q.M.Stores.	RATIONS	ANIMALS
Anson Battalion	660	11
189th.L.T.M.Bty.	60	1
Water Tins	48	6

The groups will be divided into sections of 5 or 6 animals each by Brigade Transport Officer.

Units other than Battalions of this Brigade will send their rations packed in tens as above, to the Q.M.Stores of their Group by 3 p.m.

Convoys will be loaded and started off under the direction of the Brigade Transport Officer.

All rations on arrival at R1.d.7.7. will be handed over to an Officer who will take charge of them until ca rying parties arrive. All parties should be given authority signed by an Officer stating number of rations to be drawn.

3. Arrangements for rationing on subsequent nights will be notified later.

L.W. Travers.
Captain.
Staff Captain.
188th. Infy. Brigade.

16/2/17

S E C R E T

B.O.82/1

A M E N D M E N T

Headquarters,
188th. Inf. Brigade.
15th. February, 1917.

With reference to 188th. Infantry Brigade Order No.82 of today's date, the following amendment is made :-

Cancel sub-paras. (a) and (b) of Para. [illegible], and substitute as under :-

" (a) The Companies of the HA[illegible] Battalion will move off from their assembly point under supervision of Officer Commanding No.2 Field Company R.E. in double file, and will be in position with the head of the leading Company 60 yards behind the second wave on the Left flank of the 1st. ROYAL MARINES by ZERO- 15. Officer Commanding No.2. Field Company R.E. will ensure that every consolidating Section has a proportion of R.E's attached to it.

These Companies will be preceded by Outpost Battle Patrols, who will move forward to be in position immediately behind the second wave on the Left flank of the 1st ROYAL MARINES. Each Patrol will be accompanied by a Lewis Gun.

After ZERO these Patrols will move following the wave in the direction of the tape line marking the Northern consolidating flank, and will take up a position to cover the frontage at about 75 yards to the North of the Line to be consolidated.

The rearmost Patrol moving out to the North immediately it has cleared the forming up tape, and those in front taking up their positions with about 80 yards between each Battle Patrol.

This Northern flank will be held by means of Strong Posts not less than 100 yards apart; this will entail at least 5 Posts on this flank. The direction of the line of consolidation on the Northern flank will be taped under the supervision of the R.E. Direction of this is on the line R.2.b.6.6., to L.32.d.[illegible].1.

These Companies will be followed by one Company of Pioneers, a selected party of whom will place knife rests in position on a line to be selected by the R.E. Officer, in front of the line of Posts. This line of knife rests will be carried round the junction of the Northern and Eastern Fronts.

(b) On the Eastern front a similar line of Posts will be constructed along the SUNKEN ROAD.

This line of Posts must subsequently be made continuous and strongly entrenched, and a new line of Posts constructed a 100 yards to the East of it.

The garrison of all Posts and Strong Points is to be 2 complete sections and one Lewis Gun, hence each Platoon Commander will be in charge of two Posts.

In addition to these lines of Posts, which will be the recognised system for the occupation of the Line, Strong Points will be required at or near, R.2.b.5.7., R.2.d.9.9., R.3.a.3.7., and R.3.c.5.8.

Officer Commanding No.2 Field Company R.E. will detail one section of R.E. and one section of Pioneers for the construction of each of the above points, who should be held in readiness to go forward as soon as the objective is captured.

As/

B.O.82.

APPENDIX. "C"

R.A. BARRAGE.

ARTILLERY. The attack of the 188th. Infantry Brigade will be supported by an Artillery Barrage, the time table of which is attached. The creeping barrage will keep 150 yards to the North of MIRAULONT ALLEY.

From Zero to Zero plus four, heavy Artillery will fire on SUNKEN ROAD. From Zero to Zero plus one hour, heavy Artillery will also fire on all hostile approached to the position.

Field howitzers will open on the SUNKEN ROAD at Zero, and at Zero plus four will lift to a line 400 yards to the East of it.

The 32nd. Divisional Artillery will co-operate with a protective barrage along our Northern flank.

A.D. Talbot-Smith

Captain.
Brigade Major.
188th. Inf. Brigade.

15/2/17.

(b) contd.

As regards these two latter, the Officer Commanding No.2 Field Company R.E. will arrange for the necessary R.E. and Pioneers to report at Battalion Headquarters of 1st ROYAL MARINES and HOWE Battalion by 4-0 p.m. on "Z" day.

These will be allotted by Battalion Commanders concerned to the Companies dealing with these two Strong Points."

2. ACKNOWLEDGE.

A.D. Taylor Smith

Captain.
Brigade Major.
188th. Inf. Brigade.

15/2/17.

Copies to :- All Units.

ARTILLERY TIME TABLE.

B.O.82.

TIME.	ARTILLERY	INFANTRY
Zero	(a) Creeping barrage of 27 18 pdrs. opens 200 yds. East of our forming up position.	Infantry starts advancing.
	(b) Standing barrage opens on the SUNKEN ROAD.	
Zero plus 4	Creeping barrage lifts 100 yards.	
Zero plus 8	Creeping barrage lifts to SUNKEN ROAD.	
Zero plus 12	All guns lift 100 yards clear of SUNKEN ROAD.	Infantry assaults SUNKEN ROAD.
Zero plus 14	All guns lifts 100 yards.	
Zero plus 16	All guns lift 100 yards and form a protective barrage down to the RIVER ANCRE.	
Zero plus 47	Protective barrage ceases for five minutes.	
Zero plus 52	Barrage re-opens.	
Zero plus 1 hr.	Barrage ceases.	

SECRET

Copy No......6

188th. INFANTRY BRIGADE ORDER No. 82.

Brigade Headquarters,
15th. February, 1917.

Reference Maps - 57D N.E. 1/20,000
BEAUMONT 57D S.E.,
1 & 2 (parts of) 1/10,000.
Special Trench map 1/5,000.

Intention. 1. The 188th. Infantry Brigade will at an early date attack and capture the SUNKEN ROAD in R.3.A and C. from MIRAUMONT ALLEY in the South to a point L.32.d.9.1. in the North, and form a defensive flank facing North from the latter point to about R.2.b.0.6.

The attack will be carried out in conjunction with one made by the 18th and 2nd Divisions on our Right.

The Left of the 18th. Division will finally rest along the Railway line to point R.9.b.2.3.

Information. 2. The position to be attacked by the Brigade is held by a Battalion of the 86th. I.R. (18th Division). Two Companies of this Regt. are in Reserve at the Western end of MIRAUMONT. One Regiment of the 18th Division is probably refitting as a result of the recent operation North of the ANCRE. The 230th R.I.R. has some troops in Reserve in the vicinity of BEAUREGARD ALLEY.

SWAN Trench is badly damaged West of the SUNKEN ROAD. The SUNKEN ROAD appears to be held continuously only immediate--ly North and South of SWAN Trench. There are however, strong points at R.2.b.95.85. (which is wired), R.3.a.1.7., and R.3.a.2.5. The enemy is probably also holding scattered Posts with machine guns between RIVER Trench and the SUNKEN ROAD..

Our Forces. 3. The following troops have placed at the disposal of G.O.C. 188th. Infantry Brigade for this operation:-

2 Battns. of 189th. Infantry Brigade.
2 Coys of 189th. Inf. Brigade as carrying parties.
190th. Machine Gun Company.
1 Company 14th. (pioneer) Battn. Worcester Regt.
No.2 Field Company R.E.

Distribution of Troops. 4. (a) The HOWE Battalion will attack on the Right with 4 Companies and the 1st ROYAL MARINES with the same number of Companies on the Left.

(b) The ANSON Battalion will hold its present Front Line with 2 Companies and will have 2 Companies in Support, ready to reinforce either the Left or Right attacking Battalions if required. One of these Companies should in addition, be ready to move out between the MIRAUMONT ROAD and the ANCRE RIVER if ordered, to affect a junction with the Left of the 18th Division and co-operate with them in capturing or killing any enemy in the Southern part of R.3.d.

(c) The 2nd. ROYAL MARINES will hold their present Front on the Northern flank of the Brigade, This Front extends from about R.2.a.0.8. to R.2.a.8.7.

(d) The HOOD Battalion will be in Reserve with :-

2 Companies in PUISIEUX TRENCH. R 2. D. 2. 8.
2 Companys in Old Post Line, R.2.c. Central.
~~1 Company in R.7.b.7.7. (in slits).~~

(c)

(e) 2 Companies HAWKE Battalion will construct and occupy Posts on a Northern flank from R.2.b.0.8., to L.32.b.8.1., a distance of 475 yards. They will be assisted by No.2/Company R.E. and a Company of 14th. Worsester Regt.
Field.

(f) 2 Companies HAWKE Battalion, and Headquarters will be in Brigade Reserve in the slits at South end of STATION ROAD.

Division of Front.

5. The dividing line between attacking Battalions will be drawn through R.2.b.3.0., and R.3.a.2.5.

Right Battalion frontage of its objective is above Line inclusive to R.3.c.4.7. on the Right.

Frontage for Left Battalion from the above Line on the Right exclusive to L.32.d.8.1. on the Left inclusiva.

Formation of the Attack.

6. (a) Each Battalion will attack in 2 (two) waves, each wave consisting of 4 half companies in line per Battalion - distance between waves 20 paces.

(b) By Zero - 15 the leading waves of the attacking Battalions will be formed up on a tape line running approx--imately from R.2.b.2.7. to R.2.d.8.5..

The Officer Commanding No.2 Field Company, R.E. will arrange to put out a tape line on which the troops can form up for the assault on "Z" night.

Preliminary Dispositions.

7. Approximately about Midnight on "Z" night, Officer Commanding HOWE Battalion will relieve the Right, Front, and Support Companies of 1st ROYAL MARINES in PUISIEUX (2) and RIVER Trenches (1) respectively, with 4 (four) Companies, and move his Battalion Headquarters to PUISIEUX TRENCH.

On relief these Companies of 1st. ROYAL MARINES will side-slip, and the Officer Commanding 1st ROYAL MARINES will make the necessary adjustment in his Line.

The HOOD Battalion will occupy the Lines as laid down in para.4. sub-para.(d).

The 2 Companies of the HAWKE Battalion for the North--ern flank will assemble in the vicinity of ARTILLERY ALLEY and PUISIEUX ROAD Juncture, together with No.2 Field Company and Company of 14th. Worcester Regiment.

Officer Commanding No.2 Company R.E. will arrange direct with Officer Commanding HAWKE Battalion regarding the location and hour of rendezvous for these two Companies.

Method of Attack.

8. (a) Directly the barrage opens the troops will get up as close to it as possible, the importance of this and of following the barrage closely, must be impressed on all concerned.

(b) Both waves will push through to the final objective and will establish a Line of Posts East of the SUNKEN ROAD, to cover the consolidation of Strong Points, as enumerated in para.9.

(c) The Left Battalion will detail special Bombing Sections for dealing with SWAN TRENCH, They will also, on "Z" night, as soon as it is dark, push out their Left Post, together with a Lewis Gun, to the North of Point R.2.b.2.7. to cover our Left flank during the deployment on the tape line.

Consolidation.

9. (a) The Companies of the HAWKE Battalion will move off from their assembly point under supervision of Officer Commanding No.2 Field Company R.E. in double file, and will be in position with the head of the leading Company sixty yards behind the second wave of the Left flank of the 1st ROYAL MARINES by Zero - 15. Officer Commanding No.2 Field Company, R.E. will ensure that every Platoon has a propor--tion of R.E's attached to it.

Four/

,Para.9 (a) contd.

Four men in each Platoon under a selected N.C.O. will be told off as Battle Patrols. These together with the Lewis Gun section as each Platoon halts to consolidate will move out to the Northern flank and form a line of outpost Patrols.

This Northern flank will be held by means of Strong Posts not less than 100 yards apart; this will entail 5 Posts on this flank. The direction of the line of consolidation on the Northern flank will be taped under the supervision of the R.E. - direction of this is on the line R.2.b.0.6. to L.32.d.8.1.

These Companies will be followed by one Company of Pion--eers, a selected party of whom will place knife rests in position on a line to be selected by the R.E. Officer, in front of the line of Posts. This line of knife rests will be carried round the jun--ction of the Northern and Eastern fronts.

This Line of Posts on the SUNKEN ROAD must subsequently be made continuous and strongly entrenched, and a new line of Posts constructed a 100 yards to the East of it.

The garrison of all Posts and Strong Points is to be 2 complete sections and one Lewis Gun, hence each Platoon Commander will be in charge of 2 Posts.

(b) On the Eastern Front a similar line of Posts will be con--structed along the SUNKEN ROAD.

In addition to these lines of Posts, which will be the recognised system for the occupation of the Line, Strong Points will be required at or near, R.2.b.3.7., R.2.b.9.9., R.3.a.3.7., and R.3.c.5.8.

Officer Commanding No.2 Field Company R.E. will detail one section of R.E's and one section of pioneers for the construction of each of the above Points, who should be held in readiness to go forward as soon as the objective is captured.

(c) In order to keep the attacking troops clear of hostile Artillery fire directed by the map, care will be taken as far as possible to avoid all trenches in selecting positions for consolidation.

(d) 2 Companies of NELSON Battalion will be available for carrying duties.

Officer Commanding No.2 Field Company, Royal Engineers, will requisition Brigade Headquarters for any assistance he requires for carrying up material for consolidation work in addition to that which can be carried up by the pioneers and R.E's.

(e) In all cases where consolidation work is going on, special attention must be paid to putting out covering parties in shell holes in front, together with a proportion of Lewis Guns.

Machine Guns and Light Trench Mortars. 10. Orders for the machine guns are issued as on Appendix "A", and orders for Light Trench Mortars as on Appendix "B".

R.A. 11. The barrage Table which regulates the progress of the attack is issued as Appendix "C".

Material. 12. The following will be carried by the attacking troops :-

Sandbags.	3. each man carried under the braces across the back.
Mill's grenades	2. each man in top pockets. These should be collected on reaching the objective and held in reserve in case of a counter-attack.
Aeroplane flares	Each man one.
Rations.	A day's ration and one iron ration.
Water.	Water-bottles filled.
Ammunition.	170 rounds per man.
Wire-cutters.	8 per Platoon if available.

Tools/.

Amendment to paras. 17 and 18.

Advanced Hdqtrs.	17.	Brigade Headquarters, Advanced Report Centre, No.4 Dug-out on East side PUISIEUX ROAD, R.7.b.7.7.
Battalion Hdqtrs. during the Attack.	18.	Right Battalion - ANSON R.8.b.c.6. Right Centre - HOWE PUISIEUX TRENCH, R.2.d.4.5. Left Centre - 1st ROYAL MARINES, PUISIEUX TRENCH, R.2.d.2.8. Left Battalion - 2nd ROYAL MARINES, R.7.a.2.3. Support Battalion HOOD Battalion, R.2.d.4.5.

Amendment to para. 10, (b).

(b) The Officer Commanding 2nd Field Ambulance is arranging for a supply of stretchers, blankets, and shell dressings at the Regimental Aid Posts (R.7.b.[illegible].1. and R.1.d.5.1.) and Bearer Posts (R.7.c.[illegible].8. and Q.18.b.5.8.) and, in addition to reinforcing bearer personnel on the routes of evacuation, will place 8 stretcher bearers at the disposal of Medical Officer of each assaulting battalion.

12 contd.

Tools. - Every man of the second wave (and the men for the defensive flank) should carry a pick or shovel in equal proportion. Tools should be carried on the back, head of tool uppermost.

S.O.S. Rockets. 2 sets per Company going forward. These are on no account to be used except in the case of hostile Infantry attack.

All Bombing squads must carry Rifle grenades, in addition to Bombs.

Contact Aeroplanes. 13. Officer Commanding No.4 Squadron, R.F.C. is providing Contact Patrols and the Infantry will show Red flares at certain fixed time; also at any other time on the demand being made by the Klaxon Horn or by dropping white lights.

Prisoners. 14. Prisoners should be sent back to Brigade Headquarters in small parties with an escort which should not exceed 5%.

Stragglers Posts. 15. Stragglers Posts will be established under arrangements to be made by the A.P.M. in the vicinity of STATION ROAD.

Medical Arrangements. 16. (a) The Officer Commanding 2nd Field Ambulance will be in charge of the evacuation of wounded in the forward area.

~~(b) The Officer Commanding 2nd Field Ambulance will arrange for a supply of stretchers, blankets, and shell dressings at each R.A.P. and Bearer Posts and, in addition to reinforcing bearer personnel on the routes of evacuation, will place 8 stretcher bearers at the disposal of the Medical Officer of each assaulting Battalion.~~

(c) Arrangemnets will be made for the supply of hot drinks and food at advanced Bearer posts (Q.18.b.5.8.), and LANCASHIRE DUMP.

(d) Walking wounded will be directed to a loading post near HAMEL, where they will be conveyed by Motor Lorry or Ambulance wagon to LANCASHIRE DUMP.

(e) M.O's of Battalions will keep the Officer Commanding 2nd Field Ambulance constantly informed of the number of casualties awaiting removal, and will ensure that the area of operations is thoroughly search for wounded.

(f) The Officer Commanding 2nd Field Ambulance will arrange for a Medical Officer to be attached to Brigade Headquarters. This Officer will keep him constantly informed of any changes in the situation

~~**Advanced H.Q.** 17. Brigade Headquarters, Advanced Report Centre, R.7.a.7.8.~~

Battalion Hdqtrs during the Attack. 18.

Right Battalion	- ANSON	R.8.b.6.6.
~~Right Centre~~	~~- HOWE~~	~~PUISIEUX TRENCH, R.2.d.2.8.~~
~~Left Centre~~	~~- 1st ROYAL MARINES~~	~~PUISIEUX TRENCH, R.2.Central.~~
~~Left Battalion.~~	~~- 2nd ROYAL MARINES~~	~~R.7.a.2.3.~~
~~Support Battalion HOOD Battalion~~		~~R.7.b.4.7.~~

Communic--ations. 19. Arrangements for Communication are shown in Appendix "D"

Miscellan--eous 20. Special attention is directed to the following points:-

i. All ranks taking part in the Assault are forbidden to carry any letters, papers, orders or sketches which in the event of their capture, would be likely to give information to the enemy.

ii. The necessity of getting back information is of utmost importance, and frequent reports as to the situation should be made.

iii. Officers, down to Company Commanders, will carry the 1/10,000 Trench Maps. Special maps have been issued from Divisional Headquarters for distribution down to Platoon Commanders.

iv.

Para.20 contd.

iv. Every Commander, however subordinate, will have an understudy told off in advance, This understudy must be made known to all concerned.

v. Nor more than 20 Officers will accompany the attacking Battalions. The ranks to be left behind have been communicated to Commanding Officers concerned.

vi. Commanding Officers will issue special instructions prohibiting souvenir hunting during the course of the operations. X Special collecting parties under reliable N.C.O's will however be detailed by Officer Commanding Companies after the taking of the objective, to systematically search all dug-outs, to collect identifications and papers. These will be placed in sacks and sent into Brigade Headquarters as early as possible.

S.O.S. 21. The S.O.S. Signal will be one Green, one Red, one Green Rocket. S.O.S. Signals on the wires will be as under:-

Right Battalion Front - S.O.S. QUARRIES.

Centre Battalion Front- S.O.S. East.
Northern Front - S.O.S. North.

Liaison. 22. Officer Commanding 2nd ROYAL MARINES will detail an Officer to act as Liaison Officer with the Brigade Headquarters on the Right, to report at 188th. Infantry Brigade Headquarters at 8-0 p.m. "Z" day for instructions

Watches, ZERO. 23. Instructions for sychronizing watches for "Z" day and for ZERO hour will be notified later.

24. Please ACKNOWLEDGE.

A.D. Tarler-Studley(?)

Captain.
Brigade Major.
188th. Inf. Brigade.

Issued to Signals at

Copies to :-
No.1. File
2. War Diary
3. 1st Royal Marines
4. 2nd Royal Marines
5. Anson Battalion
6. Howe Battalion
7. 188th. L.T.M.Battery
8. 188th. M.G.Company
9. 2nd Field Ambulance
10. 2nd Field Company
11. 63rd (RN) Division. (6 copies)
12. 14th. Worcesters.
13. 190th. M.G.Company
14. 190th. Inf. Brigade
15. 189th. Inf. Brigade
16. "G" R.A. Group
17. C.R.A.
19. C.R.E.
20. A.D.M.S.
21. Hawke Battalion
22. Hood Battalion
23. 18th. Division.
24. 54th. Inf. Brigade
25. Nelson Battalion.
26. Brigade Major
27. Staff Captain.
28. Intelligence Officer
29. Liaison Officer.
[illegible handwritten entries]

B.O. 82.

APPENDIX "D".

Commun-ications. 1. The arrangements for communications are as follows:-

An advanced Brigade Signal Office and Report Centre has been situtadestablished at R.7.b.7.7., linked up as follows.:-

FORWARD. Two lamp visual Stations at Points R.2.d.2.8. and R.2.d.0.10., working DD messages to R.20.c.2.5.

2. WIRELESS. Set at R.7.b.4.6. in direct communication with Brigade Headquarters, linked up with R.C. by short lines.

3. LISTENING SET. At R.7.b.4.6.
Power buzzer at R.2.d.2.8., and R.8.b.6.6.

4. PIGEONS. Battalions to carry two extra pigeons.

5. LINES. BACK.
i. Back from R.C. to No.1 Test Point (R.7.a.7.9.), to No.2 Test Point (Q.12.b.2.7.) to Brigade Headquarters by Divisional track.
ii. R.C. to Runner Post R.7.a.2.3., straight back to Brigado Headquarters.
iii. R.C. to R.7.c.9.5., to Brigade Headquarters.
iv. R.7.c.9.5., to Brigado O.P. (R.20.c.2.5.).

LINES FORWARD FROM R.C.

v. R.C. to Pt. R.2.d.4.5.
vi. R.C. to Pt. R.2.d.2.8.
vii. R.C. to Pt. R.8.b.6.6.

LATERAL WIRES.

viii. Pt. R.2.d.2.8. to Pt. R.2.d.4.5., to Pt. R.8.b.6.6

ix. No.1 Test Post to R.7.a.2.3., to Post R.7.c.9.5.

6. RUNNERS. - 12 at Report Centre.
12 at Point R.7.a.3.2.
These runners are all to be provied with the issued badges, i.e., Blue, White, Blue.

A.D. Telfer-Smollett
Captain.
Brigade Major.
188th. Inf. Brigade.

15/2/17.

S E C R E T

B.O.82/2.

A M E N D M E N T

Headquarters,
188th. Inf. Brigade.
15th. February, 1917.

With reference to Brigade Order No.82 of today's date, the following amendment is made :-

Para. 1, line 2, for R.3.c. and d., read
R.3.a. and c.

2. Please ACKNOWLEDGE.

A D [illegible]

Captain.
Brigade Major.
188th. Inf. Brigade.

Copies to all units concerned.

Copy No 4

SECRET.

B.O.82/5

AMENDMENT

With reference to 188th. Infy. Brigade Order No. 82, dated 15th. Feb. 1917, the following amendment is made in the appendix re "RATION SUPPLY".

Para. 2, line 4, for :-

"The rations of the first three groups being sent to "
"R1.d.7.7., (Left forward dump), and of the fourth to "
"R7.b.8.1., (Right forward dump)," substitute :-

"The rations of the first two groups being sent to "
"R1.d.7.7., (Left forward dump), and of the third and "
"fourth to R7.b.8.1.(Right forward dump)"

Para.2, sub_para. (A) and (B), delete :-

"Howe Bn. Q.M.Stores", etc., from sub-para.(A) and embody in sub-para.(B).

[signature]
Captain.
Staff Captain.
188th. Infy. Brigade.

16/2/17.

S E C R E T

Copy. No.... 1

B.O.82/3.

Headquarters,
188th. Inf. Brigade.
16th. February, 1917.

1. With reference to 188th. Infantry Brigade Order No.82 of 15th. inst., "Z" Day will be 17th. February, 1917.

The exact hour of "ZERO", which will be early in the morning will be notified later, by the word "CHICKEN"-

2. The Infantry will show Red flares at Zero plus 35 and at Zero plus 1 hour 45 minutes. Also at any other time on demand being made from the Contact Aeroplanes by sounding of Klaxon horns or dropping White lights.

3. Watches will synchronized by telephone from Brigade Headquarters at 3-15 p.m., and 6-15 p.m. today, 16th. February, 1917.

4. Please ACKNOWLEDGE.

A D Tafler-Smallbutt

~~Captain.~~
Brigade Major.
188th. Inf. Brigade.

Issued to Signals at 12 - 15 p.m.

Copies to :-

No.1. 1st Royal Marines
2. 2nd Royal Marines
3. Anson Battalion
4. Howe Battalion
5. 188th. L.T.M.Battery
6. 188th. M.G.Company
7. No.2 Signal Section.
8. 63rd (RN) Division.
9. 2nd. Field Ambulance
10. 2nd Field Company
11. 14th. Worsesters
12. 190th. M.G.Company
13. 190th. L.T.M.Battery
14. 190th. Inf. Brigade
15. 189th. Inf. Brigade
16. 189th. M.G.Company
17. 189th. L.T.M.Battery
18. "G" Group, R.A.
19. C.R.A.
20. C.R.E.
21. A.D.M.S.
22. Hawke Battalion
23. Nelson Battalion
24. Hood Battalion.
25. 54th. Inf. Brigade
26. 53rd Inf. Brigade
27. Liaison Officer
28. Brigade Major.
29. Intelligence Officer
30. Staff Captain.
31. 18th. Division.
32. File
33. War Diary

SECRET   B.O.82/4.

AMENDMENT

Brigade Headquarters,
16th. February, 1917.

1. With reference to 188th. Infantry Brigade Order No.82 of 15th. February, 1917, 1½ Companies of the 2nd. ROYAL MARINES, from the Support and Reserve Companies, will perform the task - at present allotted to 2 Companies of the HAWKE Battalion - of consolidating the Northern Flank, and pf providing the Battle Patrols on that Flank during consolidation.

2. The 2 Companies HAWKE Battalion will replace the 1½ Companies of 2nd. ROYAL MARINES in the positions at present occupied by the latter, and will come under the orders of the Officer Commanding 2nd. ROYAL MARINES. To be in position 2 hours before ZERO.

3. All references to the 2 Companies HAWKE Battalion should be amended to read " Companies 2nd. ROYAL MARINES" accordingly.

4. ACKNOWLEDGE.

A D [illegible]
Captain.
Brigade Major.

Issued to Signals at 2.10pm

Copies to all recipients of Brigade Order 82.

"C" Form

Army Form C. 2123.
(In books of 100.)

MESSAGES AND SIGNALS.

No. of Message ....

Prefix SM Code FL Words 21

£ s. d.

Charges to collect

Service Instructions. RH 11

Received From .... By ....

Sent, or sent out At ....m. To .... By ....

Office Stamp. R O 4 15/2/17

Handed in at .... Office ....m. Received ....m.

TO QUEEN

*Sender's Number	Day of Month	In reply to Number	AAA
BM 319	15		

Ref	para	21	of	BC
862	AAA	This	still	holds
good	at	present		

FROM CHESS

PLACE & TIME 7 pm

* This line should be erased if not required.

(B 8070) Wt. w. 7496—M857 250,000 Pads. 10/16 H & S (E436.) Forms/C.2123/3.

Instructions regarding War Diaries and Intelligence Summaries are contained in F. S. Regs., Part II. and the Staff Manual respectively. Title pages will be prepared in manuscript.

WAR DIARY
or
~~INTELLIGENCE SUMMARY.~~
(Erase heading not required.)

Army Form C. 2118.

MARCH 1917 HOWE Battn R.N.D.

Vol. 10

Place	Date	Hour	Summary of Events and Information	Remarks and references to Appendices
	MARCH		A Coy went to VARENNES to be attached to R.E. for work.	
HEDAUVILLE	1st		SUB LIEUTS J.F. BUNCE and H.M. GRAHAM have been awarded the Military Cross in connection with the reconnaissance on FEB 5th	
	2nd – 9th	March	A Coy at VARENNES under the R.E. working on the making of trench boards	
			C+D " " " ballasting the railway near ACHEUX.	
			B " - HEDAUVILLE employed on various fatigues. No training possible as all men are employed as above.	
	10th		C+D Coys finished the ballasting of the line and commenced the unloading of trucks at VARENNES	
	11th		C.O. went to attend a short course at 5th Army School DOMART which is being attended by all C.Os of the R.N.D.	
			C+D Coys billeted at VARENNES	
			The following decorations have been awarded to the Battn in connection with the recent operations N. of the ANCRE D.S.O. Lieut Commander C.S. WEST RNVR. M.C. Lieut E.A. SPRANGE R.N.V.R. and SURGEON F.H.L. CUNNINGHAM R.N. MILITARY MEDAL CZ 1702 A.B. R. ESSON KX P.O. T. COXON, T.Z. 6578 P.O. R.B. MILLS KX 164 P.O. F.B. KELLY. BZ 283 A.B. A. WILLIAMS T.Z. 3045 A.B. J. RAMSDEN K.W. 284 P.O. J.W. NORTH, C.Z. 3182 A.B. G. COOK, K.X 564 A.B (AB) J.D. STEEL K.W 167 A.B F. LYONS C.Z 4616 A.B. W. CLUNE T.Z. 232 A.B. J. BEST W.Z 1809 AB W.H. DAVIES (attd 189 L.T.M.B.) S.3894 Pte D. EDMUNDSON Med. UNIT. ORDER of CROWN of ITALY BRONZE MEDAL FOR MILITARY VALOUR P.O. F.B. KELLY	[signature] Commanding Howe Battn R.N.D. 1/4/17

1577 Wt. W10791/1773 500,000 1/15 D. D. & L. A.D.S.S./Forms/C. 2118.

Instructions regarding War Diaries and Intelligence Summaries are contained in F. S. Regs., Part II. and the Staff Manual respectively. Title pages will be prepared in manuscript.

WAR DIARY
or
~~INTELLIGENCE SUMMARY~~.
(*Erase heading not required.*)

Army Form C. 2118.

MARCH 1917

Place	Date	Hour	Summary of Events and Information	Remarks and references to Appendices
HEDAUVILLE	12-18	March	Batt^n employed during this period as stated above	
RUBEMPRE	19	"	marched at 9.15 am to RUBEMPRE picking up A. C & D Coys at VARENNES. Billetted. (10 miles)	
GEZAINCOURT	20	"	" " 8.30 am to GEZAINCOURT (14 miles) and billetted. Roads in very bad condition.	
LIGNY	21	"	" " 10 a.m. " LIGNY (14 miles) " "	
HERNICOURT	22	"	" " 9 a.m. " HERNICOURT (12 miles) " "	
"	23		Remained at HERNICOURT resting and cleaning up	
BAILLEUL-LES-PERNES	24		Marched at 9 am and billetted at the two villages of AUMERVAL and BAILLEUL les PERNES (10 miles)	
LES PRESSES	25		" " 9 am " " " LES PRESSES (6 miles)	
LE CORNET MALO	26		" " 11 a.m " " " LES CORNET MALO (12 miles)	
NOEUX les MINES	27		" " 10.45 am " " " NOEUX les MINES (10 ~~miles~~) and billetted – men in huts on South side of the town. During last 9 days batt^n has marched 88 miles.	
"	28		Spent the day cleaning up and reorganizing.	
"	29		Started course of training in all branches – ~~[illegible]~~ particular attention being paid to specialist. Received complimentary signal from G.O.C. 2nd Corps as to our work since JANUARY.	
"	30		Training continued. B. Coy fired on the 30 yard range	
"	31		" " C " " " "	H. G. [illegible] Commander R.N. O.C. Howe 1/4/17

1577 Wt. W10791/1773 500,000 1/15 D. D. & L. A.D.S.S./Forms/C. 2118.

Instructions regarding War Diaries and Intelligence Summaries are contained in F. S. Regs., Part II. and the Staff Manual respectively. Title pages will be prepared in manuscript.

WAR DIARY
or
INTELLIGENCE SUMMARY.
(Erase heading not required.)

Army Form C. 2118.

HOWE Batt. R.N.D.

Vol XI

Place	Date	Hour	Summary of Events and Information	Remarks and references to Appendices
	April 1917			
NOEUX les MINES	1st–10th		Training continued according to programme. Firing with rifle and Lewis gun every day on the 30 yard range. All officers & most P.O.s reconnoitred the section of the VILLAGE LINE between HULLUCH & LOOS as the batt. is reserve to the troops holding that sector in the event of a hostile attack. After 5.30 am on the 9th which was zero hour for the ARRAS offensive we were ordered to be ready to move at 2 hours notice.	
	11th		Marched at 11.15 am with Brigade group - less ANSON & 1RM. Billetted at DIEVAL (10 miles)	
	12–13th		Remained at DIEVAL. 4 inches of snow on the ground.	
	14th		Marched at 9.30 am about 18 miles to huts S of ECOIVRES	
ECOIVRES	17–21st		Batt. employed on a 2,000 yard stretch of the MONT. St ELOY - ARRAS road - widening, cleaning and improving. Officers & N.C.O.s have been reconnoitring the line opposite GAVRELLE. On the 20th we moved to billets at MAROEUIL.	
MAROEUIL				
IN THE LINE	22nd		At 3.45 pm the batt. marched via St Catherines to relieve the HOOD Batt. which is occupying the old German 2nd system S of ROCLINCOURT. Owing to the HOOD not having yet moved out the batt. had to wait till about 11 pm in the open.	
	23rd		At 4.45 am the 189th brigade attacked and carried GAVRELLE which they held against repeated counter attacks.	

[illegible] R.N.
O.C. HOWE

1577 Wt. W10791/1773 500,000 1/15 D. D. & L. A.D.S.S./Forms/C. 2118.

Instructions regarding War Diaries and Intelligence Summaries are contained in F. S. Regs., Part II. and the Staff Manual respectively. Title pages will be prepared in manuscript.

WAR DIARY
or
~~INTELLIGENCE SUMMARY.~~
(Erase heading not required.)

Army Form C. 2118.

HOWE Batt. R.N.D.

Place	Date	Hour	Summary of Events and Information	Remarks and references to Appendices
	APRIL	1917		
	23rd		At midday, the Batt. received orders to move up & occupy the "J" trenches in the neighbourhood of Point du JOUR where we came under the orders of the G.O.C. 189th Bde.	
			At 4pm orders were received that we should relieve the HOOD in front of GAVRELLE at dusk.	
GAVRELLE		9pm	Moved up in small parties through fairly heavy hostile shelling which caused some casualties. The Batt. occupied about 400 yards of front running partly in front of & partly through the eastern houses of the village – 3 platoons being kept behind in reserve at Batt. H.Q. in the old German front line. A fairly quiet night.	
	24th		During the morning about 60 Germans emerged from cellars and surrendered. During the early forenoon hostile artillery became active and by noon the bombardment was intense and included all guns up to 8". At 2-40pm a signal was sent to brigade asking for special observation for hostile infantry attack in view of probable breakdown of communications.	
		2.55 pm	Rifle + M.G. fire broke out on the front and 5 minutes later a runner reported that the enemy was advancing to the attack. The S.O.S. was sent and promptly answered. The enemy barrage now began to creep back to the old German front line. By 5-40pm the situation cleared and the enemy who had attacked in very strong force was completely driven back. The Lewis guns played an important	

[illegible] Comdr. R.N. O.C. Howe Bn.

1577 Wt. W10791/1773 500,000 1/15 D. D. & L. A.D.S.S./Forms/C. 2118.

Instructions regarding War Diaries and Intelligence Summaries are contained in F. S. Regs., Part II. and the Staff Manual respectively. Title pages will be prepared in manuscript.

WAR DIARY
or
INTELLIGENCE SUMMARY.
(Erase heading not required.)

Army Form C. 2118.

HOWE BATT^N. R.N.D.

Place	Date	Hour	Summary of Events and Information	Remarks and references to Appendices
	APRIL 1917			
GAVRELLE			part in the enemy's repulse firing 10-15,000 rounds. At one point an advanced party of the enemy who had gained a footing in an orchard were driven out by rifle grenade fire. Much rifle fire took place and proved very effective. Our casualties were about 100 and were caused chiefly by shell fire.	
			Communication proved difficult and chief reliance had to be placed on runners. The Power Buzzer was most useful as a means of sending signals from Batt^n. H.Q. to Brigade. In the evening the remaining 3 platoons in reserve were sent up to fill a gap which had occurred between our left and the "Nelson" Batt^n. After dusk we relieved the NELSON and DRAKE and a company of the 1/R.M. was sent up to act as support. A fairly quiet night.	
	25th		Heavy shelling during the day especially in the neighbourhood of Batt^n. H.Q. Much difficulty was experienced in getting forward rations, water and ammunition.	
		9 pm	The firing line reported about 8 platoons of enemy moving up the GAVRELLE - FRESNES road. The S.O.S was sent and nothing further developed	
	26		Intermittent bombardment during the day. After dusk the ANSON relieved and we moved back to the "J" trenches (Point du Jour) getting in about 4 am.	
POINT DU JOUR	27		Remained in the POINT du JOUR trenches during the day.	

W. J. Jameson [illegible]
Comdr. R.N.
O.C. Howe.

Instructions regarding War Diaries and Intelligence Summaries are contained in F. S. Regs., Part II. and the Staff Manual respectively. Title pages will be prepared in manuscript.

WAR DIARY
or
~~INTELLIGENCE SUMMARY.~~
(Erase heading not required.)

Army Form C. 2118.

HOWE BATTⁿ RND

Place	Date	Hour	Summary of Events and Information	Remarks and references to Appendices
APRIL		1917		
NEAR GAVRELLE	28th		The remainder of the brigade attacked at 4.25 am. in co-operation with the 2nd DIVⁿ + CANADIAN CORPS further to the North.	
		10 am	Orders were received to move forward to hold Hill 80 a report having been received that the enemy was advancing. Lost some men through shell fire on the way up. On arrival the battⁿ was disposed for defence but no attack developed. In the evening 2 companies were sent up to GAVRELLE but this was subsequently countermanded and the companies returned to Hill 80.	
	29		Remained at Hill 80. After dusk moved back to huts S.E. of ROCLINCOURT.	
	30		Marched at 10.30 + billetted at BRAY. Our casualties during the recent operations number about 130 including 4 officers.	

W. G. [illegible] Commdr RN
O.C. HOWE

1577 Wt. W10791/1773 500,000 1/15 D. D. & L. A.D.S.S./Forms/C. 2118.

Instructions regarding War Diaries and Intelligence Summaries are contained in F. S. Regs., Part II. and the Staff Manual respectively. Title pages will be prepared in manuscript.

WAR DIARY
or
~~INTELLIGENCE~~ SUMMARY.
(Erase heading not required.)

Army Form C. 2118.

Vol 12

HOWE Batt. R.N.D

Place	Date	Hour	Summary of Events and Information	Remarks and references to Appendices
			May 1917	
CAUCOURT	1st	9am	Marched to CAUCOURT and billetted	
"	2nd	4pm	G.O.C. RND spoke to the officers, complimenting the batt. on the recent operations.	
"	3rd-7th		At CAUCOURT carrying out training though facilities are none too good. Most attention devoted to training of specialists. Firing on 30 yards range. A considerable number of new officers have joined also a number of reinforcements of other ranks - returned sick and wounded.	
Mont St Eloy	8th	9am	Marched to MONT St ELOY (6 miles) and billetted in huts.	
Roclincourt	9th	1pm	Marched to huts in G5b S.E. of ROCLINCOURT. Brigade is in Corps reserve & ready to move at 15 minutes notice	
	10th		Carried out training	
	11th		Moved to another camp in G4d	
	12	8pm	Batt. moved up to POINT du JOUR ridge and started work on a 2,000 yards line of new trench - working for 5 hours and returning about 3.30 am.	
	13		ditto	
	14		Length of line wiring is now shortened down to 1,000 yards.	
	15		Instead of digging commenced wiring and made good progress	W. J. [illegible] Comdg. Howe Bn. R.N.D. O.C. HOWE 4/6/17

1577 Wt. W10791/1773 500,000 1/15 D. D. & L. A.D.S.S./Forms/C. 2118.

Instructions regarding War Diaries and Intelligence Summaries are contained in F. S. Regs., Part II. and the Staff Manual respectively. Title pages will be prepared in manuscript.

WAR DIARY
or
INTELLIGENCE SUMMARY.
(*Erase heading not required.*)

Army Form C. 2118.

HOWE Battn. RND

Place	Date	Hour	Summary of Events and Information May 1917	Remarks and references to Appendices
ROCLINCOURT	16-18		Digging and wiring cancelled. Carried out training	
	19th	7.30pm	Battn. moved to the trenches in the GAVRELLE sector & relieved 4th Battn. of the D.L.I. Relief complete at 2.20am. Battn. has 3½ coys in front line & ½ coy in immediate support & covers a front of about 1200 yds. Front line is for the most part a continuous fire trench. Battn. H.Q. in FEEBLE Trench. Relief passed off without special incident - a certain amount of shelling causing 1 or 2 casualties	
GAVRELLE	20th		Enemy shelling has much decreased since battn. was last in this sector, most attention being paid to GAVRELLE itself where there are no troops & to forward communications especially at night. Very little falls near the front line which is very quiet. At night worked on improvement of front line which is still far from being satisfactory	
	21st		A quiet day - our snipers were active & had some successes. Busy at night connecting up posts & establishing 3 new posts South of the GAVRELLE - FRESNES road. Enemy busy on their wire N of the road. Lewis guns opened bursts on them.	
	22nd		A quiet day. At night enemy sweeps our parapet from time to time with M.G. fire. The bringing up of water & rations is a matter of difficulty owing to the bad communications	
	23rd	1.30am	Enemy fired about 50 gas shells into the neighbourhood of Battn. H.Q. No harm. Enemy aircraft has been busy during the last few days and does not seem to meet with much	

1577 Wt. W1079/1773 500,000 1/15 D. D. & L. A.D.S.S./Forms/C. 2118

Instructions regarding War Diaries and Intelligence Summaries are contained in F. S. Regs., Part II. and the Staff Manual respectively. Title pages will be prepared in manuscript.

WAR DIARY
or
~~INTELLIGENCE SUMMARY.~~
(Erase heading not required.)

Army Form C. 2118.

HOWE Batt. R.N.D.

Place	Date	Hour	Summary of Events and Information May 1917	Remarks and references to Appendices
GAVRELLE	23rd		interference from our own. Day passed off quietly. At night ANSON relieved us.	
	24th	2.45 am	Relief complete. Marched back to trenches W of RAILWAY CUTTING in H.I.C. Day spent in resting + cleaning up.	
	25-27		Remained as Brigade reserve batt: carrying out various fatigues and a certain amount of training	
	28	9.15 pm	Proceeded to GAVRELLE trenches to relieve "ANSON". Relief passed off without incident	
	29	1.50 am	Relief complete. A pretty quiet night followed by an equally quiet day. Aircraft busy during the evening. During night wired and improved trenches	
	30	1.35 am	Enemy carried out a 10 min bombardment of C. Coy lines near the windmill. No casualties & very little damage. During afternoon heavy rain came on + the trenches were flooded causing much inconvenience + necessitating much repair work.	
	31st		Quiet day – very little shelling. Apparently as a result of this the brigade on our left reported an apparent intention to withdraw on the part of the enemy. As a consequence the whole Corps sent out strong patrols at night + in all cases found the enemy's line normally + strongly held. We sent out 3 patrols + obtained a certain amount of valuable information.	[illegible]

1577 Wt. W10791/1773 500,000 1/15 D. D. & L. A.D.S.S./Forms/C. 2118.

Instructions regarding War Diaries and Intelligence Summaries are contained in F. S. Regs., Part II. and the Staff Manual respectively. Title pages will be prepared in manuscript.

WAR DIARY
or
~~INTELLIGENCE SUMMARY.~~
(Erase heading not required.)

Army Form C. 2118.

Vol 13

HOWE Batt. RND

Place	Date	Hour	JUNE 1917 Summary of Events and Information	Remarks and references to Appendices
GAVRELLE	1st		A quiet day. Improving trenches at night	
	2nd	4.30am	Enemy barraged our line in reply to a barrage which our artillery put over. More shelling than usual during the day. In evening were relieved by ANSON	
		11.48pm	Relief completed. A very quick relief thanks to the moon + absence of shelling.	
	3-6		Back in former trenches W of the BOIS de la MAISON BLANCHE.	
	7	9.30pm	Moved up to relieve ANSON in the line. Quiet relief.	
	8		Fairly quiet day - got through a fair amount of work on the trenches.	
	9		Hurricane bombardments have been the order of the day of late. Enemy replies in the same way. Have had about 12 casualties during the 2 days. At night were relieved by 16 West YORKS. Relief complete at 12.25am when we marched back to	
	10th		trenches near ROCLINCOURT	
BRAY		5pm	Marched to BRAY + billeted.	
	11-12		Resting, cleaning + re-equipping	
St AUBIN	13	6am	Started a 10 day course of training. In evening moved to St AUBIN + billeted	
	14-15		Training from 7-10.30am every morning and an hour in the evening	
MAROEUIL	16		In the afternoon marched to MAROEUIL and went under canvas	Charles S. West Lieut Cmdr RNVR C/o HOWE

1577 Wt. W10791/1773 500,000 1/15 D. D. & L. A.D.S.S./Forms/C. 2118.

Instructions regarding War Diaries and Intelligence Summaries are contained in F. S. Regs., Part II. and the Staff Manual respectively. Title pages will be prepared in manuscript.

WAR DIARY
or
INTELLIGENCE SUMMARY.
(Erase heading not required.)

Army Form C. 2118.

Place	Date	Hour	JUNE 1917 Summary of Events and Information HOWE BATT^N RND	Remarks and references to Appendices
MAROEUIL	20th		Training has continued. Today Lord BERESFORD inspected the brigade by battalions	
ROCLINCOURT	22nd	7.45 am	Marched to camp near ROCLINCOURT. In evening 3 companies went to HILL 80 to dig on N. TYNE ALLEY Communication trench	
	28th		Batt^n has dug for 6 nights - 3 companies every night - on communications in the OPPY sector.	
		4pm	Moved to BRAY where we are to do 4 more days further training.	
	29th-30th		Carried out training, chief attention being devoted to Lewis guns, rifle bombers, trench to trench attack and movement generally	
				Charles [illegible] Lieut-Com^dr RNVR C/O HOWE.

1577 Wt. W10791/1773 500,000 1/15 D. D. & L. A.D.S.S./Forms/C. 2118.

Instructions regarding War Diaries and Intelligence Summaries are contained in F. S. Regs., Part II. and the Staff Manual respectively. Title pages will be prepared in manuscript.

WAR DIARY
or
INTELLIGENCE SUMMARY.
(*Erase heading not required.*)

Army Form C. 2118.

Howe Bn

Vol 14

Place	Date	Hour	Summary of Events and Information (JULY)	Remarks and references to Appendices
BRAY	1st/7		Continued training.	
ST. CATHRINE	2nd	2-00PM	Batt. moved to ST. CATHERINE arriving at 4-15PM.	
GAVRELLE	3rd	7-30PM	Batt moved into the line relieving the 18th WEST YORKS and 18th DLI. The four Companies going into front line	
	4th		Relief completed at 2-00AM.	
			Throughout the Batt's time in the line hostile activities were below normal. No infantry actions took place on our immediate front, hostile shelling was also below normal. At 1-30AM on the morning	
	8th	1-30AM	of the 8th a deserter came into our lines. Deserter belongs to 128th Prussian Regiment which was relieving a Bavarian regiment night 7th/8th.	
RESERVE	11th		Night of the 10th/11th the Batt. was relieved by the ANSON Batt. and moved into ~~SUPPORT~~ RESERVE. Relief completed at 12-45AM. The Batt had three casualties all of which were very slight.	
			While in ~~SUPPORT~~ RESERVE the usual parades and inspections are being carried out. B and D COY'S training for their offensive action, A and C COY.S furnishing the fatigues as required.	
	17th	9-35PM	The Batt. moved up the Front line, relieving the ANSON Batt.	
GAVRELLE	18th	12-50AM	Relief complete.	
"	19th		From 8h 15m AM to 9.15AM Enemy shelled front line and immediate SUPPORT with 4.2 and 5.9. Again at 10-55 he opened on front line. 5 minutes of intense barrage after	Charles S. Ward [illegible] Cmdr [illegible]

1577 Wt. W10791/1773 500,000 1/15 D. D. & L. A.D.S.S./Forms/C. 2118.

Instructions regarding War Diaries and Intelligence Summaries are contained in F. S. Regs., Part II. and the Staff Manual respectively. Title pages will be prepared in manuscript.

WAR DIARY
or
INTELLIGENCE SUMMARY.
(Erase heading not required.)

Army Form C. 2118.

Place	Date	Hour	Summary of Events and Information	Remarks and references to Appendices
GAYRELLE	July 19th		which 15 minutes of intermittent fire on front line followed. 11-30 AM enemy ceased fire.	
	"	10-56 pm.	One company of ANSON Batt. relieved our Right COY.	
		11-20	The tape which was to mark the raiders jumping off place was laid by D COY.	
	July 20th	12-45	Raiders in position on tape	
		1-00 AM	ZERO Barrage opened and raid commenced. Copy ~~of raid~~ report on raid (CO's report) attached herewith. Casualties in raid: 5 Killed 19 wounded.	
		3 30	All raiders - minus casualties - all in and settled in NAVAL (SUPPORT) trench.	
		4-00	One other company of ANSON in ~~position~~ in CHICO SUPPORT.	
		10-10 PM.	The relief of our ~~remaining~~ two Companies in front line by ANSON was completed.	
SUPPORT	"	10-10 PM.		
	July 20th/25th		While in Support Batt. had to furnish various fatigues - carrying parties - ration parties and a trench was commenced from WIDON leading to No B and C wells.	
	July 25th		The Batt relieved the ANSON Batt in front line	
		[illegible]-30 PM	Relief commenced	
		[illegible]0-20	Relief complete.	

Instructions regarding War Diaries and Intelligence Summaries are contained in F. S. Regs., Part II. and the Staff Manual respectively. Title pages will be prepared in manuscript.

WAR DIARY
or
INTELLIGENCE SUMMARY.
(*Erase heading not required.*)

Army Form C. 2118.

Place	Date	Hour	Summary of Events and Information	Remarks and references to Appendices
GAYRELLE	July 26th		Nothing of importance to note. Hostile artillery normal, rifle and machine gun fire a little above normal during the night.	
	July 27th	3 A.M.	Engineers discharged gas from behind our right COX sector 140 drums of gas were to be discharged on enemy's line however 13 misfired and 127 drums only went over. No retaliation followed.	
	" 28th		During night 27/28th Hostile artillery was very active on front line, communication trenches and back areas. Throughout the day hostile artillery fire was normal.	
	" 29th	12-30 A.M.	A raid commenced by the Division on our right. Enemy retaliated freely, also on our front and support lines, paying particular attention to CHICO SUPPORT line and WIDOW. At 3-30 P.M. 400 rounds of 6" how's were fired on WIDE TRENCH.	
	30th		Both our and hostile artillery fire was very below normal, due probably to very poor visibility. Night 30/31st the Batt. was relieved by the DRAKE BATT.	
	31st	6.00 A.M.	The Batt. arrived at their billets in St. AUBIN.	[signature illegible] Comdr. RNVR

1577 Wt. W1079 /1773 500,000 1/15 D. D. & L. A.D.S.S./Forms/C. 2118.

Instructions regarding War Diaries and Intelligence Summaries are contained in F. S. Regs., Part II. and the Staff Manual respectively. Title pages will be prepared in manuscript.

WAR DIARY
or
INTELLIGENCE SUMMARY.
(Erase heading not required.)

Army Form C. 2118.

Place	Date	Hour	Summary of Events and Information	Remarks and references to Appendices
St AUBIN	July 31st		Men rested, bathing took place in the afternoon - followed by the usual inspections. Total Casualties during this period of in line was 12 killed - 2 died of wounds and 40 wounded.	[illegible]

H.Q.
188th Brigade

Sir, I beg to report as follows on the raid at 1 am. on the night of the 19th/20th inst.

1. Preliminary Arrangements and relief. All these worked without a hitch and raiders were assembled in their trench in good time. The tape was ~~placed~~ laid very well by Sub Lieut JOYCE. Raiders had been fully equipped as arranged

2. Forming up on tape. This commenced at 12.20 am. and was completed by 12.45, the intervals between men being regular. The enemy made no attempt to interfere. His observation was hindered by a fresh westerly wind which blew his Very lights back over his own lines. Carrying parties protected this part of the programme returning through the raiders at 12.45 am.

3. Time Table. The following was the time table as observed from Battn H.Q.

zero (1 am.) Artillery, T.M's, M.G's etc opened simultaneously – the synchronization appearing to be excellent.

zero + 1½ Many German twin red + single red lights fired – apparently S.O.S.

zero + 4½ Slight enemy shelling on front. Great display of red, green & golden rains by enemy.

zero + 7½ Bursts of hostile M.G fire overhead.

zero + 8½ Hostile barrage considerable on front + left flank.

zero + 20 Red lights from 3 of our 4 light posts – signal for withdrawal. (One of our light posts had been blown in shortly after zero) 2 forward phones reported ditched.

zero + 30¼ Golden rain rocket from left company light post (all D Coy in)

zero + 40¾ Phone message received from close support station that all right Coy was believed to be in.

zero + 41½ Battn H.Q. fired 3 golden rains.

zero + 45 Hostile retaliation practically ceased.

4. Our barrage. All officers and men report most favourably on its accuracy and efficiency.

5. Thermite fired apparently with great effect completely smothering hostile M.G. from right flank.

6. Stokes mortars From evidence of Sub Lt GEDEN + others some of these appear to have fallen among our men S of the DITCH inflicting casualties and temporarily deflecting the party.

7. Enemy infantry action (128th Regt). At many points he bolted & probably got caught in our barrage. Lieut MARLOW made prisoners of 2 of these by shouting "HALTE" in German. Some of retiring enemy were shot by raiders. At sap on right 2 of enemy opened rifle fire. 2nd Lt GEDEN shot both. About the centre of the line on a 30 yard front enemy wire was thick and he bombed the raiders. Raiders appear to have killed 2 of these but were unable to drive all out before withdrawal. At all other points trench was cleared.

8. Enemy wire Except at point mentioned in para 7 it provided no obstacle

9. Enemy trench About 4 foot deep, in bad condition, several fork holes no dugouts, no duckboards, many stick bombs along parap. No sign of tunnel under road. Hardly any sandbags.

10. R.E. Exploded ammonal charge in a fire bay near road. They sustained no casualties.

11. Enemy M.G. There is a conflict of evidence as to whether there was a M.G. at point mentioned in para 7 but I think it was somewhere in rear. It fired throughout but appears to have done no damage. This was practically the only M.G. fire.

12. Withdrawal signals Red lights worked well & were easily seen. French horns were a failure – not strong enough.

13. Force engaged – 6 officers + 180 O.R. appears to have been of about right strength. Formation – 2 waves – proved satisfactory. Excellent alignment was kept during the advance.

14. Shell holes beyond trench near ditch. These were reached as rehearsed and enemy bolted.

15. Enemy Equipment His bayonets were not fixed and in many cases he was wearing no equipment.

16. Enemy Casualties 11 prisoners were brought in and about 20 killed in and around trench.

17. Raiders Casualties 3 killed – 4 missing (believed killed) 1 officer and 16 wounded. Total 24. Of these several occurred after return to our trench. Only one hit by bullet.

18. General Raid proved conclusively the value of thorough detailed rehearsal.

19. Suggestion. The use of Thermite ~~incendiaries~~ for this type of operation appears highly desirable.

I am rather doubtful about the value of oil drums.

Stokes should fire further off the flanks especially in a wind.

20. Apart from the very dashing and capable manner in which the raiders carried out their work I attribute much of the success of the raid to the carefully thought out and admirably executed ~~carried out~~ programme of cooperation by the various other arms concerned, the artillery in particular.

Charles S. West
Comdr. R.N.V.R.
O/c Horse

20/7/17

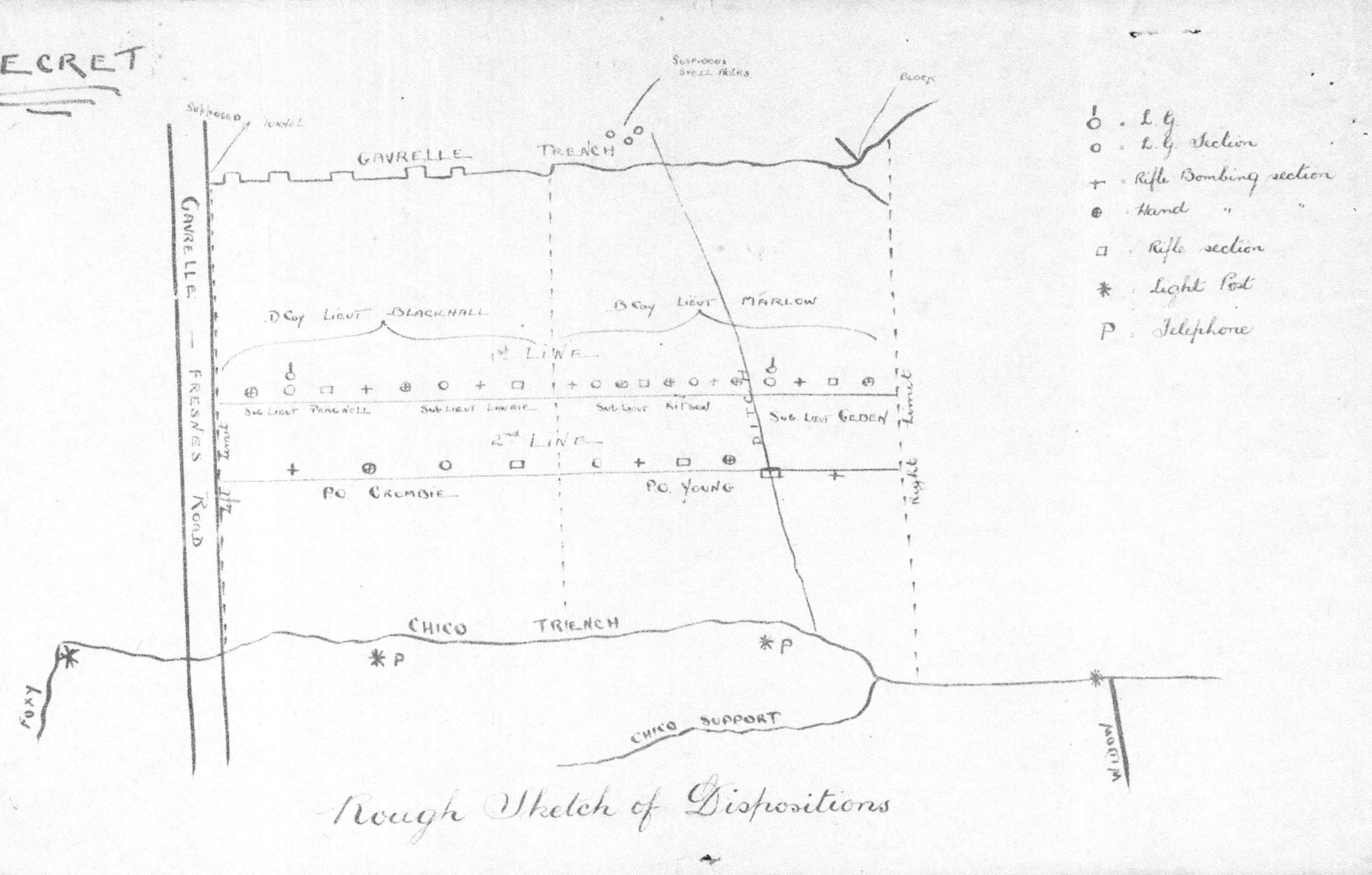
SECRET
SUPPOSED TUNNEL
SUSPICIOUS SHELL HOLES
BLOCK
GAVRELLE TRENCH
L.G.
L.G. Section
Rifle Bombing section
Hand "
Rifle section
Light Post
Telephone
D Coy LIEUT BLACKNALL
B Coy LIEUT MARLOW
1st LINE
SUB LIEUT PRAGNELL
SUB LIEUT LAWRIE
SUB LIEUT KITSON
SUB LIEUT GEDEN
2nd LINE
P.O. CROMBIE
P.O. YOUNG
DITCH
Left Limit
Right Limit
GAVRELLE — FRESNES ROAD
CHICO TRENCH
CHICO SUPPORT
FOXY
WIDOW
Rough Sketch of Dispositions

Instructions regarding War Diaries and Intelligence Summaries are contained in F. S. Regs., Part II. and the Staff Manual respectively. Title pages will be prepared in manuscript.

WAR DIARY
or
INTELLIGENCE SUMMARY.
(*Erase heading not required.*)

Army Form C. 2118.

Howe Bn
Vol 15

Place	Date	Hour	Summary of Events and Information	Remarks and references to Appendices
St. AUBIN	Aug 1st	AM.	Bathing continued also inspections - indents and reorganization.	
		PM.	Troops were employed in musketry and bayonet fighting.	
			While the Batt was in rest - July 31st to Aug 8th training continued, as far as the weather would permit it, particular attention having been paid to the training of LG crews. On Sunday Aug 5th a special parade service was held at 1st ARMY HQ. 2 Off. and 20 O.R attended from the Batt.	
			Aug 3rd 9.00 PM. A short march in gas masks took place.	
			Great attention has also been paid to musketry HQ and the four companies doing grouping and application practices at the two hundred yard range. A pool shoot took place at 2.30 pm on Aug 6th. A team consisted of 1 Off and 9 O.R. Five such teams entered, a prize of 50 frcs being given to the winning team. Our C Coy team won.	
MAISON BLANCHE	Aug 8th	4-30	The Batt. moved forward into RESERVE at MAISON BLANCHE.	
	" 8th	11th	Batt was in RESERVE, during which time particular attention having been paid to the improvement of mens shelters. Six new shelters having been partly completed, when finished each will accomodate 16 men. Nightly, two companies furnished fatigues improving the RED LINE.	
				[signature] OC HOWE Lt Cmdr RNVR

1577 Wt. W10791/1773 500,000 1/15 D. D. & L. A.D.S.S./Forms/C. 2118.

Instructions regarding War Diaries and Intelligence Summaries are contained in F. S. Regs., Part II. and the Staff Manual respectively. Title pages will be prepared in manuscript.

WAR DIARY
or
INTELLIGENCE SUMMARY.
(Erase heading not required.)

Army Form C. 2118.

Place	Date	Hour	Summary of Events and Information	Remarks and references to Appendices
Reserve	Aug 11th	8-30PM.	Batt. moved forward, relieving the ANSON Batt. in the Front Line. A C D COY's going into the Front Line, B Coy into close SUPPORT.	
GAYRELLE	11th/12	11-30PM	Relief complete.	
	12th	12-12AM	A tremendous explosion occurred in the back area which shook the whole country for miles. Hostile artillery was very active during this night, particular attention having been paid to our front and immediate SUPPORT LINES.	
do	13th	11-10PM	A rather foggy night - after 11-00 PM a thick bank of fog over "NO MANS LAND" was taken for gas or smoke. The enemy opened heavy rifle and MG fire on our parapet followed by his artillery on FRONT and SUPPORT LINES. Our left COY suffered mostly - having 10 casualties including the Coy Comm who remained on duty however. Casualties during this night 3 Killed and 7 wounded. (4-50PM all quiet)	
	14th		Quiet throughout the day hostile artillery normal but T M very active during the night.	
	15th	11-25PM	The Batt was relieved by the ANSON Batt and came into SUPPORT.	T. true [illegible] 12 NVI2 O.C. HOWE

Instructions regarding War Diaries and Intelligence Summaries are contained in F. S. Regs., Part II. and the Staff Manual respectively. Title pages will be prepared in manuscript.

WAR DIARY
or
INTELLIGENCE SUMMARY.
(Erase heading not required.)

Army Form ~~C. 2118~~.

Place	Date	Hour	Summary of Events and Information	Remarks and references to Appendices
SUPPORT			One Coy in the RED LINE – Three in NAVAL TRENCH.	
	Aug 15th/19th		While in SUPPORT Coys. were employed in the upkeep of their trenches and furnished fatigues as required. Casualties – Nil – during this period.	
GAVRELLE	19th	5-30 PM	Commenced relieving the ANSON in front line. The three Coys in NAVAL TRENCH relieving in day light. RED LINE COY after dark. 9-00 P.M. Relief complete.	
"	19th/24th		Hostile artillery below normal throughout this period. T.M. activities, however, very much increased. CHICO and WILLIE SUPPORT LINES being shelled with heavy Minenwerfers. These Minnies were active nights only. On the whole the Batt experienced a quiet time.	
"	24th/25th	PM	The Batt was relieved by the DRAKE Batt and proceeded to ST. AUBIN by tram. 12-00 Midnight Relief complete. Total Casualties while in the line. 4 Killed – 13 wounded.	J. L. Price Lieut Comdr RNVR OC HOWE
ST. AUBIN	25th		4-00 A.M. Arrived at Billets.	

1577 Wt. W10791/1773 500,000 1/15 D. D. & L. A.D.S.S./Forms/C. 2118.

Army Form C. 2118.

Instructions regarding War Diaries and Intelligence Summaries are contained in F. S. Regs., Part II. and the Staff Manual respectively. Title pages will be prepared in manuscript.

WAR DIARY
or
INTELLIGENCE SUMMARY.
(Erase heading not required.)

Place	Date	Hour	Summary of Events and Information	Remarks and references to Appendices
ST AUBIN	25/26		The whole of the 25th and 26th were spent in given the men a rest – baths and a general clean up. Reorganization of Coys. also took place.	
	27th – 31st		Commenced and carried on training according to training scheme. One company working each day on MAROEUIL RANGE. Commander C S WEST DSO. RNVR went on leave on 27th. 157 Reinforcements joined during period 30–31st, making the ration strength of the battalion 780 a greater number than it had been for a very long time	

[signature] Price
Lt Com RNVR.
Commanding
Howe Bn

1577 Wt. W10791/1773 500,000 1/15 D. D. & L. A.D.S.S./Forms/C. 2118.

Instructions regarding War Diaries and Intelligence Summaries are contained in F. S. Regs., Part II. and the Staff Manual respectively. Title pages will be prepared in manuscript.

WAR DIARY
or
~~INTELLIGENCE SUMMARY.~~
(Erase heading not required.)

Army Form C. 2118.

Howe Bn
Vol 16

Place	Date	Hour	Summary of Events and Information	Remarks and references to Appendices
St AUBIN	1/9/17		Bathing of all companies & preparation for move 32 reinforcements arrived	
	2/9/17		Church parade in morning & at 4.0 pm the battalion moved to Reserve at MAISON BLANCH	
RESERVE	3/9/17 to 6/9/17		Training of New Drafts & Lewis Gunners. Improvement of Billets. In evening 100 men working on RED LINE under R.E's. Work on billets &c. various working parties on RED LINE and heavy working party.	[illegible]
	6/9/17 to	7.30 pm	Relieved 2nd Marines in NAVAL TRENCH relief completed at 10.5 pm	
SUPPORT	9.9.17		While in SUPPORT the ~~Battalion~~ Battalion furnished usual carrying & working Parties & were engaged in carrying up wire for new defence scheme	
GAVRELLE	9.9.17	5.0 pm	Relieved ANSON Battalion in front line. The relief was commenced at 5.0 pm ~~[illegible]~~ with three Coys in NAVAL TRENCH. The company in RED LINE relieved after dark.	
	10.9.17 to 17.9.17		The Battalion was in holding the front line from Sept 10th – Sept 17th. During this period the enemy artillery	

1577 Wt. W10791/1773 500,000 1/15 D. D. & L. A.D.S.S./Forms/C. 2118.

Instructions regarding War Diaries and Intelligence Summaries are contained in F. S. Regs., Part II. and the Staff Manual respectively. Title pages will be prepared in manuscript.

WAR DIARY
or
INTELLIGENCE SUMMARY.
(Erase heading not required.)

Army Form C. 2118.

Place	Date	Hour	Summary of Events and Information	Remarks and references to Appendices
GAVRELLE	10-9.17 to 17-9.17		were remarkably quiet. During the time the Battalion was in the line our casualties were very slight. One pineapple however dropped in the trench killing 4 men of B Company. The Battalion was relieved by the DRAKE Bttn at commencing at 4 pm on 17th and relief was completed by 7.30 pm.	
ROCLINCOURT	18.9.17 to 21-9.17		The Battalion went into rest at AUBREY CAMP where it re-organised & commenced training during this period it furnished two companys daily for work on RED LINE	
	22.9.17		The Battalion moved to MONCHY-LE-BRETON moving in motor lorries & where it went into billets	
	23.9.17		Church parade in the morning.	
	24.9.17 to 30.9.17		Commenced training by Platoons especially as regards attacking strong points & "Pill boxes". During this period a Battalion Sports meeting was held ~~with~~ at which	

Instructions regarding War Diaries and Intelligence Summaries are contained in F. S. Regs., Part II. and the Staff Manual respectively. Title pages will be prepared in manuscript.

WAR DIARY
or
INTELLIGENCE SUMMARY.
(Erase heading not required.)

Army Form C. 2118.

Place	Date	Hour	Summary of Events and Information	Remarks and references to Appendices
			the Band of the RMA attended	
			Charles [illegible] Commander RNVR O. C. HOWE Battn	

1577 Wt. W10791/1773 500,000 1/15 D. D. & L. A.D.S.S./Forms/C. 2118.

63

Instructions regarding War Diaries and Intelligence Summaries are contained in F. S. Regs., Part II. and the Staff Manual respectively. Title pages will be prepared in manuscript.

WAR DIARY
or
INTELLIGENCE SUMMARY.
(Erase heading not required.)

188/63 Howe Bn Vol 17

Army Form C. 2118.

Place	Date	Hour	Summary of Events and Information	Remarks and references to Appendices
Monchy le Breton	1.10.17		Orders having been received for the Battalion to move preparations were made accordingly	
	3-10-17		Battalion entrained at TINCQUES at 4 30 am for HOPOUTRE arriving at 2 pm from whence it marched to DIRTY BUCKET CAMP 1¾ miles SSW of ELVERDINGHE.	
DIRTY BUCKET CAMP.	4.10.17		Carried out training	Charles R. West [illegible] 11.17
	5.10.17		The Battalion entrained for HERZEELE at 12.30 pm arriving at destination at 5.30 pm.	
HERZEELE	6th-10-17 – 10th-10-17		Battalion engaged in training Platoons in new formation of the attack. Lt Comdr T.L. PRICE to HOSPITAL. - Lt ALAN CAMPBELL MC joined from 188th STOKES Batty as 2nd in Command.	
	11th-10-17		Company training in the attack	
	12-10-17		Battalion training in the attack. 2 coys Baths - ~~[illegible]~~	
	13-10-17		Companies in the attack	
	14-10-17		Church Parade - 2 coys Baths.	

1577 Wt. W10791/1773 500,000 1/15 D. D. & L. A.D.S.S./Forms/C. 2118.

Instructions regarding War Diaries and Intelligence Summaries are contained in F. S. Regs., Part II. and the Staff Manual respectively. Title pages will be prepared in manuscript.

WAR DIARY
or
INTELLIGENCE SUMMARY.
(Erase heading not required.)

Army Form C. 2118.

Place	Date	Hour	Summary of Events and Information	Remarks and references to Appendices
HERZEELE	15.10.17		Companies parade in battle order. Attack carried out on training ground. Night operation	
	16.10.17		Practised attack on strong points - Intensive digging practice.	
	17.10.17 to 20.10.17		Battalion in the attack	
	21.10.17		Church Parade	
	22.10.17		Night operations with gas masks. - STORES for the attack drawn from Quarter-masters STORES.	
	23-10.17	11 am	Companies embussed for REIGERSBURG AREA.	
REIGERSBURG	24.10.17	1.30 am	moved to IRISH FARM Camp. Battalion Resting before attack.	
IRISH FARM	25.10.17	6.30 pm	Bn moved up to line. Headquarters at ALBATROS FARM.	
	26.10.17		188th Inf. Brigade attacked with the 8th Bde 3rd Canadian Division on the RIGHT and the 58th Division on the left ZERO 5.40 am. ANSON Bn to take 1st objective on RIGHT sub-sector. HOWE Bn to take 2nd objective on 1st objective being taken and consolidated. ANSON gained part of their objective but got held up in the centre and HOWE Bn could not get forward. Officer Casualties	See Operation Order attached

1577 Wt. W10791/1773 500,000 1/15 D. D. & L. A.D.S.S./Forms/C. 2118.

Army Form C. 2118.

Instructions regarding War Diaries and Intelligence Summaries are contained in F. S. Regs., Part II. and the Staff Manual respectively. Title pages will be prepared in manuscript.

WAR DIARY
or
INTELLIGENCE SUMMARY.
(Erase heading not required.)

Place	Date	Hour	Summary of Events and Information	Remarks and references to Appendices
	27.10.17		Lt JACKSON Sub Lts DOUGLAS, HINDE, – KILLED. Sub Lt [redacted] SHAW missing. Sub Lts DYSON, WITHNELL, TRENHOLM wounded. NIGHT of 26th/27th Bn was relieved from advanced posts & took up a position as counter-attack battalion near ADLER FARM	
IRISH CAMP	28.10.17		NIGHT of 27th/28th Bn withdrew to IRISH FARM arriving about 8.30 pm	
DAMBRE CAMP	29.10.17		Bn moved at 10.30 am to DAMBRE CAMP. CLEANING UP and indenting for stores clothing etc	
ditto	30.10.17		Reorganisation. Coys Bathe.	
	31.10.17		Reorganisation. Lt Commander S~~B~~RANGE M.C. proceeded to ENGLAND from XIX Corps REINFMENT CAMP	

Charles [illegible] ~~D.S.O.~~
Commander RNVR.
Commanding
HOWE Bn

1577 Wt. W10791/1773 500,000 1/15 D. D. & L. A.D.S.S./Forms/C. 2118.

OPERATION ORDERS

SECRET. by Commander C. S. West. D.S.O. R.N.V.R.

Intention. The Battalion will carry out an attack on a date and at at time to be notified later.
The Battalion will be on the right of the Brigade Sector, and will capture the second objective.
2½ Coys will take part in the actual attack.
A on the left. C on the right and ½ of B in the centre.
D Coy will be in reserve, remaining ½ of B will act as carrying ½ Coy.
A and C Coys will each have 2 platoons in the front and 2 in close support.

Battalion Boundaries. LEFT. A line drawn from V. 28. a. 2. 3 to the PADDEBEKE at V. 28. a. 5. 5 thence by S side of [illegible] track to V. 28. b. c. 9.
RIGHT. A line drawn from N Corner of the Cemetery to E end of SOURCE FARM.
Frontage of objective approx 800 yards.

Objectives: C. Coy. 2 pieces of traverse trench at V.28.C.95.70. ½ platoon.
SOURCE FARM 2 platoons.
Shaft V.28.d.3.8 ½ platoon.
About V.28.d.8.6 ½ platoon.
About V.28.d.3.5 ½ platoon.
A Coy. Traverse trench with 3 concrete dug-outs V.28.a.9.2. 2 platoons.
Cross Roads V.28.b.0.9. 1 platoon.
About V.28.a.9.6 ½ platoon.
About V.28.a.7.4 ½ platoon.
½ B Coy TOURNANT FARM.

Flanks On our right will be the 8th Brigade of the 3rd CANADIAN DIVISION.
On our left the MARINE BATTALIONS.

The Attack. The attack will be carried out in 2 stages by the right half Brigade.
The ANSON Battn will attack at zero as far as the general line V.28.a.2.3 to V.29.d.1.3.
The HOWE advancing through ANSON at zero + 1 hour.

Forming up. On Y/Z night the Battalion will ~~move from CHEDDAR VILLA CAMP at 8.30 pm via MOUSETRAP track and assemble~~

At zero the Battalion will move forward in lines of columns of ½ platoons in file, to about ~~200~~ 150 yards E of first assembly line (INCH HOUSES — CEMETERY)

Zero + 1 hour Battalion will move forward and form up under the Stationary barrage just beyond limit of first objective ready to attack.

8 minutes before the barrage lifts the barrage fire will become intense.

The reserve Company at this point will remain about 200 yards in rear of the junction of A & C Coys and will await further orders from the Battalion Commander unless the situation demands immediate action on the part of the Coy Commander.

<u>Liason Party</u> D Coy will detail 1 section to establish touch with a similar party from the Brigade on our right; this section will move out to gain touch on the forward right flank of the objective.

The object of this party is to ascertain whether the troops on our right are in touch with us.

Battalion Headquarters. During Y/Z night and until the Battalion objectives are captured Headquarters will be N of ALBATROS FARM (D.2.d.2.6.)
It will then move to VARLET FARM

Compass Bearing. The general bearing of the advance from the furthest limit of the first objective is 60°
All Officers must be in possession of Compasses and know the magnetic variation.

Documents. No orders, secret maps, documents, or letters, likely to be of use to the enemy, are to be taken into action.

Synchronisation of Watches. The arrangements for this will be notified later.

R.E. Party. B Coy will detail 4 men from the carrying ½ Coy to report at Battalion H.Q. on Y/Z night for carrying mobile charges.

Cautionary. All ranks are to be warned that the word 'retire' does not exist. If it is necessary to withdraw from any position the order will only be given by an Officer who will be called upon later to justify his action.

Aeroplanes. A contact aeroplane will fly over at a time to be notified later.

Watson Fans will be shown but not until the plane sounds a Klaxon horn or drops a white light.

A machine will be up continually to detect counter attacks.

When the enemy is seen moving to counter attack the machine will drop a smoke bomb over the front towards which the enemy is moving.

The smoke bomb will burst (about 100 feet below the aeroplane) into a white parachute flare which descends slowly leaving a trail of brown smoke about 1 foot broad.

Communications. Sometime after zero the signal section will run a wire from VARLET FARM to PILLBOX at V. 28. a. 95. 10. and thence to Coy Headquarters.

Medical Arrangements. The R.A.P. will first be at ALBATROS FARM but will be established later further forward.

probably at YARLET FARM or INCH HOUSES.
The stretcher bearers of the attacking Companies will remain with the reserve Coy until the objectives have been reached.

Dress and Equipment. Jerkins will be worn over tunics. Each man will carry 220 rounds of ammunition; 10 rounds in magazine.

2 Sand bags
1 Bomb
1 Shovel per 3 men will be carried.
1 Rifle Grenade per 3 men " " "
21 magazines per Lewis Gun " "
3 men in each Rifle Grenade Section and
2 men in each Bombing section will be equipped as Rifle Grenadiers and bombers respectively.

23/10/17

[signature] Edwards
Lieut RNVR.
Adjutant

Ref Operation Order

Delete Para. Forming Up: from "C 11/Z [illegible] to "track and assemble" and substitute

On 7/Z night the battalion will move from present area via MOUSE TRAP TRACK and will form up on a line the right at D 3 a 7 2 (ADLER FARM) left at about D 3 a 7 7 on a frontage of 250 yds

C on the right A Coy on left

Forward ½ Coy of B in close support at junction of A & C Coys

D Coy in reserve immediately behind H.Q. & Company ½ Coy of B. in rear

Os. Coys will send a runner to Bn H.Q. to report when they are in position

Bn H.Q. will be located at ALBATROS FARM.

~~Ar. Zero [illegible]~~

Utmost care must be taken in checking bearings and to ensure arrival at right place when the cups move off at Zero

~~[illegible]~~.

Howe Bn
63 RN Div

WAR DIARY
or
INTELLIGENCE SUMMARY.

(Erase heading not required.)

Army Form C. 2118.

Howe Bn
Vol 18

Instructions regarding War Diaries and Intelligence Summaries are contained in F. S. Regs., Part II. and the Staff Manual respectively. Title pages will be prepared in manuscript.

Place	Date	Hour	Summary of Events and Information	Remarks and references to Appendices
	1917			
DAMBRE CAMP	1 Nov		3 days spent in improvement of camp, reorganisation & refitting. Many of the men thought	
"	3 Nov		missing from the operations 26/10/17 were traced during this period to C.C.S.	
"	4 Nov		Service by Rev Kennett. Chaplain McCardel being on leave. The remainder of the day spent in preparation for moving to the line.	
Line	5 Nov.		Moved from DAMBRE CAMP to the line, entraining at BRIELEN SIDING and detraining at ST JEAN	
	7 Nov		2 coys B & C attached to the ANSON BN in front. The remaining 2 coys and Bn HQ at CALIFORNIA TRENCH.	
	Night 7/8		The 2 coys attached to ANSON were relieved & proceeded to IRISH FARM. Rest of the Battalion remained in CALIFORNIA TRENCH	
SCHOOL CAMP	8th		Battalion entrained at ST JEAN for a siding W of POPERINGHE and occupied SCHOOL CAMP. the whole brigade close at hand	
"	9 10 11		Remained at SCHOOL CAMP cleaning up &c. Camp found in very dirty condition	
WINNEZEELE	12		Marched to WINNEZEELE and passed the night in tents with much mud. Surplus personnel which had been left out of the attack on 26-10-17 rejoined	
RUBROUCK	13		Marched to RUBROUCK AREA and billeted there. Plenty of room in the billets but extremely scattered	Alan Campbell RNVR Cmdr

1577 Wt. W10791/1773 500,000 1/15 D. D. & L. A.D.S.S./Forms/C. 2118.

Howe Bn
63 RN Div

Instructions regarding War Diaries and Intelligence Summaries are contained in F. S. Regs., Part II. and the Staff Manual respectively. Title pages will be prepared in manuscript.

WAR DIARY
or
INTELLIGENCE SUMMARY.
(Erase heading not required.)

Army Form C. 2118.

Place	Date	Hour	Summary of Events and Information	Remarks and references to Appendices
RUBROUCK	14 Nov		Commander C.S. WEST DSO RNVR proceeded on a months leave to England.	
			Battalion settled down in billets improving where possible.	
"	15 Nov 16 17 Nov		Continued training 9-12 and 1.30-2.30 About 300 reinforcements arrived bringing the Battalion almost to full strength again.	
			Regt. A Band played near H.Q. Mess during afternoon of 16th.	
"	18 Nov		Divine Service in morning. Sermon preached by Deputy Chaplain General (Bishop of Khartoum)	
	19 Nov		The Battalion prepared to move to the forward area on the morning of the 20th but word was received that the battalion would not move. Padre returned from leave with band instruments	
"	20 Nov		Transport moved by road to the forward area halted for the night at a camp just W of POPERINGHE ROAD CAMP. Orders received late at night that the battalion would not move till 22nd	
"	21 Nov		Capt BACKHOUSE RN late G.O.C. 2nd RN Bde visited the battalion area and inspected one Coy. (C)	
REIGERSBURG	22 Nov		Battalion moved by bus to forward area arriving at REIGERSBURG CAMP at about 2.30 and found a camp of tents erected on a site covered with mud	
	23 Nov		Battalion attached to the C.R.E 1st Div for work carrying duckboards towards front line first party left at 1 p.m. Indented for material for improvement of the Camp	[illegible] Lt Cdr [illegible]

1577 Wt. W10791/1773 500,000 1/15 D. D. & L. A.D.S.S./Forms/C. 2118.

Instructions regarding War Diaries and Intelligence Summaries are contained in F. S. Regs., Part II. and the Staff Manual respectively. Title pages will be prepared in manuscript.

Howe Bn
63rd RN Div

WAR DIARY
or
INTELLIGENCE SUMMARY.
(Erase heading not required.)

Army Form C. 2118.

Place	Date	Hour	Summary of Events and Information	Remarks and references to Appendices
REIGERSBURG	24/11/17		The 1st Div relieved by 32nd Div and Battalion came under the orders of C.R.E. 32nd Div working for the 206th & 219th Fld Coys.	
"	25 Nov – 30 Nov		Working Parties carrying duckboards; parties of 200 men being required in the morning and about 150 in the evening. The work extremely exhausting owing to the long distances to be traversed. Casualties on 27th. 7 ORs wounded. On 29th a shell burst in the camp killing one man and wounding another.	

Alan Campbell
Lt Comdr RNVR

1577 Wt. W10791/1773 500,000 1/15 D. D. & L. A.D.S.S./Forms/C. 2118.

Instructions regarding War Diaries and Intelligence Summaries are contained in F. S. Regs., Part II. and the Staff Manual respectively. Title pages will be prepared in manuscript.

HOWE BN
R.N.D.

WAR DIARY
or
~~INTELLIGENCE SUMMARY~~. Dec 1917

(*Erase heading not required.*)

Army Form C. 2118.

Vol 19

Place	Date	Hour	Summary of Events and Information	Remarks and references to Appendices
REIGERSBURG	Dec 1		Carrying Party of 200 men working under 206 Field Coy R E worked from 6 0 a m No party in evening	
	2		400 men employed carrying duckboards after the attack made by the 32nd Div	
	3 - 5		Remained at REIGERSBURG CAMP and employed the days cleaning up and a certain amount of drill.	
SCHOOL CAMP.	6		Moved by Route march to School CAMP. starting at 10 30 a m orders received that we were to entrain on 9th destination unknown	
	7		Cleaning up and camp improvement 2 coys bathed in afternoon G O C. Bde visited camp in morning and notified postponement of move	
	8		Battalion prepared for the move and rested.	
	9	1 30 a.m.	B, C & D Coys marched to PESELHOEK STN where they entrained on arrival and left at 4 40. A Coy marched off 4 hrs later & caught the 8.43 train B, C, D Coy arrived at ACHIET LE GRAND at 2 p m and marched to F Camp BEAULENCOURT with the exception of D Coy which remained behind as detraining coy.	

D. M. W. Beak
Lt Comdr
Comdg HOWE Bn

1577 Wt. W10791/1773 500,000 1/15 D. D. & L. A.D.S.S./Forms/C. 2118.

Instructions regarding War Diaries and Intelligence Summaries are contained in F. S. Regs., Part II. and the Staff Manual respectively. Title pages will be prepared in manuscript.

Howe Bn.

WAR DIARY
or
~~INTELLIGENCE SUMMARY.~~
(Erase heading not required.)

December 1917

Army Form C. 2118.

Place	Date	Hour	Summary of Events and Information	Remarks and references to Appendices
BRANCOURT	10		A Coy arrived at 12.30 a.m. The day spent in resting & cleaning up camp.	
	11		D Coy arrived, having detrained the brigade, and carried on cleaning up.	
			The rest of the battalion trained under coy arrangements.	
	12		Training. In afternoon HOWE defeated ANSON at football	
	13		Training. Warning order received to move at 9.0 a.m. 14th to ETRICOURT.	
ROCQUIGNY	14		Battn marched to Rocquigny & billeted in Huts. Arrived 3.30 p.m. stayed night	
ETRICOURT	15		Battn marched to ETRICOURT, arrived at 12 noon. Stayed night in Tents	
LECHELLE	16		Battn marched to LECHELLE arrived at 11.30 a.m. Billetted in Huts.	
	17 to 19		Battn training during forenoon & recreational Training in afternoon	
	20		Celebrated Xmas	
	21		Continued Training	
VILLIERS PUICH	22		Battn moved to METZ at 10 a.m. had dinner there & moved to SUPPORT LINE at 4.30 p.m.	
	23		Battn were in SUPPORT LINE 3 Companies A.B.D. at VILLIERS	
	–		PUICH & C Co in LINCOLN AV. Working parties were	
	26		digging trenches in SUPPORT LINE.	

D. M. W. Beak
Lt Condr
Comdg HOWE BN

1577 Wt. W10791/1773 500,000 1/15 D. D. & L. A.D.S.S./Forms/C. 2118.

Army Form C. 2118.

Instructions regarding War Diaries and Intelligence Summaries are contained in F. S. Regs., Part II. and the Staff Manual respectively. Title pages will be prepared in manuscript.

WAR DIARY
or
~~INTELLIGENCE SUMMARY~~.

(Erase heading not required.)

Place	Date	Hour	Summary of Events and Information	Remarks and references to Appendices
VILLIERS POICH	27		Battn relieved ANSON BATTN in FRONT LINE. A & B Companies in PRENTICE TR. B in CORNWALL & CORNER TR. rest	
	–		C & D Cos in close support	
	30	6.35	Enemy launched an attack on our left front Co after heavy barrage. He obtained a footing in CORNER TRENCH & WELSH SUPPORT. B Co established a block in CORNWALL TRENCH.	
		7.10	Commander WEST & Lt Com CAMPBELL killed by shell.	
		4.30	2 Companies of ANSON BATTN counter attacked & most of lost ground was retaken. O C 'B' Co & 2 other Officers missing.	
	31		BATTN was relieved by ANSON BATTN on morning of 31st inst stayed in vicinity of VILLIERS POICH till 4.30pm then marched to METZ arrived there at 6-30 billetted in HUTS & shelters	

D. M. W. Beak
Lt Comdr.
Comdg. Howe Bn

1577 Wt. W10791/1773 500,000 1/15 D. D. & L. A.D.S.S./Forms/C. 2118.

S E C R E T.

AMENDMENT to 188th Inf. Brigade Order No. 158.

Réf.para.2. Timesof passing the Starting Point are amended to read as follows:--

2/R.M.L.I. -----	10.45 am.
1/R.M.L.I. -----	11 am.
Anson Battn. ---	11.15 am.
Howe Battn. ---	11.30 am.

Para.3. is cancelled and the following substituted:--
"188th M.G.Company will move indepedently - head of Company to reach Road junction H.3.d.2.3. at 11 am".

Para.5. last line for"9.50 am" read"11.50 am".

R.A.R. Neville
~~Major~~, Lieut.
A/Brigade Major,
188th Inf. Brigade.

5/12/17.
Copies to:-
1st R.M.L.I.
2nd R.M.L.I.
Anson Battn.
Howe Battn.
188th M.G.Coy.

S E C R E T.

Reference attached Warning Order.

The composition of the 188th Inf. Brigade Group for entrainment will be as follows:-

1st R.M. Battalion.
2nd R.M. Battalion.
Anson Battalion.
Howe Battalion.
188th M.G. Company.
188th L.T.M. Battery.
247th Field Coy. R.E.
148th Field Ambulance.
14th Worc. Regt. (Pioneers).
No.2 Coy. Divl. Train.

A D Tufnell Smollett

Major,
Brigade Major,
188th Inf. Brigade.

B.M.1828/1.
5th December, 1917.

SECRET.

WARNING ORDER.
-:-:-:-:-:-:-:-:-:-:-:-:-:-

Brigade Headquarters
5th December, 1917.

1. B.M. 1828 of 4th inst is cancelled.

2. The following Units of the 188th Infantry Brigade Group will be held in readiness to move by march route to vicinity of SCHOOLS CAMP, on the 6th inst.

1st R.M. Battalion.
2nd R.M. Battalion.
Anson Battalion.
Howe Battalion.
188th M.G. Company.
148th ~~150th~~ Field Ambulance.

Transport will move with Units.

3. Detailed orders for march will be issued later.
Remaining Units of Brigade Group will stand fast until further orders in their present locations.

4. Entraining Station will be PESELHOEK.

5. Date of entrainment probably 8th inst.

6. ACKNOWLEDGE.

[signature]
Lieut RNVR.
for Major,
Brigade Major.

B.M. 1828/1.

Copies to:-
1st R.M. Battalion.
2nd R.M. Battalion.
Anson Battalion.
Howe Battalion.
188th M.G. Company.
188th L.T.M. Battery.
~~223rd M.G. Company.~~
148th ~~150th~~ Field Ambulance.
No.2. Coy. Divl. Train.
247th Field Company R.E.
14th Worc Regt.

SECRET.   Copy No. 7

188th INFANTRY BRIGADE ORDER No. 158.

Brigade Headquarters,
5th December, 1917.

Reference Maps:-
Sheet 28 N.W. - 1/20,000.
Sheet 27 - 1/40,000.

1. Units of the 188th Infantry Brigade will move by March route to SCHOOLS CAMP to-morrow 6th inst. Dress - full marching order, Steel helmets will be worn.
1st Line transport will move with units.
Transport of 1st R.M.L.I. will join the column in rear of their Battalion at junction of roads at H.3.d.2.3.

2. Units will pass the Starting point - road junction at BRIELEN (B.29.c.8.9.) as follows:-

2nd R.M.Battalion	---	9.0 am.
1st R.M.Battalion	---	9.15 am.
Anson Battalion	---	9.30 am.
Howe Battalion	---	10 am.

ROUTE. BRIELEN - VLAMERTINGHE road as far as road junctions in H.3.d.2.3. - thence via Switch road to main VLAMERTINGHE - POPERINGHE road at H.8.b.4.9 - road junction at G.3.c.7.3. - Switch Road - POPERINGHE - WATOU Road.

3. The 188th M.G.Company will move independently and will clear road junction at H.3.d.2.3. by 9.15 am.

4. East of the VLAMERTINGHE - ELVERDINGHE road Units will move in file, not fours. They will close up into fours when clear of road junctions at H.3.d.2.3.
The following intervals will be maintained on the March:-

200	yards	between	Companies.
500	"	"	Battalions.
100	"	"	Units & their Transport.
25	"	"	every 6 vehicles.

5. The usual halts will be observed i.e. at ten minutes to the Clock hour, march being resumed at the hour. First halt will be 9.50 am.

6. Each Battalion will detail a party, under an Officer, to clear up Camp after departure of Units. Officer in charge will, before leaving, obtain a certificate from Camp Adjutant that Camp has been left in a satisfactory condition.

7. Attention is drawn to Brigade Standing March Orders, instructions contained therein will be strictly adhered to.

18

8. Actual destinations of Units are not yet known, but Billeting Parties will report to Camp Adjutant SCHOOLS CAMP at 2.30 pm - 6th inst. Above parties will meet their units at junction of POPERINGHE - PROVEN and POPERINGHE - St. JANTER BIEZEN roads L.4.b.8.2.

9. On arrival in billets Units will send a bicycle orderly to Brigade Headquarters to report arrival in billets, location of Battalion Headquarters, and number of men who have fallen out.

10. Brigade Headquarters will remain at POPERINGHE.

11. Acknowledge.

Major,
for Brigade Major.

Issued to Signals at 4 pm.

Copies to:-
No. 1 File
2 War Diary.
3 Staff Captain.
4 1st R.M. Battalion.
5 2nd R.M. Battalion.
6 Anson Battalion.
7 Howe Battalion.
8 188th M.G. Company.
9 188th LTM Bty.
10 No.2 Signal Section.
11 Bde. Transport Officer.
12 Bde. Supply Officer.
13 No.2 Coy. Divl. Train.
14 148th Field Ambulance.
16 247th Field Coy. R.E.
17 14th Worc. Regt.
18 63rd (R.N.) Divn. "G".
19 63rd (R.N.) Divn. "Q".
20 A.D.M.S. do.
21 C.R.E. do.
22 C.R.A. do.
23 189th Inf. Bde.
24 190th Inf. Bde.

S E C R E T.

AMENDMENT No.2 to 188th Infantry Brigade Order No.159 - 6/12/17.

-:-

1. Origianl Time-table issued with 188th Brigade Order 159 stands good, except that for dates Dec. 8th and 9th. read Dec. 9th and 10th. Amended Time Table is attached.

2. All other orders with reference to move by train remain unaltered.

3. Units will hand to Entraining Officer certificates, if possible signed by Camp Adjutant, that Camps were left in a satisfactory condition. Entraining Officer will forward these certificates to 188th B.H.Q. on completion of move.

4. The Detraining Officer will be Lieut. CURTIS. R.M.

5. One blanket per man will be carried.

6. A bicycle orderly from each Unit in Brigade Group will report to B.H.Q. with all gear and rations for 9th inst., and bicycle at 6 pm to-night. These orderlies will rejoin their Units at the Station.

7. ACKNOWLEDGE.

Captain,
Brigade Major,
188th Inf. Brigade.

8/12/17.
To all Units of Brigade Group.

S E C R E T.

AMENDMENT No.1 to 188th Infantry Brigade Order No. 159.- 6/12/17.

-:-

The Time-table issued with the above order is cancelled.

Fresh dates and times will be notified later.

A D Mfr. Smollett

Major,
Brigade Major,
188th Inf. Brigade.

7/12/17.

To all Units of Brigade Group.

Plan to accompany 188th Brigade Order No 159

Peselhoek Station

Howe

1 Train

30 Covered Trucks
[37 men to each]
or 8 horses
17 Flat Trucks
1 Officers Coach

Troops must not use Chinese latrine at *

Units entrain at positions as marked opposite entrainment rail

H. P. Thompson Capt
Brigade Major

"A" Form.

Army Form C. 2121.
(In pads of 100.)

MESSAGES AND SIGNALS.

No. of Message..............

Prefix............Code..............m. | Words. | Charge.

Office of Origin and Service Instructions.

Sent
At..............m.
To..............
By..............

This message is on a/c of:
.... *Service.*
(Signature of "Franking Officer.")

Recd. at.........m.
Date..............
From..............
By..............

TO { 1 Horse Bn

Sender's Number.	Day of Month.	In reply to Number.	AAA
BM 789	8/12		

Warning Order. Entrainment will commence midnight night 8th/9th. Further instructions will ~~will~~ be issued later.

From 188 Inf Bde.
Place
Time

AD Tufp Sndlewold Capt
Bde Major
188 Inf Bde

The above may be forwarded as now corrected. (Z)

Censor. Signature of Addressor or person authorised to telegraph in his name.

* This line should be erased if not required.

(3796.) Wt. W 492/M1647. 650,000 Pads. 5/17. H.W. & V., Ld. (E. 1187.)

AMENDED TIME TABLE to accompany 188th Brigade Order 159.

DATE.	No. of TRAIN.	TIME.	ENTRAIN AT	SERIAL NUMBER.	DESCRIPTION.
Dec. 9th.	3	4.43	PESELHOEK.	6314.	Howe Bn. (less 1 Coy., 1 Cooker & Team).
9th.	6	8.43	"	(6310 (6315 (6316 (6317 (6314a	Brigade Headquarters. Brigade Signal Section. 188th M.G.Company. 188th L.T.M.Battery. 1 Coy., 1 Cooker & Team of Howe Battn.
9th.	9	12.43	"	(6376 (6381	No.2 Coy. Divl. Train. 247th Field Coy. R.E.
9th.	12	16.43	"	6311	1st R.M.L.I.Battn.
9th.	15	20.43	"	6312	2nd R.M.L.I.Battn.
10th.	18	-.43	"	6304	14th Bn.Worc.Regt.(less 1 Coy 4 G.S.Wagons. Cooker & Teams.)
10th.	21	4.43	"	(6386 (6304a ((6313a (	148th (RN) Field Ambulance. 1 Coy. 4 G.S.Wagons. Cooker & Teams of 14th Worc.Regt. 1 Coy. 1 Cooker & Team of Anson Battn.
10th	24	8.43	"	6313	Anson Bn.(less 1 Coy. 1 Cooker & Team).

SECRET

No. 10

63rd (R.N.) DIVISION ADMINISTRATIVE INSTRUCTIONS NO. 6
with reference to 63rd Divn. Order No. 185.

Map Reference. Sheet 27 and 28.

1. The Division will entrain in accordance with Time Table which will be issued later. ✗ herewith Entrainment will probably commence 4 a.m. on 8th December 1917.
Attached is a Table marked "A" showing Serial Numbers.

2. The Entrainment Stations will be as follows :-

188th Inf. Brigade Group - PESELHOEK
189th Inf. Brigade Group - HOPOUTRE
190th Inf. Brigade Group - GODEWAERSVELDE.

The following will entrain with the 189th Infantry Brigade Group:-

Gas School; D.M.G.O. and his personnel;
H.Q., 63rd Divl Engineers, H.Q. 63rd Divl. Train
and 253rd D. E. C.
D.H.Q., H.Q. Signal Coy., and No. 1 Sec. Signal Coy. will entrain with 190th Infantry Brigade Group.

3. The Routes to the Station will be as follows :-

188th Inf. Bde. Group. - SCHOOL CAMP via ST. JAN DER BIEZEN, and SWITCH ROADS.

14th Worc. Regt. - From POPERINGHE along PESELHOEK Road.

189th Inf. Bde. Group - ST. JAN DER BIEZEN, SWITCH ROAD West of POPERINGHE to HOPOUTRE.

190th Inf Bde. Group - No restrictions.

D. H. Q., H.Q. Div. Sig.Coy. and No. 1 Sec.- Div. Sig.Coy. - via PROVEN ROAD, Western SWITCH Road, ABEELE, Cross Roads in K.35.d. to GODEWAERSVELDE.

4. Arrangements are to be made by Brigades to Control Traffic on the Road approaches to the Entraining Stations and no Troops, or Transport to be allowed, to enter the Stations Yards until the R.T.O. is ready.
Units will send an Officer to their Entraining Stations to ascertain the Entrainment situation, one hour before the first portion of their Unit is due to arrive.
The A.P.M. will make arrangements to see that there is no congestion of Traffic on the roads.

5. ENTRAINING OFFICER.
Brigades will detail an Officer to superintend the Entrainment of the Brigades Groups.

ENTRAINING PARTIES.
Brigades will detail 2 Officers 100 Other Ranks to assist Units in the loading. Those parties and the Entrainment Officer together with 6 Police to report to their respective R.T.O. 3½ hours before the first train is due to leave. They will entrain on the last train of their Group and therefore should be drawn from the Units comprising last Train and thus prevent overcrowding.

6. DETRAINING PARTIES.
Brigades will detail one Officer to superintend the Detrainment and a party of 2 Officers and 100 Other Ranks plus 6 Police as Detraining Parties. They will be found from the personnel of the first train from each Entraining Station and report to the R.T.O. on arrival. They will rejoin their Units on completion of Detrainment.

7. Transport of Battalions including Mounted Personnel will arrive at Entraining Stations 3 hours and dismounted personnel $1\frac{1}{2}$ hours before each train is due to depart. Units other than Battalions will arrive complete 3 hours before departure of the trains.

8. ADVANCED BILLETING PARTIES.
Brigade Groups will have the following Advanced Billeting Parties detailed ready to move at an hours notice.

	Offrs.	N.C.Os.
Each Battn. including Pnrs. ...	1	5
Each M.G. Coy.		1
Brigade H.Q. and T.M.B. ...		1
Each Fd. Coy. R.E. ...		1
Each Fd. Ambce.		1
Each Coy. Divl Train ...		1

One bicycle per Unit will be taken.

Additional personnel considered necessary for Billeting are to proceed in the first train from each Station.

9. WATER.
Water Carts and Water Bottles will be entrained full; horses to be watered before entraining. There are watering facilities at all three Entraining Stations.

10. BREAST ROPES.
Breast ropes for horses will be provided by Units, one breast rope per 4 animals. Should an animal get cast and it be impossible to release head chain, head collar is to be undone or cut.

Ropes for lashing vehicles on the flat trucks will be provided by the Railway.

11. AMBULANCE CARS.
The A.D.M.S. will arrange for 1 Motor Ambulance to be on duty at each Entraining Station.

12. SUPPLY AND BAGGAGE WAGONS will accompany their Units in every case.

13. SUPPLIES.
There will be a double refil for all Units on the 7th December. Rations for consumption on the 10th will be loaded up on the Supply Wagons on the 8th for all Units proceeding after noon on that date

Supply Wagons will travel loaded.

14. MECHANICAL TRANSPORT.
All Mechanical Transport including Motor Bicycles will proceed by Road.
The Signal, Electric Light Lorry and Motor Bicycles of Divisional Signal Coy. will proceed under orders to be issued by O.C. Div. Signal Company. The Motor Ambulance Wagons will proceed under orders of the A.D.M.S.
The Supply Vehicles of the 63rd Divisional Supply Column will move under orders to be issued by the Second Corps.

15. AMMUNITION.
Units will entrain with Mobile Reserve complete.

16. ENTRAINING STATES.
Entraining States for each Unit or part of Unit showing bicycle number of personnel, animals and nature, vehicles (four-wheeled and two-wheeled) are to be handed to the R.T.O. 3 hours before departure of the train; duplicate copy being given to the Entraining Officer who will hand same to Lieut. W.S. DAVIS.

17. LIGHTS.
Entraining and Detraining Parties are to be provided with Lanterns.

18. RENDEZVOUS.
Brigades will select adjacent to each Station RENDEZVOUS, notifying them to all concerned.
Brigades will also issue necessary orders re Sanitation, and the leaving of the Rendezvous in a clean condition.

19. The Entrainment of all Units must be completed ½ hour before departure of Train.

20. PICQUETS.
Picquets are to be provided at all stops for each end of the Train to prevent Troops leaving.
All doors of covered trucks and carriages on the right hand side of the Train are to be kept closed.

21. Lieut. E.C.B. COLLINS, R.N.V.R., and Lieut. C.E. HOPKINSON, with 3 Motor Cyclist Orderlies will proceed in advance of the Division to arrange billets, etc. in the New Area. Their address will be notified later.
Lieut. W.S. DAVIS and 2nd Lieut. H. CHURCHILL SMITH, R.M., will be on duty during the Entrainment - Address c/o Town Major POPERINGHE.
The O.C., Div. Signal Company will place 2 Motor Cyclists at the disposal of these Officers.

22. The 63rd Divl. Artillery and No. 1 Company Divl. Train will rejoin the 63rd (R.N.) Division under orders to be issued by II Corps.

23. ACKNOWLEDGE.

R Foster

5/12/17

Lieut.Colonel, A.A. & Q.M.G.,
63rd (R.N.) Division.

(Distribution P.T.O.)

DISTRIBUTION

Copies to :-

"G"	1 - 3
A.A. & Q.M.G.	4
D.A.A.G.	5
D.A.Q.M.G.	6
War Diary	7 - 8
188th Inf.Bde.Group.	9 - 21
189th -do-	22 - 34
190th -do-	35 - 47
14th Worcs.	48
C.R.E.	49
Div.Sig.Coy.	50
Div.Train	51
S.S.O.	52
D.M.G.O.	53
D.S.C.	54
D.A.D.O.S.	55
D.A.D.V.S.	56
D.E.C.	57
A.P.M.	58
A.D.M.S.	59
Div. Gas Offr.	60
R.T.O. PESELHOEK	61
" HOPOUTRE	62
" GODEWAERS-VELDE	63
Traffic Offr. HAZEBROUCK	64
File	65
Spare	66 - 67
II Corps "Q"	68) For
63rd Div.Arty.	69) information.
Camp Commandant	70

TABLE "A" Issued with 63rd (R.N.) Division Administrative Instructions No. 6.

"A"

SECRET

63rd (R.N.) DIVISION (LESS ARTILLERY)

UNIT.	Serial Number	DESCRIPTION.
DIVISIONAL UNITS.	6301	Divisional Headquarters
	6302	
	6303	H.Q. Divl. Engineers
	6304	14th Bn. Worc. R.(Pnrs) less 6304 a
	6304a	1 Coy. 4 G.S.Wgns./cooker and Teams of 14th Worcester Regt.
	6305	H.Q. & No. 1 Sect. Div.Signals.
	6308	223rd Machine Gun Company.
	6309	253rd Div. Employment Company.
188th INFANTRY BRIGADE	6310	Brigade Headquarters
	6311	1st R.M. Battn.
	6312	2nd R.M. Battn.
	6313	Anson Battn. less 6313a.
	6313a	1 Coy. 1 Cooker and Team of Anson Bn.
	6314	Howe Battn. less 6314a
	6314a	1 Coy. 1 cooker & Team of Howe Bn.
	6315	Bde. Sig.Sect.
	6316	Bde. Machine Gun Company.
	6317	Bde Trench Mortar Battery (Light)
189th INFANTRY BRIGADE	6320	Brigade Headquarters
	6321	Drake Bn. less 6321a
	6321a	1 Coy., 1 cooker & team of Drake Bn.
	6322	Hawke Bn. less 6322a
	6322a	1 Coy. 1 cooker & team of Hawke Bn.
	6323	Hood Bn. less 6323a
	6323a	1 Coy., 1 cooker and Team of Hood Bn.
	6324	Nelson Bn. less 6324a.
	6324a	1 Coy., 1 cooker & Team of Nelson Bn.
	6325	Brigade Signal Section
	6326	Brigade Machine Gun Company
	6327	Brigade Trench Mortar Battery (Light)
190th INFANTRY BRIGADE	6330	Brigade Headquarters
	6331	7th Roy.Fus. (Ex.S.R.)
	6332	4th Bed. Regt. (Ex.S.R.)
	6333	1/4 K.S.L.I. less 6333a.
	6333a	1 Coy. 1 Cooker & Team of 1/4 K.S.L.I.
	6334	1/28th London Regt.
	6335	Brigade Signal Section
	6336	Brigade Machine Gun Company
	6337	Brigade Trench Mortar Battery (Light)

P.T.O.

UNIT.	Serial Number	DESCRIPTION.
DIVISIONAL TRAIN	6375	H.Q. Divisional Train
	6376	No. 2 Company
	6377	No. 3 Company
	6378	No. 4 Company
DIVISIONAL ENGINEERS	6381	247th Field Company R.E.
	6382	248th Field Company R.E.
	6383	249th Field Company R.E.
MEDICAL UNITS	6386	148th (RN) Field Ambulance
	6387	149th (RN) Field Ambulance
	6388	150th (RN) Field Ambulance.
VETERINARY UNIT	6390	53rd Mobile Veterinary Section

NOTICE

(a) All Trains consist of 1 Officers carriage; 17 flat trucks: 30 covered trucks.

(b) (i) Each flat truck will take an average of 4 axles.
(ii) Each covered truck will take 6 H.D. Horses
or 8 L.D. Horses or Mules.
or 40 men.

(c) No personnel or stores will be allowed in the brake vans at each end of the Train, or on the roofs of the trucks.
No covered trucks should be used for baggage as it restricts space available for personnel.

SECRET. Copy No. 7

188th INFANTRY BRIGADE ORDER No. 159.

-:-:-:-:-:-:-:-:-:-:-:-:-:-:-:-:-:-:-:-

Reference Maps:-
Sheet 28 N.W. - 1/20,000.
Sheet 27 - 1/40,000.

Brigade Headquarters,
6th. December, 1917.

1. The 188th Infantry Brigade will entrain in accordance with attached Time-table on the 8th and 9th inst.

2. Entrainment will be carried out in accordance with X "63rd Divisional Administrative Instructions" issued with this order.

3. With reference to "Administrative Instructions":-

Para.5. ENTRAINING OFFICER. Captain ELIOT - 2/R.M.L.I. Assisted by Lieut. NEVILLE, 2/R.M.L.I.

Entraining Parties and 6 Police. To be furnished by Anson Battn. (Serial No.13), will be accommodated night 7th/8th Dec. at PESELHOEK Station to report to R.T.O. at 4 pm. 7th inst.

Para.6. Detraining Parties. To be furnished by Howe Battn. (Serial No.14).

Para.8. Advanced Billeting Parties. Seperate instructions have already been issued.

Attention is drawn to paras. 7, 9, 10, - the instructions contained therein will be strictly adhered to.

Para.13. Supply waggons will join Units at the Station.

Para. 16. Entraining States. Officers Commanding are reminded that the personnel, animals and vehicles of baggage and supply waggons must be included.

Para.18. Rendezvous. - open piece of ground in the Station yard - guides will be posted at entrance to Station to show Units exact positions.

4. ROUTE to the STATION:- St.JANTER BIEZEN - POPERINGHE Road - SWITCH ROAD to A.25.d.4.1. thence to road junction at A.20.d.3.1; from this point dismounted personnel will proceed by right fork and Transport by left fork to Station which is situated in A.20.b. and A.21.a.

The above route will be reconnoitred beforehand by all Units.

5. ACKNOWLEDGE.

[signature]
Major,
Brigade Major.

Issued to Signals at 4 pm.

Copies to - See overleaf.

X "ADMINISTRATIVE INSTRUCTIONS" only issued to Brigade Group.

Copies to:--
No. 1 File.
2 War Diary.
3 Staff Captain.
4 1st R.M.Battalion.
5 2nd R.M.Battalion.
6 Anson Battalion.
7 Howe Battalion.
8 188th M.G.Company
9 188th L.T.M. Battery.
10 No.2 Signal Section.
11 Bde. Transport Officer.
12 Bde. Supply Officer.
13 No. 2 Coy. Divl. Train.
14 148th Field Ambulance.
15 247th Field Coy. R.E.
16 14th Worc. Regt.
17 63rd (R.N.) Divn "G".
18 63rd (R.N.) Divn "Q".
19 A.D.M.S. do.
20 C.R.E. do.
21 C.R.A. do.
22 189th Inf. Bde.
23 190th Inf. Bde.

TIME TABLE to accompany Brigade Order No.159.

Date.	No of Train.	Time.	Entrain at.	Serial Number.	DESCRIPTION.
Dec. 8th.	3.	4.43.	PESELHOEK.	6314.	Howe Bn. (less 1 Coy., 1 Cooker & Team)
8th.	6.	8.43.	" -	(6310 (6315. (6316 (6317. (6314a.	Brigade Headquarters. Brigade Signal Section 188th M.G.Company 188th L.T.M.Battery. 1 Coy., 1 Cooker & Team of Howe Bn.
8th	9.	12.43.	" -	(6373. (6381.	No 2 Coy.Divl.Train. 247th Field Coy.R.E.
8th	12.	16.43.	" -	6311.	1st R.M.L.I. Bn.
8th	15.	20.43.	" -	6312.	2nd R.M.L.I. Bn.
9th.	18.	- .43.	" -	6304.	14th Bn.Worc.Regt. (less 1 Coy. 4 G.S. Wagons. Cooker & Teams.)
9th.	21.	4.43.	" -	(6388. (6304a ((6313a	148th (RN) Field Ambulance. 1 Coy.4 G.S.Wagons.Cooker & Teams of 14th Worc.Regt. 1 Coy 1 Cooker & Team of Anson Bn.
9th.	24.	8.43.	"	6313.	Anson Bn. (less 1 Coy. 1 Cooker & Team)

LORRIES.

1. 6 Lorries have been allotted to the Brigade for the transport of Blankets, Stores, etc. to the Entraining Station.
2. These lorries will be at the disposal of Units as under :-

TABLE A. 8th inst.

Lorry No	Unit.	From	To	Remarks.
1	Bde H.Q.	p.m. 8th.	8 a.m., 9th.	Then reports to 2nd R.M.L.I.
2.	188th M.G.C.	do.	do.	do.
3.	188th L.T.M's	do.	do.	do.
4.	Howe Bn.	do.	4 am., 9th.	then reports to 1/R.M.L.I
5.	do.	do.	do.	do.
6.	do.	do.	do.	do.

TABLE B. 9th inst.

1.	2/R.M.L.I.	8 am.	3 pm.	then reports to Anson.
2.	do.	do.	do.	do. Bn.
3.	do.	do.	do.	do.
4.	1/R.M.L.I.	4 am.	3 pm.	then reports to 14th
5.	do.	do.	do.	do. Worc.Rgt.
6.	do.	do.	do.	then reports to 148th Field Amb.

TABLE C. 9th inst.

1.	Anson Bn.	3 pm.	8 am 10th.	Returns to Park.
2.	do.	do.	do.	do.
3.	do.	do.	do.	do.
4.	14th Worcs.	do.	11 pm 9th.	do.
5.	do.	do.	do.	do.
6.	148th Fd.Amb.	do.	4 am 10th.	do.

TABLE D.

3. Locations:-
188th Inf.Bde.Hdqrs. 6. Rue de Pots. POPERINGHE.
1/R.M.L.I. - 2/R.M.L.I. Anson Bn.)
Howe Bn. 188th M.G.C 188th L.T.M's) SCHOOLS CAMP.
14th Worc.Regt. Rue de Ballance. POPERINGHE.
148th Field Ambulance. TUNNELING Camp.

4. To ensure that lorries go to the right places Units in Tables B& C will send 1 representative per lorry to report to-night to H.Q. unit concerned to remain on their lorry till it becomes available.

e.g. 1 Representative from both 2/R.M.L.I & Anson Bn. to report Bde Hdqrs.
1 " " both 2/R.M.L.I & Anson Bn. to report 188th M.G.Coy. etc.

5. Lorries are in each case to be sent on to the next unit by time laid down.

6. Gear will have to be dumped at the Station and guard left to look after it to enable this to be done.

7. Copies of these orders have been issued to the lorry drivers.

H.C. Barlow
Lieut, R.N.V.R.
A/Staff Captain,
188th Inf.Brigade.

S.C.Q. 522.
8/12/17.

To All Units of Brigade Group.

to all units of Brigade Group

RATIONS.

(i) Rations for consumption 9-12-17 issued 7-12-17
" " " 10-12-17* " 8-12-17
" " " 11-12-17 " :- a and b.

a. Units entraining before noon on 9th.
viz. 188th.B.H.Q.) Will be ~~issued~~ delivored
188th.L.T.M.B.) after detrainment in new
188th.M.G.C.) area from A.R.P.
Howe Battn.) To be notified on arrival 10-12-17.

b. Units entraining after noon on the 9th.
viz. Remaining units) Will be loaded on supply wagons
of Brigade Group.) which will entrain with units.

* The 188th.L.T.M.Battery rations are loaded with 188th.B.H.Q. for this date.

(2) Supply wagons of units under a. are to report to B.H.Q. 9 a.m. 10th., when guide will be sent from No 2 Coy.Train.
Remaining supply wagons should report to No 2 Coy.Train.
Location of No 2 Coy.Train and 188th.B.H.Q. should be obtained from R.T.O. BAPAUME. on arrival.

S.C.Q 523.
8-12-17

Lieutenant R.N.V.R.
A/Staff Captain
188th.Infantry Brigade

SECRET.   Copy No. 9

188th INFANTRY BRIGADE ORDER No. 160.

-:-:-:-:-:-:-:-:-:-:-:-:-:-:-:-:-:-:-

Reference Map:-
FRANCE 57c - 1/40,000.

Brigade Headquarters,
13th December, 1917.

1. The 188th Infantry Brigade Group will move on the 14th December to ETRICOURT (V.8.), where it will be in III Corps Reserve.

2. Route will be:- VILLERS---AU---FLOS -- BARASTRE -- BUS -- LECHELLE.

3. Starting Point will be:- Road junction at N.18.a.1.0.

4. Units will pass starting point in following order:-

Brigade Headquarters at 9.0 am.
Howe Battalion --- at 9.3 am.
Anson Battalion --- at 9.11 am.
2nd R.M.Battalion - at 9.19 am.
1st R.M.Battalion - at 9.27 am.
14th Worc. Regt. - at 9.35 am.
* 188th L.T.M.Bty. - at 9.43 am.
* 188th M.G.Company.- at 9.46 am.
247th Field Coy. - at 10.0 am.
148th Field Amb. - at 10.0 am.
No.2 Coy.Divl. Train will move independently.
* Will join column at Camp.

5. Following distances will be maintained:-

Between Units	100 yards.
" Headquarters and leading Company etc.	Nil.
" Companies etc.	50 yards.
" Companies etc. and Transport.	50 yards.

6. The following Billeting parties will report to Town Major - ETRICOURT at 9 am on 14th December:-

Each Battalion - 1 officer and 4 N.C.Os.
Other units - 1 N.C.O.
Billeting states will be brought.

7. Extra transport will be notified later.

8. Usual certificates, that Camps have been left in a satisfactory condition, will be obtained from Area Commandant and forwarded to B.H.Q.

9. The usual halts on Line of March will be observed - first halt will be at 9.50 am.

/10.

10. Brigade Headquarters will close at BEAULENCOURT at 8.30 am. and will open at ETRICOURT at 12 noon.

11. ACKNOWLEDGE.

H. P. Thornhill [signature]

Captain,
Brigade Major.

Issued to Signals at 12.30 p.m.

Copies to:--
No. 1 G.O.C.
2 B.M.
3 S.C.
4 War Diary.
5 File.
6 1st R.M.Battn.
7 2nd R.M.Battn.
8 Anson Battn.
9 Howe Battn.
10 188th M.G.Coy.
11 188th L.T.M.Bty.
12 14th Worc.Regt.
13 247th Field Coy.
14 148th Field Amb.
15 No.2 Coy.Divl.Train.
16-17 63rd (R.N.) Division.
18 189th Inf.Brigade.
19 190th Inf.Brigade.
20 Area Commandant BEAULENCOURT.
21 Town Major ETRICOURT.
22 Bde. Signal Officer.
23 Intelligence Officer.
24 Bde. Supply Officer.
25 A.D.M.S. 63rd Divn.
26 C.R.E. - do.
27 Brigade Transport Officer.

S E C R E T.   Copy No.

188th Infantry Brigade Order No. 161.

Brigade Headquarters,
14th December, 1917.

Reference Map:-
57c. 1/40,000.

1. The 188th Infantry Brigade Group will move to ROCQUIGNY to-day via LE TRANSLOY - WINDMILL MOUND.

2. Starting Point SUGAR FACTORY N.24.b.1.0. Order of march and times of passing starting point are as in Order No.160 except that the hour is 2pm instead of 9.0 am. ~~247th~~ 148th Field Ambulance will join column at Camp.

3. Billeting representatives to report to Town Major ROCQUIGNY before 12 noon to-day.

4. All other details as in Order No. 160.

5. The Brigade Group will march to-morrow to ETRICOURT starting at 9 am.

6. Brigade Headquarters will close at BEAULENCOURT at 1.30 pm and open at ROCQUIGNY at 3 pm to-day.

7. Acknowledge.

8. Transport is not to be on the BAPAUME - LE TRANSLOY Road before Units move to the Starting Point.

H J P Thompson
Captain,
Brigade Major,
188th Inf. Brigade.

To all Units of Brigade Group.

SECRET.

W A R N I N G   O R D E R.

-:-:-:-:-:-:-:-:-:-:-:-:-:-:-:-

1. 1st R.M.Battalion, Howe Battalion, 188th L.T.M.Battery and 188th M.G.Company will be prepared to move on 16th December to LECHELLE.

2. 2nd R.M.Battalion and Anson Battalion will probably move on 17th December to METZ EN COUTURE.

3. Detailed orders will be sent later.

for [illegible] Lieut
~~Captain~~,
Brigade Major.

B.M. 1860.
15/12/17.

Issued to Signals at 4 pm.

Copies to:--
No.1 G.O.C.
2 B.M.
3 S.C.
4 Brigade Signal Section.
5 & 6 63rd (R.N.) Divn.
7 1st R.M.Battalion.
8 2nd R.M.Battalion.
9 Anson Battalion.
10 Howe Battalion.
11 188th L.T.M.Battery.
12 188th M.G.Company.

S E C R E T.   Copy No. 5

188th INFANTRY BRIGADE ORDER No. 163.

Brigade Headquarters,
15th December, 1917.

Reference Map:-
FRANCE 57c - 1/40,000.

1. Headquarters-- 188th Inf. Bde., 1st R.M.Battn., Howe Battn., 188th L.T.M.Bty. and 188th M.G.Coy. will move on 16th December to LECHELLE.

2. Units will move in accordance with the following March Table:-

UNIT. (in order of march)	STARTING POINT.	TIME.	ROUTE.
Howe Battn.	Cross Roads V.2.b.0.2.	10.45 am.	Road junction P.32.d. thence by Road N.W. to LECHELLE.
1st R.M.Battn.	ditto.	10.55 am.	
188th M.G.Coy.	Cross Roads V.13.c.5.4.	10.25 am.	V.7.d. - ETRICOURT - BEET ROOT FACTORY - thence as above.
188th L.T.M.Bty.	ditto.	10.35 am.	
188th B.H.Q.	ditto.	10.38 am.	

3. Transport will accompany Units. Distances will be kept as in to-day's march. The first halt will be at 11.50 am.

4. Usual billeting representatives will meet Lieut. NEVILLE at Area Commandant's Office - LECHELLE at 10 am.

5. 2nd R.M.Battn. and Anson Battn. will move at mid-day 17th December to METZ EN COUTURE, where they will relieve 2 Battalions of 190th Inf.Bde. On completion of relief these Battalions will be in Divisional Reserve and under orders of G.O.C. 63rd (R.N.) Division. Advance parties will proceed to METZ on 16th December to ascertain accommodation and locations from units now occupying area. Detailed orders follow.

6. Brigade Headquarters close at MANANCOURT at 10 am and open at LECHELLE at 12 noon.

7. Acknowledge.

H.J. Thompson
Captain,
Brigade Major.

Issued to Signals at 7.30 pm.

Copies to:-
No.1 G.O.C.
2 B.M.
3 S.C.
4 Bde. Signal Section.
5 Howe Battalion.
6 Anson Battalion.
7 1st R.M.Battalion.
8 2nd R.M.Battalion.
9. 188th L.T.M.Bty.
10. 188th M.G.Company.
11&12. 63rd (R.N.) Divn.
13. No.2 Coy. Divl.Train.
14. Brigade Supply Officer.
15. 190th Inf. Brigade.
16. A.D.M.S.
17. A.P.M.
18. Lieut. NEVILLE.

S E C R E T.

AMENDMENT No.1 to 188th Inf.Bde. Order No. 164 - 16/12/17.

Ref. Para.1 - for Q.29.d. read Q.19.d.

Captain,
Brigade Major.

A.B.O./164/1.
17/12/17.

To all recipients of above order.

SECRET. Copy No. 7

188th INFANTRY BRIGADE ORDER No. 104.

Reference Map:-
FRANCE 57c - 1/40,000.

Brigade Headquarters,
16th December, 1917.

1. 2nd R.M.Battalion and Anson Battalion will move to METZ to-morrow to quarters in Q.20.c. and Q.[illegible].d. respectively, where they will be in Divisional Reserve.

2. Battalions will march independently, 2nd R.M.Battalion leaving Camp at 12 noon and Anson Battalion at 12.30 pm.

3. Route will be via EQUANCOURT - thence by road running North-east through V.4.[illegible] and P.35.central to METZ.

4. 200 yards distance will be kept between Companies.

5. Steel helmets will be worn.

6. Travelling kitchens and water-carts will accompany Battalions. All other transport will move at 11.30 am under orders of Brigade Transport Officer to LECHELLE where accommodation will be arranged by Staff Captain.

7. 2 Motor Lorries per Battalion will report at 7 am. These will be used to carry all stores required at METZ, where Quartermaster's Stores will be established.

8. Divisional Ammunition dump is at Q.20.b.4.[illegible].

9. Usual certificates will be obtained from Camp Commandant - ETRICOURT and forwarded to B.H.Q.

10. After arrival at METZ - 1 Officer per Company will carry out reconnaissance of following routes:--

(a) Track running East from TRESCAULT to ridge in R.7.
(b) TRESCAULT - BEAUCAMP - VILLERS PLOUICH Road.

11. ACKNOWLEDGE.

H.G.P. Thompson
Captain,
Brigade Major.

Issued to Signals at 8 pm.

Copies to:--
No. 1. G.O.C.
2. B.M.
3. S.C.
4. 1st R.M. Battn.
5. 2nd R.M. Battn.
6. Anson Battn.
7. Howe Battn.
8. 188th M.G.Company.
9. 188th L.T.M.Battery.
10.& 11. 63rd (R.N.) Divn.
12. Bde. Signal Section.
13. Bde. Supply Officer.
14. A.P.M.
15. 189th Inf. Bde.
16. 190th Inf. Bde.

S E C R E T

Copy No. 11.

W A R N I N G   O R D E R.

Reference Maps:-
57c - 1/40,000.
57c S.E. - 1/20,000.

1. The 188th Infantry Brigade and 188th L.T.M. Battery will relieve units of the 61st Division in the line on the night 22/23rd December.

2. The limits of the Sector to be taken over are roughly R.21.c.7.0. and R.15.c.6.9.

3. The line will be held as follows:--

FRONT LINE (Right) --- 2nd R.M. Battalion.

" " (Left) --- Anson Battalion.

Close Support --- Howe Battalion.

Reserve (probably in METZ) --- 1st R.M. Battalion.

4. As soon as detailed orders are received the G.O.C. will hold Conferences of C.O's at Bde. H.Q. LECHELLE and at 2nd R.M. Battalion Headquarters at METZ.

5. Orders for 188th M.G. Company will be issued separately.

6. Acknowledge.

[illegible]
Captain,
Brigade Major.

B.M.4.
19/12/17.

Copies to:-
No.1 G.O.C.
2 B.M.
3 S.C.
4 Bde. Signal Officer.
5 Intelligence Officer.
6 Bde. Supply Officer.
7 No.2 Coy. Divl. Train.
8 1st R.M. Battalion.
9 2nd R.M. Battalion.
10 Anson Battalion.
11 Howe Battalion.
12 188th M.G. Company.
13 188th L.T.M. Battery.

cw

Copy No. 9

SECRET.

188th INFANTRY BRIGADE ORDER No, 165.

Reference Maps:-
57c - 1/40,000.
GOUZEAUCOURT - 1/20,000.

Brigade Headquarters,
20th December, 1917.

1. The 63rd (R.N.) Division is extending its right and taking over the line held by the 61st Division; relief to be completed by the morning of the 23rd December.

2. 188th Infantry Brigade will relieve the 183 Infantry Brigade and 1 Company of Hood Battalion on night 22nd/23rd December in accordance with attached Table.

3. (a) On completion of relief the 188th Inf.Bde. boundaries will be as under:--

Southern (Divisional boundary) R.20.d.2.0. - R.19.central - Q.24.central.

Northern (Inter-Brigade boundary) R.15.c.1.2. - R.15.a.0.5. - R.14.b.2.2. - Q.18.b.0.4.

(b) The 16 Inf Bde. 9th Divn. will be on our right, the 189th Inf.Bde. on our left.

4. All other details of the relief will be arranged by O.C's concerned.

Trench Standing Orders will be strictly observed so far as they affect the relief.

5. A lorry will leave Bde.H.Q. at 8.30 am on Dec. 21st to take reconnaissance parties to the line - vacancies are allotted as follows:-

Brigade Headquarters	---	2
1st R.M.Battalion --	---	4
Howe Battalion ---	---	15
188th L.T.M.Battery	---	4

2nd R.M.Battalion and Anson Battalion will carry out reconnaissance under their own arrangements.

6. All Defence Schemes, Trench Stores, Aeroplane Photographs, Secret Maps etc. will be taken over by the relieving units.

7. Administrative Instructions will be issued separately.

8. On completion of relief the Command will pass to G.O.C. - 188th Inf. Brigade.

9. Completion of relief will be reported to Brigade Headquarters by code word - "CHRISTMAS".

10. ACKNOWLEDGE.

H P Thompson
Captain,
Brigade Major.

Issued to Signals at 8 pm.

P.T.O.

Copies to :-

1 G.O.C.
2 B.M.
3 S.C.
4 File.
5 War Diary.
6 1st R.M. Battalion.
7 2nd R.M. Battalion.
8 Anson Battalion.
9 Howe Battalion.
10 188th M.G. Company.
11 188th L.T.M. Battery.
12 Bde. Signal Officer.
13 Bde. Supply Officer.
14 Bde. Transport Officer.
15 189th Infantry Brigade.
16 190th Infantry Brigade.
17 183rd Infantry Brigade.
18 23th Infantry Brigade.
19 63rd R.N. Division "G".
20 do. "Q".
21 A.D.M.S. 63rd R.N. Divn.
22 C.R.E. do.
23 C.R.A. do.
24 A.P.M. do.

TABLE TO ACCOMPANY 188th INFANTRY BRIGADE ORDER No.165.

UNIT.	FROM	TO.	RELIEVING.	ROUTE.	STARTING POINT.	TIME	REMARKS.
nd R.M.Bn.	METZ.	Front Line right. H.Q.R.14.c.5.0.	A Battalion 183rd Inf.Bde.	To be arranged by C.O.			Will relieve by daylight if weather is misty.
nson Bn.	METZ.	Front Line Left. H.Q.R.14.c.5.0.	"B" Battalion 183rd Inf.Bde. & 1 Coy. HOOD Bn.	do.	do.		do.
Howe Bn.	LECHELLE	Support.	"C" & "D" Battns. 183rd Inf. Bde. in FUSILIER Reserve & LINCOLN Avenue.	YTRES - NEUVILLE - BOURJONVAL - METZ.	N.W. Limit of Camp P.25.b.6.2.	10.0 am.	Will halt for Dinners in quarters Vacated by Anson Bn. in METZ.
188th.L.T.M Battery.	LECHELLE	Line.	183rd L.T.M.B.	do.	do.	10.15 am.	do.
1st R.M.Bn.	LECHELLE	Reserve in METZ.	2nd R.M.Bn.	do.	do.	10.20 am.	
Bde. H.Q.	LECHELLE	Line R.13.d.9.5.	183rd Inf.Bde.	do.	do.	10.35 am.	Rear H.Q. in METZ.

NOTES. (1) Distances E. of METZ will be :-
200 yards between Companies.
100 yards between Platoons.

W. of METZ :-
100 yards between Companies.
200 yards between units.

(2) Respirators will be worn at the 'ALERT' E. of METZ.

Officer Commanding,
~~1/R.M.L.I.Bn.~~
~~2/R.M.L.I.Bn.~~
~~Anson Bn.~~
Howe Bn.
~~M.G.Coy.~~

Reference 188th Inf.Bde Ord r No 165 of 20/12/17.

The 1st Line Transport of the Brigade will move to-morrow to V.6.b.7.2., as under :-

1/R.M.L.I. 10.40. am.-(less cookers,lewis gun limbers,mess & medical cart, which will accompany Bn.)
Howe Bn. 10.45. am.
2/R.M.L.I. 10.50.am.
Anson Bn. 10.55. am.
M.G.Coy. 11.00 am.

The Brigade Transport Officer will issue these orders to Transport Officer of 2/R.M.L.I and Anson Bns direct.

Quarter Master Stores will also move to V.6.b.7.2. to-morrow - lorries will report as under :-

1/R.M.L.I.)
Howe Bn.) - 7.30 am.
M.G.Coy.)

1 each

2/R.M.L.I) - 10.00 am.
Anson Bn.)

Baggage wagons will not be available. Lorries to be returned to their unit on completion of move.

The Brigade Transport Officer will arrange with Transport Officers concerned to take advanced party to draw and erect tents and shelters for Q.M.Stores and Transport personnel.

Captain,
Staff Captain,
188th Inf.Brigade.

S.C.Q. 551.
21/12/17.

MOVE ORDERS

By Commander C.S.West, D.S.O., R.N.V.R.
In the Field, 21/12/17

REVEILLE 6.45 a.m.

1. INTENTION — The Battalion will move by route march to the line to-morrow (22nd) to relieve ----------Bde.

2. ORDER OF MARCH — Hqrs, A. B. C, D 100 yards between Coys west of METZ. 200 yards between Coys and 100 yards between Platoons East of METZ.

3. STARTING POINT — North West limit of Camp. P. 25. B. 6. 2.

4. TIME — Coys will be ready to pass starting Point at 10 a.m. The Battalion will halt at METZ for dinner.

5. DRESS — Full marching order, less haversacks, steel helmets to be worn, water bottles filled. C and D Coys will carry one blanket per man. Each man will carry 120 rounds of ammunition. Box Respirators will be worn at Alert Position East of METZ.

6. TRANSPORT — Transport and Q.M.Stores will move to V. 6. b. 7. 2. at 10.45 a.m and 7.30 respectively. Field kitchens, ration limbers (with camp kettles) and Lewis Gun limbers behind their own Companies. Officers' packs and mess gear will be carried on limber.

7. BLANKETS, VALISES, SPARE MESS GEAR and HAVERSACKS — These will be at Q.M.Stores by 9 a.m. Blankets to be neatly rolled in tight bundles of 10. Haversacks to be marked.

8. BILLETS — Billets will be left scrupulously clean. Coy Commanders will render a certificate to Adjt before moving off to that effect.

9. SURPLUS PERSONNEL — They will accompany the Battalion to METZ, after dinner they will proceed to transport line.

(Signed) M.M.Hirschfeld
Sub Lieut, R.N.V.R.
Act Adjt.

S E C R E T. Copy No. 11

188th INFANTRY BRIGADE ORDER NO.166.

-:-:-:-:-:-:-:-:-:-:-:-:-:-:-:-:-:-:-:-

Brigade Headquarters,
24th December, 1917.

1. On night 26th/27th December, 1st R.M. Battalion will relieve 2nd R.M. Battalion in right sector, and Howe Battalion will relieve Anson Battalion in left Sector.

2. Reliefs will be carried out by daylight if visibility is poor.

3. Anti-Aircraft Lewis Gun Posts will be handed over.

4. Trench Stores, Schemes of work, Aeroplane photographs and Secret Maps will be handed over and receipts forwarded to 188th Bde. H.Qs. by 12 noon, December 27th.

5. 63rd R.N. Division Trench Standing Orders as far as they affect the relief will be strictly observed.

6. All other details of the relief will be arranged by C.O's concerned.

7. On relief, 2nd R.M. Battalion will move to quarters vacated by 1st R.M. Battalion in METZ, Anson Battalion will take over quarters vacated by Howe Battalion and will be in support with H.Q's and 3 Companies near VILLERS PLOUICH, and 1 Company in LINCOLN TRENCH.

8. Completion of relief will be reported by code word:- BOXING DAY.

9. ACKNOWLEDGE.

H P Thornhill [signature]
Captain,
Brigade Major,

Issued to Signals at 7.30 pm.

Copies to :-
1 G.O.C.
2 B.M.
3 S.C.
4 Intelligence Officer.
5 & 6. 63rd R.N. Divn.
7 D.M.G.O. do.
8 1st R.M. Battalion.
9 2nd R.M. Battalion.
10 Anson Battalion.
11 Howe Battalion.
12 188th M.G. Company.
13 188th L.T.M. Battery.
14 26th Inf. Brigade.
15 189th Inf. Brigade.
16 Brigade Supply Officer.
17 Brigade Signal Officer.
18 File.
19 War Diary.

Relief Complete 7 0 p.m 26.12.17

SECRET.

RELIEF ORDERS.

By Commander C. S. WEST. D.S.O., R.N.V.R.

1. INTENTION. The Battalion will relieve the ANSON as LEFT Battalion on night of 26/27th. Advance Parties have already been sent to their respective Sectors.

2. GUIDES. Guides from ANSON at the rate of 1 per Platoon will be at Battalion H.Q. at 4.30 pm.

3. ROUTE. B. Coy and D. Coy will move via WELSH Road and POPE AVENUE.
A. Coy via VILLAGE Road.
C. Coy will leave LINCOLN AVENUE as soon as safe from observation. Route via VILLERS PLOUICH to Battalion H.Q. where Guides will be picked up. Coy will move to its Sector via VILLAGE Road.

4. TIME. A. and B. will move at 4.30 pm.
D. will follow B.
Battalion H.Q. will move after C. Coy has gone forward.

5. ORDER OF MARCH. Platoons at 100 yards interval.

6. LOCATION. On relief Battalion H.Q. will be at E. end of Farm Ravine R.20.a.8.8.

7. RELIEF. Relief complete will be communicated by phone. Code word REST CAMP.

8. DISPOSITION. Coy Commanders will send in a map showing disposition of their Coy in the Line before 10 am. on the 27th.

RATIONS.W While in Front Line, Rations will be delivered by Limber at junction of VILLAGE Road and SURREY Road R.14.c.3.1. The Support Coys will be responsible for carrying rations to to their respective Front Coy. To-morrow night H.Q. and each Coy will leave a Guard at R.14.c.3.1. to guard rations until Coys send back Ration Parties after relief has been completed.

WATER. All water bottles filled.
A.B. and D. will each hand over to ANSON Representatives 25 full tins of water.
C. Coy will hand over 15 FULL tins.
Support Coy will supply Front Coy with water under arrangements between O.C.Coys.

COOKING. Cooking will be done in Camp Kettles in the Line. Fires can be lighted but great care must be taken that there is no smoke.

REGIMENTAL AID POST. Map Reference R.20.a.7.7.

In the Field. 25/12/17.

R Hirschfeld Sub-Lieut. R.N.V.R.
A/Adjutant.

S E C R E T.   Copy No. 10.

188th INFANTRY BRIGADE ORDER No.167.

-:-:-:-:-:-:-:-:-:-:-:-:-:-:-:-:-:-

Brigade Headquarters,
29th December 1917.

1. On night 30th/31st December, 2nd R.M. Battalion will relieve 1st R.M. Battalion in right sector, and Anson Battalion will relieve Howe Battalion in Left sector.

2. Reliefs will be carried out by daylight if visibility is poor.

3. Anti-Aircraft Lewis Gun Posts will be handed over. The Post of 2nd R.M. Battalion at 63rd R.N. Div. H.Q. YTRES will be relieved by 2 Lewis Guns and teams of Howe Battalion by 10.30 am. on 30th. The Lewis Guns of Howe Battalion will be relieved by a unit of 189th Inf. Brigade by 12 noon on January 1st.

4. Trench Stores, Schemes of work, Aeroplane photographs and Secret Maps will be handed over and receipts forwarded to 188th Bde. H.Q's. by 12 noon, December 31st.

5. 63rd R.N. Division Trench Standing Orders as far as they affect the relief will be strictly observed.

6. All other details of the relief will be arranged by C.O's concerned.

7. On relief, Howe Battalion will move to quarters vacated by 2nd R.M. Battalion at METZ, 1st R.M. Battalion will take over quarters vacated by Anson Battalion and will be in Support with H.Q's and 3 Companies at VILLERS PLOUICH and 1 Company in LINCOLN TRENCH.

8. Completion of relief will be reported by code word :- SOUP.

9. ACKNOWLEDGE.

H P Thompson
Captain,
Brigade Major,

Issued to Signals at 4 pm.

Copies to :-
1 G.O.C.
2 B.M.
3 S.C.
4 Intelligence Officer.
5 Bde. Signal Officer.
6 Bde. Supply Officer.
7 1st R.M. Battalion.
8 2nd R.M. Battalion.
9 Anson Battalion.
10 Howe Battalion.
11 188th L.T.M. Battery.
12 188th M.G. Company.
13 & 14 63rd R.N. Divn.
15 189th Inf. Brigade.
16 26th Inf. Brigade.
17 D.M.G.O. 63rd Divn.
18 M.G. Group Commander.
19 R.A. Group Commander.
20 Town Major, METZ.
21 War Diary.
22 File.

SECRET. **M O V E   O R D E R S.**

By Lieut. J. COOTE" R.N.V.R. In the Field.
31/12/17.

---

1. INTENTION. The Battalion will move to METZ tonight.

2. TIME. H.Q. will move ogf at 4.30 pm.

3. ORDER OF MARCH. H.Q....B....D....C....A.
Platoons at 100 yards interval.

4. ROUTE. via VILLERS PLOUICH to R.13.a.9.3. thence by Sunken Road to Q.23.b.8.3. thence by track to Q.21.b.7.8.then Main Road TRESCAULT to METZ.

5. LEWIS GUNS. Coys will dump all Lewis Guns and L.G. Amm at 3 pm by Battalion H.Q. Sub-Lieut NIEL will be in charge of party detailed by him to be left behind.

6. MESS GEAR OFFICERS PACKS. These will be dumped with L.Gs at 3 pm.

7. DIXIES. All dixies and cooking gear will be dumped at same place at 3 pm.

8. ADVANCE PARTY. Each Coy will send ahead at least one servant to see about Officers Valises.

9. BOX RESPIRATORS. Box Respirators will be worn at ALERT position E. of METZ.

[signature] Sub-Lieut, R.N.V.R
A/Adjutant.

Instructions regarding War Diaries and Intelligence Summaries are contained in F. S. Regs., Part II. and the Staff Manual respectively. Title pages will be prepared in manuscript.

WAR DIARY or INTELLIGENCE SUMMARY.

(Erase heading not required.)

Army Form C. 2118.

Howe Bn

January 1918

Vol 20

Place	Date	Hour	Summary of Events and Information	Remarks and references to Appendices
METZ	1		Day spent in cleaning up after coming out of the Line	
"			Our Casualties were about 140 all together	
	1		~~[illegible]~~ Lt Comdr Beak assumed Command of the Battn	
	2		Paraded in morning & Comdr Beak read out letter from the G.O.C. expressing his appreciation of what the Battn had done. B Co bathed	
		3 p.m.	The bodies of Comdr WEST & Lt Comdr CAMPBELL were buried	
	3		Morning spent in training. A.B.D. Companies bathed in afternoon. 129 O.R. arrived from Dunkirk	
	4		Morning spent in getting ready for the Line. Battn moved off at 3.30 p.m. & relieved the 2nd R.M. BATTN in the right	
VILLERS PLUICH			sector. Relief complete 9.30. Situation quiet	
	5th		Holding right sub sector. Owing to extreme cold & subsequent thaw sickness	
	6th		rose to a high level. State of trenches very bad. GAME SUPPT being 2–3 ft	
	7th		deep in water. Lt J. Cole RNVR appd 2nd i/c 6th inst.	
	8th		Relieved by Anson & moved into Support in VILLERS PLUICH. Relief complete by 8.30 p.m.	
	9th		Resting in support.	
	10th		Relieved 2/RMLI in left sub. sector. Relief complete by 9 p.m. Condition of [illegible]	

Instructions regarding War Diaries and Intelligence Summaries are contained in F. S. Regs., Part II. and the Staff Manual respectively. Title pages will be prepared in manuscript.

WAR DIARY
or
~~INTELLIGENCE~~ SUMMARY.
(Erase heading not required.)

Army Form C. 2118.

January 1918

Place	Date	Hour	Summary of Events and Information	Remarks and references to Appendices
VILLERS PLOUICH	10th		very bad indeed. Front line 1 to 4 ft deep in water throughout. Movement very difficult & the carrying up of hot food a long & arduous process.	
	11th			
	12th		Holding left sub sector. Condition of trenches getting worse in spite of all efforts	
	13th		owing to the continued thaw & rain. Sick since 5th inst number 180.	
	14th		Relieved by Anson & moved into support in Villers Plouich relief complete 8.50 pm.	
	15th		Resting by day, working ~~on~~ HOLLY SUPP? at night. Condition of men very	
	16th		bad many being unable to put on boots owing to swollen feet	
METZ	17th		Moved to Bde. Reserve in METZ arriving there 8 p.m.	
	18th, 19th 20th		METZ Resting, cleaning & refitting	
VILLERS PLOUICH	21st		Relieved 2/RMLI in Right Sub sector disposition:- 2 Coys in front line in posts 1 Coy in VILLERS PLOUICH & 1 Coy in Quarry. The posts have now been drained but communication except over the top impossible	
	22nd ~~23rd~~		Holding line. Very little activity & no casualties. Weather warmer	
METZ	23rd		Relieved by 22nd Royal Fusiliers & proceeded to METZ relief complete 8 p.m.	
	24th		Moved by train to Camp at ROCQUIGNY into Corps Reserve.	

T2134. Wt. W708—776. 500000. 4/15. Sir J. C. & S.

Instructions regarding War Diaries and Intelligence Summaries are contained in F. S. Regs., Part II. and the Staff Manual respectively. Title pages will be prepared in manuscript.

WAR DIARY
or
~~INTELLIGENCE SUMMARY.~~

(Erase heading not required.)

Army Form C. 2118.

January 1918

Place	Date	Hour	Summary of Events and Information	Remarks and references to Appendices
RULQUIGNY	25th. 26th. 27th.		Resting, Reorganising & Cleaning.	
	28th.		Training started. Duk Bath.	
	29th.		Training & Bathing	
	30th.		All hands working on protection of huts against E.A. attack.	
	31st.		Training & work. Duk Bath.	

Dhu W. Beak
Commander R.N.V.R.
Comdg. HOWE Bn.

T2134. Wt. W708–773. 500000. 4/15. Sir J. C. & S.

Army Form C. 2118.

Howe Bn
Vol 21

Instructions regarding War Diaries and Intelligence Summaries are contained in F. S. Regs., Part II. and the Staff Manual respectively. Title pages will be prepared in manuscript.

WAR DIARY
or
~~INTELLIGENCE SUMMARY.~~

(Erase heading not required.)

Place	Date	Hour	Summary of Events and Information	Remarks and references to Appendices
ROCQUIGNY	Feb. 1		Continued Training	Ceased
"	2		(Sunday) Church Parade Games in afternoon	
"	3		Training. – All Gas Helmets tested by Div Gas Officer	
"	4		Training.	
"	5		Training	
"	6		Training Draft of 5 Off & 100 O.R. transferred to ANSON BN. including the 2nd in Command Lt Cmdr J. COOTE.	
"	7		Training & Camp Fatigues. continued protection of all Huts	
"	8		Training	
"	9		(Sunday) Church Parade. The Battn played the 188th T.M.B at football in the afternoon.	
"	10		6 Officers & 120 men transferred to 2nd R.M.L.I 12 Officers & 250 men transferred to 1st R.M.L.I	
"	11		Reorganization & Training.	
"	12		Training	
"	13		Training	

Army Form C. 2118.

Instructions regarding War Diaries and Intelligence Summaries are contained in F. S. Regs., Part II. and the Staff Manual respectively. Title pages will be prepared in manuscript.

WAR DIARY
or
INTELLIGENCE SUMMARY.
(Erase heading not required.)

Place	Date	Hour	Summary of Events and Information	Remarks and references to Appendices
LECHELLE	Feb 14th		Moved from ROCQUIGNY to LECHELLE by route march started 10.45 a.m. arrived PIONEER CAMP 11.50 a.m.	
	15th		Training & Protection of HUTS.	
	16th		(Sunday) Church Parade. A Working Party of 2 Officers & 100 O.R. was sent up the line to work under the 189th Bde. Arrived at TRESCAULT (by train from YTRES) & waited for guides for nearly 3 hours. No guides turning up Working Party entrained TRESCAULT at 12 midnight. arrived camp 2 a.m.	
	17		A Working Party of 2 Off & 100 O.R was provided to work for 189th Inf Bde	
	18		Training	
	19		Similar Working Party as on the 17th was provided	
	20/21		Training	
	22		A Draft of 6 Off & 326 O.R was transferred to the 7th Entrenching Battn.	
RUYAULCOURT	22		Surplus of Bn moved to RUYAULCOURT	

1577 Wt. W10731/1773 500,000 1/15 D. D. & L. A.D.S.S./Forms/C. 2118.

Instructions regarding War Diaries and Intelligence Summaries are contained in F. S. Regs., Part II. and the Staff Manual respectively. Title pages will be prepared in manuscript.

WAR DIARY

or

~~INTELLIGENCE~~ SUMMARY.

(Erase heading not required.)

Army Form C. 211

Place	Date	Hour	Summary of Events and Information	Remarks and references to Appendices
RUYAULCOURT	23		Reorganization of Surplus	
	24		The C.O. held Divine Service	
	25		Training	
	26		do	
	27		do	
	28		Surplus of Howe Bn transferred to the 7th Entrenching Battn.	

[illegible] Adjt

HOWE

1577 Wt. W10791/1773 [illegible]/15 D. D. & L. A.D.S.

Howe Batt

www.ingramcontent.com/pod-product-compliance
Lightning Source LLC
Chambersburg PA
CBHW080850230426
43662CB00013B/2069